Unlocking the Spectrum: A Comprehensive Guide to Understanding and Thriving with Autism

Travis Breeding

Published by Travis Breeding, 2024.

While every precaution has been taken in the preparation of this book, the publisher assumes no responsibility for errors or omissions, or for damages resulting from the use of the information contained herein.

UNLOCKING THE SPECTRUM: A COMPREHENSIVE GUIDE TO UNDERSTANDING AND THRIVING WITH AUTISM

First edition. February 20, 2024.

ISBN: 979-8224554263

Written by Travis Breeding.

Also by Travis Breeding

Harmony in Flux: Navigating Bi-Polar Brilliance

The Friendship Rainbow

The Great Kindergarten Adventure: A Story about Going to School with Autism

The Magic Forest Adventure

Unlocking Brilliance: Navigating Autism and Applied Behavior Analysis Towards a Radiant Future

Decoding Love: Navigating Dating and Relationships on the Autism Spectrum

Echoes of a Late Diagnosis: Unveiling the Spectrum Within

From Theory to Practice: Implementing Effective Autism Interventions St

The Amazing Adventures of Aiden and His Asperger's Superpowers

The Magical Adventures of Lily and the Enchanted Forest

Unlocking Potential: A Journey Of Discovery Through ABA Therapy

Unlocking Potential: Navigating Employment for Neurodiverse Talent

Unlocking the Spectrum: A Journey through Applied Behavior Analysis from an Autistic Perspective

Unlocking The Spectrum: Navigating The Complexity Of Autism With Advanced Strategies And Insights

Beyond The Spectrum: Insights From Autistic Adults

Beyond The Stereotypes

Breaking Barriers: Navigating Autism With Therapeutic Insight

Celebrating Neurodiversity
Embracing Differences
From Diagnosis To Treatment
From Dreams To Reality: The Young President
Living With Autism: A Journey Of Triumph And Challenges
Neurodiversity Unveiled: Navigating The Spectrum Of Inclusion
Sunshine At Disney World
The Art Of Reinforcement
The Magical School Bus Ride: A Journey Of Understanding
ThroughThe Spectrum Of Love
Dancing With Shadows: How To Turn Your Fears Into Powerful
Allies
From Chaos To Control: How To Develop Strong Executive
functioning Skills
From Misunderstood To Mainstream
Unlocking the Spectrum: A Comprehensive Guide to
Understanding and Thriving with Autism
Unraveling The Mind: Understanding OCD, Autism, And
Obsession
Rise: Mastering Confidence, Mindfulness, And Self-Esteem
Twice Exceptional: Navigating Life with Autism and Gomez Lopez
Hernandez Syndrome
Unlocking The Spectrum: A Journey Of Discovery With Gomez
Lopez Hernandez Syndrome

Watch for more at breedingautismconsulting.com.

Table of Contents

Chapter 1: The Ultimate Guide to Executive Functioning: Strategies for a More Organized Life

Executive functioning is a set of cognitive processes that are responsible for managing and regulating our thoughts, actions, and emotions. It plays a crucial role in our daily lives, influencing our productivity, success, and overall well-being. From planning and organizing tasks to staying focused and managing time effectively, executive functioning skills are essential for navigating the complexities of modern life.

Understanding Executive Functioning: What is it and Why is it Important?

Executive functioning refers to a collection of mental processes that enable us to set goals, plan and organize tasks, manage time, regulate emotions, and make decisions. It involves higher-order cognitive functions such as working memory, attention control, inhibitory control, cognitive flexibility, and problem-solving. These skills are crucial for managing complex tasks, adapting to new situations, and achieving our goals.

The importance of executive functioning in daily life cannot be overstated. It is the foundation for effective self-regulation and self-control. Without strong executive functioning skills, it becomes challenging to stay organized, manage time effectively, prioritize tasks, and make sound decisions. Executive functioning also plays a significant role in social interactions, as it helps us understand others' perspectives, regulate our emotions in social situations, and communicate effectively.

The Role of Executive Functioning in Daily Life: How it Affects Your Productivity and Success

Executive functioning skills have a direct impact on our productivity and success in various areas of life. For example, in the workplace, strong executive functioning skills enable individuals to manage their time effectively, prioritize tasks based on importance and urgency, stay focused on their work, and adapt to changing demands. This leads to increased productivity and better job performance.

In academic settings, executive functioning skills are crucial for students to succeed. They help students manage their time effectively to meet deadlines, organize their study materials, plan their assignments and projects, stay focused during lectures or study sessions, and regulate their emotions during exams or presentations. Students with strong executive functioning skills are more likely to achieve higher grades and perform well academically.

In personal life, executive functioning skills are essential for managing household tasks, organizing personal finances, maintaining healthy relationships, and making informed decisions. For example, individuals with strong executive functioning skills are better able to manage their schedules, balance work and personal life, set and achieve personal goals, and communicate effectively with their loved ones.

Common Executive Functioning Challenges: Identifying Your Weaknesses and Areas for Improvement

While executive functioning skills are crucial for success in various areas of life, many individuals struggle with certain aspects of executive functioning. Some common challenges include difficulty with planning and organizing tasks, managing time effectively, staying focused and avoiding distractions, regulating emotions, and making decisions.

To identify your weaknesses and areas for improvement in executive functioning, it is essential to reflect on your daily experiences and observe patterns of behavior. Pay attention to situations where you feel overwhelmed or struggle to stay organized or focused. Keep a journal or use a task management app to track your tasks and deadlines. This will help you identify areas where you may need to improve your executive functioning skills.

Developing Self-Awareness: The First Step to Improving Executive Functioning

Self-awareness is a crucial aspect of improving executive functioning skills. It involves being conscious of your thoughts, emotions, behaviors, strengths, and weaknesses. By developing self-awareness, you can gain a better understanding of how your executive functioning skills impact your daily life and identify areas for improvement.

There are several strategies you can use to develop self-awareness. One effective approach is mindfulness meditation, which involves paying attention to the present moment without judgment. This practice can help you become more aware of your thoughts, emotions, and bodily sensations. Another strategy is journaling, where you can reflect on your experiences and emotions. Additionally, seeking feedback from others can provide valuable insights into your strengths and weaknesses in executive functioning.

Planning and Prioritizing: Strategies for Organizing Your Tasks and Time

Effective planning and prioritizing are essential for managing tasks and time efficiently. By breaking down larger tasks into smaller, manageable steps and setting realistic deadlines, you can ensure that you stay on track and complete your tasks on time.

One strategy for effective planning and prioritizing is creating a to-do list. Write down all the tasks you need to accomplish, and then prioritize them based on importance and urgency. Another helpful technique is using a planner or calendar to schedule your tasks and allocate specific time slots for each task. This will help you stay organized and ensure that you have enough time to complete your tasks.

Setting Goals and Objectives: How to Stay Focused and Motivated

Setting goals and objectives is an important aspect of executive functioning. Goals provide a sense of direction and purpose, while objectives break down goals into specific, measurable, achievable, relevant, and time-bound (SMART) targets.

To stay focused and motivated, it is important to set goals that are meaningful to you. Reflect on your values, passions, and long-term aspirations to identify goals that align with your personal vision of success. Break down these goals into smaller objectives that can be achieved within a specific timeframe. Regularly review your goals and objectives to stay on track and make adjustments as needed.

Time Management Techniques: Maximizing Your Productivity and Efficiency

Time management is a critical skill for improving executive functioning. By managing your time effectively, you can maximize your productivity, reduce stress, and achieve a better work-life balance.

One effective time management technique is the Pomodoro Technique, which involves working in focused bursts of 25 minutes followed by short breaks. This technique helps improve focus and prevents burnout. Another technique is the Eisenhower Matrix, which involves categorizing tasks based on their urgency and importance. This helps prioritize tasks and allocate time accordingly.

Managing Distractions and Procrastination: Tips for Staying on Task

Distractions and procrastination can significantly impact executive functioning and productivity. It is important to identify common distractions and develop strategies to manage them effectively.

Common distractions include social media, email notifications, noise, and multitasking. To manage distractions, consider turning off notifications on your phone or computer, creating a designated workspace free from distractions, and using time-blocking techniques to allocate specific time slots for focused work. Additionally, practicing mindfulness can help you stay present and avoid getting caught up in distractions.

Improving Memory and Recall: Techniques for Retaining Information

Memory and recall are essential aspects of executive functioning. By improving your memory and recall skills, you can retain information more effectively and apply it when needed.

One technique for improving memory is using mnemonic devices, such as acronyms or visual imagery, to associate information with memorable cues. Another technique is spaced repetition, which involves reviewing information at regular intervals over time to reinforce memory retention. Additionally, practicing active listening and engaging in regular mental exercises, such as puzzles or brain games, can help improve memory and recall.

Effective Communication: How to Communicate Clearly and Confidently

Effective communication is a crucial aspect of executive functioning. It involves expressing your thoughts and ideas clearly, listening actively, understanding others' perspectives, and adapting your communication style to different situations.

To improve communication skills, it is important to practice active listening by giving your full attention to the speaker, asking clarifying questions, and summarizing what you have heard. Additionally, practice expressing your thoughts clearly and concisely by organizing your ideas before speaking or writing. Pay attention to nonverbal cues such as body language and tone of voice to enhance your understanding of others' emotions and intentions.

Coping with Stress and Overwhelm: Strategies for Maintaining Balance and Well-Being

Stress and overwhelm can significantly impact executive functioning skills. It is important to develop strategies for managing stress and maintaining balance in your life.

One effective strategy is practicing self-care, which involves engaging in activities that promote physical, mental, and emotional well-being. This can include exercise, meditation, spending time in nature, pursuing hobbies, and maintaining a healthy work-life balance. Additionally, developing healthy coping mechanisms such as deep breathing exercises, journaling, or talking to a trusted friend or therapist can help manage stress and overwhelm.

Improving executive functioning skills is a lifelong journey that requires self-awareness, practice, and perseverance. By understanding the importance of executive functioning in daily life and implementing strategies to improve these skills, you can enhance your productivity, success, and overall well-being. Remember to be patient with yourself and celebrate small victories along the way. With dedication and effort, you can develop strong executive functioning skills that will serve you well in all areas of life.

Chapter 2: Sensory Overload: How to Recognize and Manage Overstimulation

Sensory overload is a condition that many people experience on a daily basis. It occurs when our senses are overwhelmed by too much stimuli, making it difficult to process and respond to our environment. This can have a significant impact on our daily lives, affecting our ability to concentrate, communicate, and engage in social activities. In this article, we will explore the concept of sensory overload, its causes, symptoms, and its impact on mental health. We will also discuss coping mechanisms and strategies for managing sensory overload in various settings, such as at work, while traveling, and in children.

Understanding Sensory Overload: What is it and How Does it Happen?

Sensory overload is a condition that occurs when there is an excessive amount of sensory information coming into the brain at once. This can happen when our senses are bombarded with too much noise, light, smells, or other stimuli. The sensory system is responsible for processing information from our environment and sending it to the brain for interpretation. When there is an overload of sensory input, the brain becomes overwhelmed and has difficulty filtering and organizing the information.

The sensory system consists of five main senses: sight, hearing, taste, smell, and touch. Each sense has its own set of receptors that detect specific types of stimuli. For example, the eyes detect light and color, while the ears detect sound waves. These receptors send signals to the brain, which then interprets the information and allows us to make sense of our surroundings.

Common Causes of Sensory Overload: Identifying Triggers in Your Environment

There are several common triggers that can lead to sensory overload. These triggers can vary depending on the individual and their specific sensitivities. Some common triggers include loud noises, bright lights, strong smells, crowded spaces, and certain textures or fabrics.

In different environments, there can be different triggers that may cause sensory overload. For example, in a busy city, the constant noise, bright lights, and crowded streets can be overwhelming for some individuals. In a shopping mall, the combination of loud music, bright lights, and the presence of many people can also lead to sensory overload.

It is important to identify your personal triggers in order to better manage sensory overload. Some individuals may be more sensitive to certain types of stimuli than others. For example, someone with a sensitivity to loud noises may find it difficult to concentrate in a noisy office environment. By identifying these triggers, you can take steps to minimize their impact on your daily life.

Signs and Symptoms of Sensory Overload: How to Recognize Overstimulation

Sensory overload can manifest in a variety of ways, and the symptoms can vary from person to person. However, there are some common signs and symptoms that may indicate overstimulation.

Physical symptoms of sensory overload can include headaches, fatigue, dizziness, increased heart rate, and muscle tension. These physical symptoms are often a result of the body's stress response to the overwhelming sensory input.

Emotional symptoms of sensory overload can include irritability, anxiety, frustration, and feeling overwhelmed. These emotional symptoms are often a result of the brain's difficulty in processing and responding to the excessive sensory information.

Behavioral symptoms of sensory overload can include withdrawal from social situations, avoidance of certain environments or activities, and difficulty concentrating or completing tasks. These behavioral symptoms are often a result of the individual's attempt to cope with the overwhelming sensory input.

The Impact of Sensory Overload on Mental Health: Anxiety, Depression and More

Sensory overload can have a significant impact on mental health. The constant bombardment of sensory stimuli can lead to increased levels of anxiety and stress. This can make it difficult for individuals to relax and engage in activities that they enjoy. Over time, this chronic stress can contribute to the development of mental health conditions such as anxiety disorders and depression.

Anxiety disorders are characterized by excessive worry and fear. Individuals with sensory overload may experience heightened levels of anxiety due to their difficulty in processing and responding to their environment. This can lead to feelings of overwhelm and a constant state of alertness.

Depression is another common mental health condition that can be associated with sensory overload. The constant stress and overwhelm can lead to feelings of sadness, hopelessness, and a loss of interest in activities. Individuals may also experience difficulty sleeping, changes in appetite, and a lack of energy.

Other mental health conditions that can be associated with sensory overload include post-traumatic stress disorder (PTSD), attention deficit hyperactivity disorder (ADHD), and autism spectrum disorder (ASD). These conditions can all be characterized by difficulties in processing sensory information and can be exacerbated by sensory overload.

Coping Mechanisms for Sensory Overload: Self-Care Strategies and Techniques

There are several self-care strategies and techniques that can help individuals cope with sensory overload. These strategies can be tailored to the individual's specific needs and sensitivities.

One self-care strategy is to create a sensory-friendly environment. This can involve making changes to your physical surroundings to minimize sensory triggers. For example, you can use noise-cancelling headphones or earplugs to reduce the impact of loud noises. You can also use dimmer switches or curtains to control the amount of light in a room. Additionally, you can use calming scents or essential oils to create a soothing atmosphere.

Another self-care strategy is to practice relaxation techniques. These techniques can help calm the nervous system and reduce stress levels. Some examples of relaxation techniques include deep breathing exercises, meditation, yoga, and progressive muscle relaxation. These techniques can be done anywhere and at any time, making them easily accessible for individuals experiencing sensory overload.

Engaging in activities that promote self-expression and creativity can also be helpful in managing sensory overload. These activities can provide a sense of control and allow individuals to focus their attention on something enjoyable. Examples of creative activities include painting, drawing, writing, playing a musical instrument, or engaging in a hobby.

Sensory Overload in Children: Recognizing and Managing Overstimulation in Kids

Sensory overload can also affect children, and it is important for parents and caregivers to recognize and manage overstimulation in kids. Children may be more sensitive to sensory stimuli than adults, and they may have difficulty expressing their feelings or understanding what is happening to them.

Some common triggers for sensory overload in children include loud noises, bright lights, strong smells, crowded spaces, and certain textures or fabrics. It is important for parents and caregivers to be aware of these triggers and take steps to minimize their impact on the child's daily life.

One way to manage sensory overload in children is to create a sensory-friendly environment. This can involve making changes to the child's bedroom or play area to minimize sensory triggers. For example, you can use blackout curtains to control the amount of light in the room. You can also provide the child with noise-cancelling headphones or earplugs to reduce the impact of loud noises.

It is also important to provide children with opportunities for sensory breaks throughout the day. These breaks can allow the child to take a break from overwhelming stimuli and engage in calming activities. For example, you can create a quiet corner in the home where the child can go to relax and unwind. You can also provide the child with sensory toys or tools that they can use to self-regulate their sensory input.

Sensory Processing Disorder: Understanding the Link to Sensory Overload

Sensory processing disorder (SPD) is a condition that affects how individuals process and respond to sensory information. It is often characterized by difficulties in regulating and organizing sensory input. Sensory overload is a common symptom of SPD, as individuals with this condition may have a heightened sensitivity to certain types of stimuli.

The link between sensory processing disorder and sensory overload is complex and can vary from person to person. Some individuals with SPD may be hypersensitive to certain types of stimuli, while others may be hyposensitive and seek out intense sensory experiences. Regardless of the specific sensitivities, individuals with SPD often experience difficulties in processing and responding to sensory information, which can lead to sensory overload.

Managing sensory processing disorder often involves a combination of therapy and self-care strategies. Occupational therapy can help individuals develop strategies for managing sensory input and improving their ability to process and respond to their environment. Self-care strategies, such as creating a sensory-friendly environment and engaging in relaxation techniques, can also be helpful in managing sensory overload in individuals with SPD.

Sensory Overload at Work: How to Manage Overstimulation in the Workplace

Sensory overload can be particularly challenging in the workplace, where individuals are often exposed to a variety of stimuli throughout the day. Common triggers in the workplace can include loud noises, bright lights, strong smells, crowded spaces, and interruptions from coworkers.

One way to manage sensory overload at work is to create a sensory-friendly workspace. This can involve making changes to your physical surroundings to minimize sensory triggers. For example, you can use noise-cancelling headphones or earplugs to reduce the impact of loud noises. You can also use task lighting or adjust the brightness of your computer screen to control the amount of light in your workspace.

Taking regular breaks throughout the day can also help manage sensory overload at work. These breaks can allow you to step away from overwhelming stimuli and engage in calming activities. For example, you can take a short walk outside or find a quiet space where you can relax and unwind.

It is also important to communicate with your coworkers and supervisors about your sensory sensitivities. By explaining your needs and preferences, you can work together to create a more supportive and understanding work environment. This may involve making adjustments to your workspace or implementing strategies to minimize sensory triggers.

Sensory Overload and Autism: Tips for Managing Overstimulation in Individuals with Autism

Sensory overload is a common experience for individuals with autism spectrum disorder (ASD). Many individuals with ASD have heightened sensitivities to certain types of stimuli, which can make it difficult for them to process and respond to their environment.

Common triggers for sensory overload in individuals with autism can include loud noises, bright lights, strong smells, crowded spaces, and certain textures or fabrics. It is important for individuals with autism and their caregivers to be aware of these triggers and take steps to minimize their impact on daily life.

One way to manage sensory overload in individuals with autism is to create a sensory-friendly environment. This can involve making changes to the individual's home or school environment to minimize sensory triggers. For example, you can use noise-cancelling headphones or earplugs to reduce the impact of loud noises. You can also provide the individual with a quiet space where they can go to relax and unwind.

It is also important to provide individuals with autism with opportunities for sensory breaks throughout the day. These breaks can allow them to take a break from overwhelming stimuli and engage in calming activities. For example, you can provide the individual with sensory toys or tools that they can use to self-regulate their sensory input.

Sensory Overload and Travel: How to Manage Overstimulation While on the Go

Traveling can be particularly challenging for individuals experiencing sensory overload, as it often involves exposure to new and unfamiliar environments. Common triggers while traveling can include loud noises, bright lights, strong smells, crowded spaces, and changes in routine.

One way to manage sensory overload while traveling is to plan ahead and research your destination. By familiarizing yourself with the environment and potential triggers, you can take steps to minimize their impact on your trip. For example, you can choose accommodations that offer quiet rooms or provide noise-cancelling headphones. You can also plan your itinerary to avoid crowded tourist attractions or busy times of day.

Taking regular breaks throughout your trip can also help manage sensory overload. These breaks can allow you to step away from overwhelming stimuli and engage in calming activities. For example, you can find a quiet park or café where you can relax and unwind. You can also schedule downtime in your itinerary to give yourself time to recharge.

It is also important to communicate with your travel companions about your sensory sensitivities. By explaining your needs and preferences, you can work together to create a more supportive and understanding travel experience. This may involve making adjustments to your itinerary or implementing strategies to minimize sensory triggers.

Seeking Professional Help for Sensory Overload: When to Consult a Doctor or Therapist

In some cases, sensory overload may be severe or persistent enough to interfere with daily functioning and quality of life. If you are experiencing significant distress or impairment as a result of sensory overload, it may be beneficial to seek professional help.

A doctor or therapist can help assess your symptoms and provide a diagnosis if necessary. They can also provide guidance and support in managing sensory overload and developing coping strategies. Treatment options may include therapy, medication, or a combination of both.

When seeking professional help for sensory overload, it is important to find a qualified doctor or therapist who has experience working with individuals with sensory sensitivities. They should have an understanding of the sensory system and be knowledgeable about the specific challenges associated with sensory overload.

Sensory overload is a condition that many people experience on a daily basis. It occurs when our senses are overwhelmed by too much stimuli, making it difficult to process and respond to our environment. Sensory overload can have a significant impact on our daily lives, affecting our ability to concentrate, communicate, and engage in social activities. However, there are strategies and techniques that can help individuals manage sensory overload and improve their quality of life. If you are experiencing significant distress or impairment as a result of sensory overload, it may be beneficial to seek professional help. Remember, you are not alone, and there is support available to help you navigate the challenges of sensory overload.

Chapter 3: The Art of Effective Communication: Mastering the Social Game

Communication is a vital life skill that affects all aspects of our lives. Whether it's in our personal relationships, professional endeavors, or social interactions, the ability to communicate effectively is crucial. Effective communication allows us to express ourselves, understand others, and build strong connections with those around us. It is the foundation for successful relationships and can lead to personal and professional success.

Understanding the Different Types of Communication

There are various types of communication that we engage in on a daily basis. Verbal communication is perhaps the most common form, involving the use of words to convey our thoughts, ideas, and emotions. Non-verbal communication, on the other hand, involves body language, facial expressions, gestures, and tone of voice. Lastly, written communication refers to the use of written words to communicate, such as through emails, letters, or text messages.

Verbal Communication: The Power of Words

Verbal communication is a powerful tool that can have a significant impact on our relationships and interactions with others. The words we choose to use can either build bridges or create barriers between individuals. It is important to choose our words carefully and consider their potential impact on others.

In addition to the words themselves, the tone and inflection we use when speaking also play a crucial role in effective verbal communication. The way we say something can completely change its meaning and how it is received by others. For example, saying "I'm fine" with a sarcastic tone can convey a completely different message than saying it with a genuine tone.

Active listening is another important aspect of verbal communication. It involves fully engaging with the speaker and giving them our full attention. Active listening allows us to understand the speaker's perspective and respond appropriately. It shows respect and empathy towards the speaker and helps build stronger connections.

Non-Verbal Communication: The Art of Body Language

Non-verbal communication is often considered the silent language that speaks louder than words. It includes body language, facial expressions, gestures, and even the way we dress. These non-verbal cues can convey a wealth of information about our thoughts, feelings, and intentions.

Understanding and interpreting non-verbal cues is essential for effective communication. For example, crossed arms and a furrowed brow may indicate that someone is defensive or closed off. On the other hand, open body language and a smile can convey warmth and approachability.

Non-verbal communication also has a significant impact on our relationships. It can help establish trust, build rapport, and create a sense of connection with others. Being aware of our own non-verbal cues and being able to read those of others can greatly enhance our communication skills.

Active Listening: The Key to Effective Communication

Active listening is a fundamental skill that is often overlooked but is crucial for effective communication. It involves fully focusing on the speaker, paying attention to both their verbal and non-verbal cues, and responding appropriately.

Listening is not just about hearing the words being spoken; it is about understanding the speaker's perspective and showing empathy. It requires setting aside our own thoughts and judgments and truly immersing ourselves in the speaker's world.

Active listening plays a vital role in building relationships. When we actively listen to someone, we show them that we value their thoughts and feelings. This creates a sense of trust and openness, which leads to stronger connections.

Improving active listening skills can be done through practice and conscious effort. Some tips for improving active listening include maintaining eye contact, nodding or using other non-verbal cues to show understanding, asking clarifying questions, and summarizing what has been said.

Empathy: The Secret Weapon of Effective Communication

Empathy is the ability to understand and share the feelings of another person. It is an essential skill for effective communication as it allows us to connect with others on a deeper level and truly understand their perspective.

Empathy plays a crucial role in building relationships. When we are able to put ourselves in someone else's shoes and understand their emotions, we can respond in a more compassionate and understanding way. This creates a sense of trust and strengthens the bond between individuals.

Developing empathy skills can be done through practice and self-reflection. It involves actively listening to others, being open-minded, and trying to understand their experiences and emotions. It also requires setting aside our own biases and judgments and approaching situations with an open heart.

Overcoming Communication Barriers

Communication barriers can hinder effective communication and create misunderstandings. Some common communication barriers include language barriers, cultural differences, distractions, and emotional barriers.

To overcome these barriers, it is important to be aware of them and make a conscious effort to address them. Strategies for overcoming communication barriers include using simple and clear language, being mindful of cultural differences, minimizing distractions, and managing emotions effectively.

Adapting our communication styles to different situations is also crucial for overcoming communication barriers. Different situations may require different approaches to communication, such as being more assertive in a professional setting or using humor in a social setting.

Building Trust Through Communication

Trust is the foundation of any successful relationship, whether it's personal or professional. Effective communication plays a vital role in building trust as it allows individuals to be open, honest, and transparent with each other.

Strategies for building trust through communication include being honest and authentic, following through on commitments, actively listening to others, and showing empathy. It is also important to be consistent in our words and actions and to communicate openly about any issues or concerns.

The impact of trust on relationships cannot be overstated. When there is trust between individuals, there is a sense of safety and security that allows for open communication and collaboration. Trust also fosters loyalty and commitment, leading to stronger and more fulfilling relationships.

Conflict Resolution: The Art of Communicating Under Pressure

Conflict is a natural part of any relationship, but effective communication is crucial for resolving conflicts in a healthy and constructive way. When conflicts arise, it is important to communicate effectively to understand each other's perspectives, find common ground, and work towards a resolution.

Effective communication in conflict resolution involves active listening, expressing emotions in a constructive way, and using "I" statements to express concerns or frustrations. It also requires being open to feedback and willing to compromise.

The impact of effective communication on conflict resolution is significant. When individuals are able to communicate their needs and concerns effectively, conflicts can be resolved in a way that strengthens the relationship rather than damaging it. Effective communication allows for understanding, empathy, and finding mutually beneficial solutions.

Mastering the Social Game: Effective Communication in Social Settings

Effective communication is not limited to professional or personal relationships; it is also crucial in social settings. Whether it's at a party, networking event, or social gathering, being able to communicate effectively can greatly enhance our social interactions.

Strategies for communicating effectively in social situations include active listening, asking open-ended questions, showing genuine interest in others, and using positive body language. It is also important to be mindful of cultural differences and adapt our communication style accordingly.

The impact of effective communication on social relationships is significant. When we are able to communicate effectively in social settings, we can build stronger connections with others, create meaningful friendships, and enjoy more fulfilling social experiences.

The Art of Effective Communication as a Life Skill

Effective communication is a vital life skill that affects all aspects of our lives. It allows us to express ourselves, understand others, and build strong connections with those around us. The ability to communicate effectively can lead to success in personal and professional relationships.

Continuous improvement in communication skills is important as communication is a lifelong process. By understanding the different types of communication, such as verbal, non-verbal, and written, and mastering skills such as active listening and empathy, we can enhance our communication abilities.

The impact of effective communication on personal and professional success cannot be overstated. It allows us to build trust, resolve conflicts, and navigate social situations with ease. By continuously working on our communication skills, we can improve our relationships, enhance our interactions with others, and lead more fulfilling lives.

Chapter 4: From Diagnosis to Progress: A Parent's Guide to Early Intervention Services

Early intervention services are crucial for children with developmental delays. These services provide support and assistance to children and their families to help them overcome challenges and reach their full potential. In this article, we will explore the importance of early intervention services, the different types of services available, and how parents can access and work with service providers to create a plan for their child's development.

Understanding Early Intervention Services: What Parents Need to Know

Early intervention services are a range of specialized services designed to support children with developmental delays from birth to age three. These services are provided by a team of professionals who work closely with the child and their family to address their unique needs and challenges. The goal of early intervention is to promote the child's development, enhance their learning abilities, and improve their overall quality of life.

To be eligible for early intervention services, a child must meet certain criteria. These criteria vary depending on the country or state, but generally include a significant delay in one or more areas of development, such as communication, motor skills, or social-emotional development. It is important for parents to be aware of these eligibility criteria and seek early intervention services as soon as they suspect their child may have a developmental delay.

The Importance of Early Intervention for Children with Developmental Delays

Early intervention services have numerous benefits for children with developmental delays. Research has shown that early intervention can lead to significant improvements in a child's development and functioning. By addressing developmental delays early on, children have a better chance of catching up to their peers and reaching their full potential.

One of the key benefits of early intervention is that it can prevent or minimize the impact of developmental delays on a child's long-term development. By providing targeted interventions and support during the critical early years, children can develop the skills they need to succeed in school and in life. Early intervention can also help prevent secondary issues that may arise as a result of developmental delays, such as behavioral problems or academic difficulties.

The Diagnosis Process: Identifying Developmental Delays in Children

Identifying developmental delays in children is an important first step in accessing early intervention services. Parents and caregivers play a crucial role in recognizing the signs and symptoms of developmental delays and seeking appropriate evaluations and assessments.

Some common signs of developmental delays include delays in reaching developmental milestones, such as sitting up, crawling, or speaking; difficulties with social interactions or communication; and challenges with motor skills or coordination. If parents suspect that their child may have a developmental delay, it is important to consult with a healthcare professional who can conduct a comprehensive evaluation.

Diagnostic tools and assessments used to identify developmental delays may include standardized tests, observations, and interviews with parents and caregivers. These assessments are designed to assess a child's development across different domains, such as cognitive, language, motor, and social-emotional development. The results of these assessments can help determine the child's eligibility for early intervention services and guide the development of an individualized intervention plan.

Types of Early Intervention Services Available for Children with Developmental Delays

There are various types of early intervention services available for children with developmental delays. These services are tailored to meet the unique needs of each child and may include therapies, educational interventions, and support services.

Some examples of specific early intervention services include speech therapy, occupational therapy, physical therapy, and behavioral therapy. Speech therapy focuses on improving communication skills, while occupational therapy helps children develop fine motor skills and daily living skills. Physical therapy focuses on improving gross motor skills and coordination, while behavioral therapy addresses challenging behaviors and promotes social-emotional development.

In addition to these therapies, early intervention services may also include educational interventions such as early childhood education programs or specialized instruction in areas such as reading or math. Support services may include counseling or support groups for parents and caregivers, as well as assistance with accessing community resources and navigating the healthcare system.

How to Access Early Intervention Services for Your Child

Accessing early intervention services for your child involves several steps. The first step is to contact your local early intervention program or agency to request an evaluation. This can usually be done by calling a toll-free number or submitting an online form.

Once the evaluation is requested, a team of professionals will conduct a comprehensive assessment of your child's development. This may involve observations, interviews, and standardized tests. The results of the assessment will determine your child's eligibility for early intervention services.

If your child is found eligible for early intervention services, the next step is to develop an individualized family service plan (IFSP). This plan outlines the specific goals and objectives for your child's development and identifies the services and supports that will be provided. It is important for parents to actively participate in the development of the IFSP and advocate for their child's needs.

The Role of Parents in Early Intervention: Working with Service Providers

Parents play a crucial role in early intervention. They are their child's best advocate and can provide valuable insights into their child's strengths, challenges, and preferences. It is important for parents to actively participate in their child's early intervention program and work collaboratively with service providers.

One of the key ways parents can be involved in early intervention is by attending meetings and discussions related to their child's development. This includes participating in the development of the IFSP, attending therapy sessions, and providing feedback on their child's progress. Parents can also ask questions, seek clarification, and share their concerns or observations with service providers.

It is also important for parents to communicate regularly with service providers and share information about their child's progress or any changes in their needs or circumstances. This open line of communication allows service providers to make adjustments to the intervention plan as needed and ensures that parents are informed and involved in their child's development.

Creating a Plan for Early Intervention: Setting Goals and Objectives

Setting goals and objectives is an important part of the early intervention process. Goals and objectives provide a roadmap for the child's development and help guide the selection of appropriate interventions and supports.

When setting goals and objectives, it is important to consider the child's unique strengths, challenges, and interests. Goals should be specific, measurable, achievable, relevant, and time-bound

(SMART). For example, a goal for a child receiving speech therapy may be to increase their vocabulary by 50 words within six months.

Objectives are the specific steps or actions that will be taken to achieve the goals. They should be concrete and measurable. For example, an objective for the same child receiving speech therapy may be to practice using new words in everyday conversations for 10 minutes each day.

It is important for parents to actively participate in the goal-setting process and provide input based on their observations and knowledge of their child. By working collaboratively with service providers, parents can ensure that the goals and objectives are meaningful and relevant to their child's needs.

Progress Tracking: How to Monitor Your Child's Developmental Progress

Tracking progress is an essential part of early intervention. It allows parents and service providers to monitor the child's development, evaluate the effectiveness of interventions, and make adjustments as needed.

There are various methods for tracking progress in early intervention. These may include formal assessments, such as standardized tests or checklists, as well as informal observations and documentation. Parents can also keep a journal or log of their child's progress, noting any milestones achieved or changes observed.

Regular communication between parents and service providers is also important for tracking progress. This includes sharing information about the child's achievements, challenges, and any changes in their needs or circumstances. Service providers can provide feedback on the child's progress and suggest strategies or interventions to support further development.

Working with Your Child's Team: Collaboration and Communication

Collaboration and communication between parents and service providers are essential for the success of early intervention. By working together as a team, parents and service providers can ensure that the child's needs are met and that interventions are effective.

Effective communication involves active listening, asking questions, and sharing information openly and honestly. It is important for parents to express their concerns, ask for clarification, and provide feedback on their child's progress. Service providers should also be responsive to parents' questions and concerns and provide clear and timely communication.

Collaboration involves working together to develop and implement the intervention plan, as well as making decisions about the child's development. This includes attending meetings, participating in discussions, and actively engaging in the decision-making process. By working collaboratively, parents and service providers can ensure that the child's needs are met and that interventions are tailored to their unique strengths and challenges.

Preparing for the Transition: Moving from Early Intervention to School-Aged Services

The transition from early intervention to school-aged services is an important milestone for children with developmental delays. It involves moving from a family-centered approach to a more school-based approach to support the child's development.

To prepare for this transition, it is important for parents to start planning early. This may involve attending transition meetings or workshops, visiting potential schools or programs, and gathering information about available services and supports. It is also important to communicate with service providers and school personnel to ensure a smooth transition.

During the transition process, it is important for parents to advocate for their child's needs and ensure that appropriate supports are in place. This may involve developing an individualized education plan (IEP) or 504 plan, which outlines the specific accommodations and services that will be provided in the school setting.

Resources and Support: Finding Help and Information for Your Child and Family

There are numerous resources and support available for families of children with developmental delays. These resources can provide valuable information, guidance, and support to help parents navigate the early intervention process and support their child's development.

Some examples of resources include support groups, advocacy organizations, and online forums or communities. Support groups provide an opportunity for parents to connect with others who are going through similar experiences and share information and resources. Advocacy organizations can provide information about rights and entitlements, as well as guidance on accessing services and supports.

Online forums or communities can also be a valuable source of information and support. These platforms allow parents to connect with others, ask questions, and share their experiences. It is important to use caution when accessing online resources and ensure that the information is reliable and evidence-based.

Early intervention services play a crucial role in supporting children with developmental delays. By providing targeted interventions and support during the critical early years, early intervention can help children overcome challenges, reach their full potential, and improve their overall quality of life. It is important for parents to be aware of the benefits of early intervention, understand the different types of services available, and actively participate in their child's development. By seeking early intervention services and working collaboratively with service providers, parents can give their child the best possible start in life.

Chapter 5: The Power of Inclusion: Supporting Individuals with Autism

Autism Spectrum Disorder (ASD) is a neurodevelopmental disorder that affects individuals' social communication and interaction skills. It is characterized by a range of behaviors and challenges, making it a complex disorder to understand and support. It is estimated that 1 in 54 children in the United States are diagnosed with ASD, highlighting the importance of understanding and supporting individuals with this disorder.

Understanding and supporting individuals with ASD is crucial for several reasons. Firstly, it allows for the creation of inclusive environments where individuals with ASD can thrive and reach their full potential. Secondly, it promotes empathy and understanding among neurotypical individuals, fostering a more inclusive society. Lastly, it ensures that individuals with ASD have access to the necessary resources and support systems to lead fulfilling lives.

Understanding Autism Spectrum Disorder: What You Need to Know

ASD is a developmental disorder that affects individuals' social communication and interaction skills. It is characterized by difficulties in social interaction, communication, and repetitive behaviors. Individuals with ASD may have challenges in understanding nonverbal cues, maintaining eye contact, engaging in reciprocal conversations, and developing friendships.

Diagnosing ASD can be complex as it is a spectrum disorder, meaning that individuals can exhibit a wide range of symptoms and behaviors. The Diagnostic and Statistical Manual of Mental Disorders (DSM-5) outlines specific criteria for diagnosing ASD, including deficits in social communication and interaction, restricted interests or repetitive behaviors, and symptoms that are present in early childhood.

The prevalence of ASD has been increasing over the years, with more children being diagnosed with the disorder. According to the Centers for Disease Control and Prevention (CDC), approximately 1 in 54 children in the United States are diagnosed with ASD. This increase in prevalence highlights the need for increased awareness, understanding, and support for individuals with ASD.

The Importance of Inclusion for Individuals with Autism

Inclusion refers to the practice of ensuring that individuals with disabilities, including those with ASD, are fully included in all aspects of society. Inclusion is crucial for individuals with ASD as it provides them with opportunities to develop social skills, build relationships, and access education and employment.

Inclusion has numerous benefits for individuals with ASD. Firstly, it promotes social interaction and communication skills, allowing individuals to develop meaningful relationships and connections. It also provides opportunities for individuals with ASD to learn from their neurotypical peers and vice versa, fostering a sense of empathy and understanding.

Exclusion and isolation can have negative effects on individuals with ASD. It can lead to feelings of loneliness, low self-esteem, and increased anxiety. Inclusive environments, on the other hand, promote a sense of belonging and acceptance, which can have a positive impact on individuals' mental health and overall well-being.

Individuals with disabilities, including those with ASD, are protected by various legal rights and protections. The Individuals with Disabilities Education Act (IDEA) ensures that individuals with disabilities have access to a free appropriate public education (FAPE) in the least restrictive environment (LRE). This means that individuals with ASD should be educated alongside their neurotypical peers to the maximum extent possible.

Common Challenges Faced by Individuals with Autism

Individuals with ASD face various challenges that can impact their daily lives and functioning. These challenges include sensory processing difficulties, communication challenges, social skills deficits, and executive functioning difficulties.

Sensory processing difficulties refer to difficulties in processing and responding to sensory information from the environment. Individuals with ASD may be hypersensitive or hyposensitive to certain sensory stimuli such as noise, light, touch, or smell. This can lead to sensory overload or sensory seeking behaviors.

Communication challenges are another common characteristic of ASD. Individuals with ASD may have difficulties in understanding and using verbal and nonverbal communication. They may have limited vocabulary, struggle with expressive language, or have challenges in understanding social cues and gestures.

Social skills deficits are also common in individuals with ASD. They may have difficulties in initiating and maintaining conversations, understanding social norms and expectations, and developing friendships. This can lead to social isolation and difficulties in forming meaningful relationships.

Executive functioning difficulties refer to challenges in planning, organizing, and completing tasks. Individuals with ASD may struggle with time management, organization, and problem-solving skills. This can impact their academic performance, daily routines, and overall independence.

Strategies for Creating an Inclusive Environment

Creating an inclusive environment for individuals with ASD requires a multi-faceted approach that addresses their unique needs and challenges. Some strategies for creating an inclusive environment include implementing universal design for learning, using positive behavior supports, adopting a collaborative team approach, and providing assistive technology and accommodations.

Universal design for learning (UDL) is an educational framework that aims to provide multiple means of representation, expression, and engagement to meet the diverse needs of learners. By implementing UDL principles, educators can create inclusive classrooms where individuals with ASD can access the curriculum and participate fully in learning activities.

Positive behavior supports (PBS) is a proactive approach to managing challenging behaviors. It focuses on teaching individuals with ASD appropriate behaviors and providing them with the necessary supports to succeed. PBS strategies include using visual supports, implementing structured routines, and providing clear expectations and consequences.

Adopting a collaborative team approach involves involving various stakeholders in the individual's life, including parents, educators, therapists, and support staff. By working together as a team, individuals with ASD can receive consistent support across different settings and have their unique needs addressed effectively.

Assistive technology and accommodations can also play a crucial role in creating an inclusive environment for individuals with ASD. Assistive technology such as communication devices or visual supports can enhance communication skills and independence. Accommodations such as preferential seating or extra time on tasks can help individuals with ASD succeed in academic and social settings.

Building Positive Relationships with Individuals with Autism

Building positive relationships with individuals with ASD is essential for their overall well-being and development. It requires a person-centered approach, empathy and understanding, positive reinforcement and praise, and active listening and communication.

A person-centered approach involves recognizing and valuing the unique strengths, interests, and needs of individuals with ASD. It involves actively involving them in decision-making processes and respecting their autonomy and preferences. By taking a person-centered approach, individuals with ASD can feel empowered and supported.

Empathy and understanding are crucial when building relationships with individuals with ASD. It involves putting oneself in their shoes, recognizing their challenges, and responding with compassion and patience. By demonstrating empathy and understanding, individuals with ASD can feel accepted and valued.

Positive reinforcement and praise are effective strategies for building positive relationships with individuals with ASD. By providing specific praise and rewards for desired behaviors, individuals with ASD can feel motivated and encouraged to continue engaging in those behaviors. This can help build their self-esteem and confidence.

Active listening and communication involve actively engaging in conversations with individuals with ASD, using clear and concise language, and providing opportunities for them to express themselves. By actively listening to their thoughts, feelings, and ideas, individuals with ASD can feel heard and understood.

The Role of Communication in Supporting Individuals with Autism

Communication plays a crucial role in supporting individuals with ASD. It involves using augmentative and alternative communication (AAC), visual supports and schedules, social stories and scripts, and clear and concise language.

Augmentative and alternative communication (AAC) refers to the use of tools or strategies to support communication for individuals who have difficulties with speech or language. AAC can include sign language, picture exchange systems, or electronic devices that generate speech. By using AAC, individuals with ASD can effectively communicate their wants, needs, and thoughts.

Visual supports such as visual schedules or visual cues can help individuals with ASD understand and follow routines and expectations. Visual supports provide a visual representation of information, making it easier for individuals with ASD to process and understand.

Social stories and scripts are narrative tools that can help individuals with ASD navigate social situations and understand social norms and expectations. Social stories provide a step-by-step guide to specific social situations, while scripts provide pre-determined responses or phrases for common social interactions.

Using clear and concise language is important when communicating with individuals with ASD. It involves using simple and concrete language, avoiding figurative language or idioms, and providing visual supports when necessary. By using clear and concise language, individuals with ASD can better understand and respond to communication.

Teaching Self-Advocacy Skills to Individuals with Autism

Teaching self-advocacy skills to individuals with ASD is crucial for their independence and self-determination. It involves teaching self-determination and decision-making skills, encouraging self-expression and self-awareness, and supporting self-advocacy in the community.

Self-advocacy refers to the ability to speak up for oneself, make decisions, and advocate for one's own needs and rights. Teaching self-determination skills involves helping individuals with ASD identify their strengths, interests, and goals, and develop the skills necessary to make informed decisions.

Encouraging self-expression and self-awareness involves providing opportunities for individuals with ASD to express their thoughts, feelings, and preferences. This can be done through various means such as art therapy, journaling, or role-playing. By encouraging self-expression and self-awareness, individuals with ASD can develop a sense of identity and agency.

Supporting self-advocacy in the community involves providing individuals with ASD with the necessary skills and resources to advocate for themselves in various settings. This can include teaching them how to communicate their needs effectively, educating them about their rights and protections, and connecting them with support networks or organizations.

Supporting Social Skills Development for Individuals with Autism

Supporting social skills development is crucial for individuals with ASD to navigate social interactions and build meaningful relationships. Some strategies for supporting social skills development include social skills training and coaching, peer-mediated interventions, social stories and role-playing, and community-based instruction and practice.

Social skills training and coaching involve teaching individuals with ASD specific social skills through structured lessons and practice. This can include teaching them how to initiate conversations, take turns, or interpret nonverbal cues. By providing explicit instruction and opportunities for practice, individuals with ASD can develop their social skills.

Peer-mediated interventions involve pairing individuals with ASD with neurotypical peers who can serve as social mentors or coaches. This allows individuals with ASD to learn from their peers and receive feedback and support in real-life social situations. Peer-mediated interventions can be implemented in various settings such as schools or community programs.

Social stories and role-playing are effective tools for teaching individuals with ASD appropriate social behaviors and responses. Social stories provide a narrative description of a specific social situation, while role-playing allows individuals to practice and rehearse appropriate behaviors. By using social stories and role-playing, individuals with ASD can develop their social skills in a safe and structured environment.

Community-based instruction and practice involve providing individuals with ASD with opportunities to practice their social skills in real-life settings. This can include community outings, volunteer work, or job training programs. By practicing their social skills in authentic contexts, individuals with ASD can generalize their skills to different situations.

Addressing Sensory Needs of Individuals with Autism

Addressing the sensory needs of individuals with ASD is crucial for their comfort and well-being. Some strategies for addressing sensory needs include sensory integration therapy, environmental modifications, sensory diets and routines, and collaborative problem-solving.

Sensory integration therapy is a therapeutic approach that aims to help individuals with ASD regulate their sensory responses. It involves engaging in activities that provide sensory input, such as swinging, jumping, or playing with textured materials. Sensory integration therapy can help individuals with ASD better process and respond to sensory stimuli.

Environmental modifications involve making changes to the physical environment to accommodate the sensory needs of individuals with ASD. This can include reducing noise levels, providing visual supports, or creating designated quiet spaces. By modifying the environment, individuals with ASD can feel more comfortable and better able to focus and engage.

Sensory diets and routines involve providing individuals with ASD with a structured schedule of sensory activities throughout the day. This can include activities that provide sensory input, such as deep pressure or movement breaks. By incorporating sensory activities into their daily routines, individuals with ASD can regulate their sensory responses and maintain optimal arousal levels.

Collaborative problem-solving involves working together with individuals with ASD to identify their specific sensory needs and develop strategies to address them. This can involve using visual supports to communicate preferences, providing choices for sensory activities, or implementing individualized accommodations. By involving individuals with ASD in the problem-solving process, their unique needs can be effectively addressed.

The Benefits of Inclusion for Neurotypical Peers

Inclusion not only benefits individuals with ASD but also has positive effects on their neurotypical peers. Some benefits of inclusion for neurotypical peers include increased empathy and understanding, improved social skills and relationships, enhanced academic and cognitive outcomes, and a positive impact on school culture and climate.

Inclusion provides neurotypical peers with opportunities to interact and build relationships with individuals with ASD. This exposure fosters empathy and understanding, as neurotypical peers learn about the unique challenges and strengths of individuals with ASD. It also promotes acceptance and reduces stigma surrounding disabilities.

Interacting with individuals with ASD can also improve neurotypical peers' social skills and relationships. It provides opportunities for them to practice patience, tolerance, and effective communication. It also encourages the development of inclusive attitudes and behaviors, which can benefit their relationships with individuals from diverse backgrounds.

Inclusive classrooms have been shown to have positive effects on academic and cognitive outcomes for neurotypical peers. Research has found that inclusive classrooms promote higher levels of engagement, motivation, and academic achievement. This is attributed to the diverse perspectives and learning styles present in inclusive classrooms.

Inclusive environments also have a positive impact on school culture and climate. They promote a sense of belonging and acceptance among all students, fostering a positive and supportive learning environment. Inclusive schools are more likely to have lower rates of bullying and higher levels of student satisfaction.

Advocating for Inclusion: How You Can Make a Difference

Advocating for inclusion is crucial for promoting the rights and well-being of individuals with ASD. There are several ways in which individuals can make a difference, including educating others about ASD and inclusion, advocating for policy and legislative changes, supporting inclusive practices in schools and communities, and volunteering and supporting organizations that promote inclusion.

Educating others about ASD and inclusion is an important first step in promoting understanding and acceptance. This can be done through sharing personal experiences, organizing awareness campaigns or events, or providing resources and information to others. By educating others, individuals can help dispel myths and misconceptions surrounding ASD.

Advocating for policy and legislative changes is another effective way to promote inclusion. This can involve contacting elected officials, participating in advocacy groups or organizations, or supporting initiatives that promote the rights of individuals with disabilities. By advocating for policy changes, individuals can help create a more inclusive society by pushing for laws and regulations that protect the rights and ensure the equal opportunities of individuals with disabilities. This can include advocating for accessible infrastructure, inclusive education, employment opportunities, healthcare access, and social inclusion. By actively engaging in policy advocacy, individuals can contribute to dismantling barriers and promoting a society that values and includes people of all abilities.

Chapter 6: Power of Cognitive Empathy: Understanding Others\' Perspectives

Cognitive empathy is a crucial skill that allows individuals to understand and relate to the thoughts, feelings, and perspectives of others. It involves the ability to put oneself in someone else's shoes and see the world from their point of view. This skill is essential for building strong relationships, improving communication, and resolving conflicts. In today's interconnected world, where understanding and empathy are more important than ever, developing cognitive empathy is crucial.

What is cognitive empathy and why is it important?

Cognitive empathy refers to the ability to understand and comprehend the emotions, thoughts, and perspectives of others. It involves being able to imagine oneself in another person's situation and understand how they might be feeling or thinking. This skill allows individuals to connect with others on a deeper level and build stronger relationships.

Cognitive empathy is important because it helps us understand others better and fosters a sense of compassion and understanding. When we can put ourselves in someone else's shoes, we are more likely to treat them with kindness and respect. It also allows us to navigate social situations more effectively by understanding the needs and desires of those around us.

The difference between cognitive empathy and emotional empathy

While cognitive empathy involves understanding someone else's perspective, emotional empathy involves actually feeling the emotions that another person is experiencing. Emotional empathy is often described as "feeling with" someone, whereas cognitive empathy is more about understanding their experience.

While both types of empathy are important, cognitive empathy can be particularly useful in situations where emotional empathy may not be appropriate or helpful. For example, in a professional setting, it may be more beneficial to understand someone's perspective without becoming overwhelmed by their emotions.

How to develop cognitive empathy skills

Developing cognitive empathy skills takes practice and effort, but it is a skill that can be learned and improved upon over time. Here are some tips for developing cognitive empathy:

1. Active listening: Pay attention to what others are saying and make an effort to truly understand their perspective. Avoid interrupting or jumping to conclusions.

2. Perspective-taking: Try to imagine yourself in someone else's situation and consider how you would feel or think in that situation. This can help you better understand their perspective.

3. Ask open-ended questions: Instead of assuming you know what someone is thinking or feeling, ask them open-ended questions to encourage them to share more about their perspective.

4. Practice empathy in everyday interactions: Look for opportunities to practice empathy in your daily life, whether it's with friends, family, or colleagues. The more you practice, the better you will become at understanding others.

The benefits of understanding others' perspectives

Understanding others' perspectives has numerous benefits, both personally and professionally. Here are some of the key benefits:

1. Improved communication and relationships: When we understand where someone is coming from, we can communicate more effectively and build stronger relationships. This leads to better collaboration and teamwork.

2. Reduced conflicts and misunderstandings: By understanding others' perspectives, we can avoid misunderstandings and conflicts that arise from miscommunication or lack of understanding.

3. Increased empathy and compassion: Understanding others' perspectives helps us develop a greater sense of empathy and compassion towards others. This can lead to a more caring and inclusive society.

The role of cognitive empathy in building stronger relationships

Cognitive empathy plays a crucial role in building stronger relationships by fostering understanding and connection. When we can understand someone else's perspective, we are better able to relate to them and build trust.

Empathy is the foundation of any healthy relationship, whether it's a romantic partnership, a friendship, or a professional relationship. When we can understand and empathize with someone else's experiences, we are more likely to treat them with kindness, respect, and understanding.

For example, imagine a couple who is going through a difficult time. If one partner can understand and empathize with the other's perspective, they are more likely to be supportive and understanding, which can help strengthen their relationship.

How cognitive empathy can improve communication

Cognitive empathy is closely linked to effective communication. When we can understand someone else's perspective, we are better able to communicate in a way that is clear and respectful.

By actively listening and trying to understand someone else's point of view, we can avoid misunderstandings and miscommunications. This leads to more productive conversations and better outcomes.

For example, in a workplace setting, if a manager can understand the perspective of their employees, they are more likely to communicate in a way that is clear and respectful. This can lead to better teamwork, increased productivity, and a more positive work environment.

The impact of cognitive empathy on conflict resolution

Cognitive empathy plays a crucial role in conflict resolution by helping us understand the perspectives of all parties involved. When we can understand where someone else is coming from, we are better able to find common ground and work towards a resolution.

By actively listening and trying to understand the underlying needs and desires of all parties involved, we can find solutions that are mutually beneficial. This leads to more effective conflict resolution and stronger relationships.

For example, imagine a disagreement between two colleagues at work. If both parties can understand each other's perspectives and actively listen to one another, they are more likely to find a resolution that satisfies both of their needs.

Cognitive empathy and workplace success

Cognitive empathy is increasingly recognized as an important skill for success in the workplace. Employers value employees who can understand and relate to the perspectives of others, as it leads to better teamwork, collaboration, and problem-solving.

By understanding the needs and desires of colleagues, employees can work together more effectively towards common goals. This leads to increased productivity, improved morale, and a more positive work environment.

For example, a manager who can understand the perspectives of their team members is more likely to be able to delegate tasks effectively, provide support and guidance, and create a positive work environment.

Overcoming biases through cognitive empathy

Cognitive empathy can help us overcome biases by allowing us to see beyond our own preconceived notions and understand the perspectives of others. By actively listening and trying to understand someone else's point of view, we can challenge our own biases and develop a more open-minded perspective.

By understanding others' perspectives, we can recognize the common humanity that we all share and develop a greater sense of empathy and compassion. This can help break down barriers and foster a more inclusive society.

For example, imagine someone who holds biased views towards a certain group of people. If they can actively listen to the experiences and perspectives of individuals from that group, they may begin to challenge their own biases and develop a more empathetic perspective.

The role of cognitive empathy in leadership

Cognitive empathy is a crucial skill for effective leadership. Leaders who can understand and relate to the perspectives of their team members are better able to inspire, motivate, and guide them towards achieving common goals.

By understanding the needs and desires of their team members, leaders can create a positive work environment that fosters collaboration, creativity, and innovation. This leads to increased productivity and success.

For example, a leader who can understand the perspectives of their team members is more likely to be able to provide support and guidance that is tailored to their individual needs. This leads to increased job satisfaction, higher employee retention rates, and better overall performance.

The future of cognitive empathy in society

Cognitive empathy has the potential to play a transformative role in society. As our world becomes increasingly interconnected, understanding and empathy are more important than ever.

By developing cognitive empathy skills, individuals can contribute to creating a more empathetic society where people understand and respect the perspectives of others. This can lead to greater social cohesion, reduced conflicts, and a more inclusive and equitable society.

Cognitive empathy can also be used to address societal issues such as discrimination, inequality, and social injustice. By actively listening to the experiences and perspectives of marginalized groups, we can work towards creating a more just and equitable society for all.

In conclusion, cognitive empathy is a crucial skill that allows individuals to understand and relate to the thoughts, feelings, and perspectives of others. It is important for building strong relationships, improving communication, resolving conflicts, and creating a more empathetic society.

By actively listening, practicing perspective-taking, and developing a greater sense of empathy and compassion, individuals can improve their cognitive empathy skills. This will not only benefit their personal relationships but also their professional success and their ability to contribute to a more inclusive and equitable society.

It is important for individuals to recognize the importance of cognitive empathy and make a conscious effort to develop this skill. By doing so, we can create a world where understanding and empathy are valued and celebrated.

Chapter 7: Navigating Life as a Neurodivergent Person: Tips for Self-Care and Success

Neurodiversity is a concept that emphasizes the importance of understanding and accepting the wide range of neurological differences that exist in the human population. It recognizes that neurodivergent individuals, who have conditions such as autism, ADHD, and dyslexia, have unique strengths and perspectives that should be celebrated and valued. In this blog post, we will explore the concept of neurodiversity in depth, discussing what it means to be neurodivergent, the challenges faced by neurodivergent individuals, self-care strategies, building a support network, advocating for oneself, finding strengths in neurodivergent traits, coping with sensory overload, navigating the workplace, managing anxiety and depression, cultivating resilience, and celebrating neurodiversity.

Understanding Neurodiversity: What It Means to be Neurodivergent

Neurodivergent individuals are those whose neurological development and functioning differ from what is considered typical or "neurotypical." This includes conditions such as autism spectrum disorder (ASD), attention deficit hyperactivity disorder (ADHD), dyslexia, and many others. Being neurodivergent means having a brain that processes information and experiences the world in a unique way.

It is important to recognize and accept neurodiversity because it challenges the notion that there is a single "normal" or "correct" way of thinking and being. Neurodivergent individuals have valuable perspectives and strengths that can contribute to society in meaningful ways. By embracing neurodiversity, we can create a more inclusive and understanding world.

Common Challenges Faced by Neurodivergent Individuals

Neurodivergent individuals often face unique challenges that can impact their daily lives. These challenges can vary depending on the specific condition and individual experiences, but some common difficulties include social difficulties, sensory overload, and executive dysfunction.

Social difficulties can manifest as struggles with communication, understanding social cues, and forming and maintaining relationships. Neurodivergent individuals may find it challenging to navigate social situations and may feel isolated or misunderstood.

Sensory overload is another common challenge. Many neurodivergent individuals have heightened sensitivity to sensory stimuli, such as loud noises, bright lights, or certain textures. This can lead to feelings of overwhelm and discomfort in environments that are not sensory-friendly.

Executive dysfunction refers to difficulties with planning, organizing, and completing tasks. Neurodivergent individuals may struggle with time management, prioritization, and staying focused on a task. This can make it challenging to meet deadlines and fulfill responsibilities.

Self-Care Strategies for Neurodivergent People

Self-care is crucial for neurodivergent individuals to maintain their well-being and manage the challenges they face. It involves taking intentional steps to prioritize one's physical, emotional, and mental health. Some self-care strategies that can be helpful for neurodivergent individuals include:

1. Sensory breaks: Taking regular breaks in a quiet and calm environment can help reduce sensory overload and provide a sense of relief.

2. Establishing routines: Creating predictable routines and sticking to them can provide a sense of stability and reduce anxiety.

3. Mindfulness practices: Engaging in mindfulness activities, such as deep breathing exercises or meditation, can help calm the mind and reduce stress.

4. Engaging in hobbies and interests: Pursuing activities that bring joy and fulfillment can be a form of self-care. Whether it's painting, playing an instrument, or gardening, engaging in hobbies can provide a sense of purpose and relaxation.

Building a Support Network: The Importance of Community

Having a strong support network is crucial for neurodivergent individuals. A support network can provide understanding, validation, and practical assistance when needed. It can consist of family members, friends, support groups, therapists, or other individuals who share similar experiences.

Community is important for neurodivergent individuals because it provides a sense of belonging and reduces feelings of isolation. It allows individuals to connect with others who understand their unique challenges and can offer support and guidance. Being part of a community also provides opportunities for social interaction and the development of meaningful relationships.

Support networks can offer practical assistance, such as helping with daily tasks, providing transportation, or offering guidance on navigating systems and accessing resources. They can also provide emotional support, offering a safe space to share experiences, express emotions, and receive validation.

Advocating for Yourself: Tips for Communicating Your Needs

Self-advocacy is an essential skill for neurodivergent individuals to develop. It involves effectively communicating one's needs, preferences, and boundaries to others. Here are some tips for advocating for yourself:

1. Use "I" statements: When expressing your needs or concerns, use "I" statements to clearly communicate your perspective and feelings. For example, instead of saying, "You never listen to me," say, "I feel unheard when..."

2. Be specific: Clearly articulate what you need or want from others. Avoid vague statements and provide concrete examples or suggestions.

3. Educate others: Help others understand your condition by providing information and resources. This can help dispel misconceptions and foster empathy and understanding.

4. Practice active listening: When engaging in conversations about your needs, actively listen to the other person's perspective and validate their feelings. This can help create a more collaborative and understanding environment.

Finding Your Strengths: Embracing Neurodivergent Traits

Neurodivergent traits can be seen as strengths rather than weaknesses. Many neurodivergent individuals possess unique qualities that can contribute to their success in various areas of life. Some examples of strengths include:

1. Attention to detail: Many neurodivergent individuals have a keen eye for detail and can spot patterns or inconsistencies that others may miss. This attention to detail can be valuable in fields such as research, design, or quality control.

2. Creativity: Neurodivergent individuals often have a rich imagination and can think outside the box. This creativity can lead to innovative ideas and solutions in fields such as art, writing, or problem-solving.

3. Hyperfocus: Some neurodivergent individuals have the ability to hyperfocus on tasks that interest them. This intense focus can lead to high levels of productivity and expertise in specific areas.

4. Empathy: Many neurodivergent individuals possess a deep sense of empathy and compassion for others. This empathy can foster strong connections with others and make them effective advocates for social justice and equality.

Coping with Sensory Overload: Practical Solutions for Daily Life

Sensory overload can be overwhelming and distressing for neurodivergent individuals. It occurs when the brain receives more sensory information than it can process, leading to feelings of overwhelm, anxiety, or discomfort. Here are some practical solutions for coping with sensory overload:

1. Create a sensory-friendly environment: Make adjustments to your environment to reduce sensory stimuli that trigger overload. This can include using noise-cancelling headphones, dimming lights, or using fidget toys to redirect sensory input.

2. Take breaks: When experiencing sensory overload, take breaks in a quiet and calm space to allow your nervous system to reset.

3. Use grounding techniques: Grounding techniques involve focusing on the present moment and your physical sensations to help calm the mind and body. Examples include deep breathing exercises, progressive muscle relaxation, or using weighted blankets.

4. Plan ahead: When possible, plan activities or outings in advance to minimize surprises or unexpected sensory triggers. Knowing what to expect can help reduce anxiety and prepare for potential challenges.

Navigating the Workplace: Accommodations and Disclosure

Navigating the workplace can present unique challenges for neurodivergent individuals. However, there are accommodations and strategies that can help create a more inclusive and supportive work environment. It is important to consider the pros and cons of disclosing one's neurodivergent condition to employers.

Pros of disclosing include:

1. Access to accommodations: Disclosing your condition can allow you to access workplace accommodations that can help you perform your job more effectively. This can include adjustments to your workspace, flexible scheduling, or additional support.

2. Increased understanding: Disclosing your condition can help educate your colleagues and supervisors about neurodiversity, fostering a more inclusive and understanding work environment.

Cons of disclosing include:

1. Stigma and discrimination: Unfortunately, there is still stigma and discrimination surrounding neurodivergent conditions in some workplaces. Disclosing your condition may lead to negative stereotypes or biases that could impact your career opportunities or relationships with colleagues.

2. Privacy concerns: Some individuals may prefer to keep their neurodivergent condition private for personal reasons. It is important to respect an individual's decision regarding disclosure and prioritize their comfort and well-being.

Managing Anxiety and Depression: Tools for Mental Health

Anxiety and depression are common mental health challenges experienced by many neurodivergent individuals. These conditions can be influenced by the unique challenges faced by neurodivergent individuals, such as social difficulties, sensory overload, or executive dysfunction. It is important to prioritize mental health and seek appropriate support when needed.

Some tools for managing anxiety and depression include:

1. Therapy: Working with a therapist who specializes in neurodiversity can provide valuable support and guidance in managing anxiety and depression. Therapists can help develop coping strategies, provide a safe space for processing emotions, and offer tools for self-care.

2. Medication: In some cases, medication may be prescribed to help manage symptoms of anxiety or depression. It is important

to work with a healthcare professional to determine the most appropriate treatment plan.

3. Support groups: Joining a support group specifically for neurodivergent individuals can provide a sense of community and understanding. It can be helpful to connect with others who share similar experiences and can offer support and guidance.

4. Self-care practices: Engaging in self-care activities, such as exercise, mindfulness, or engaging in hobbies, can help manage symptoms of anxiety and depression. It is important to prioritize self-care and find activities that bring joy and relaxation.

Cultivating Resilience: Overcoming Obstacles and Building Confidence

Resilience is an important trait for neurodivergent individuals to cultivate. It involves the ability to bounce back from challenges, adapt to change, and maintain a positive outlook. Cultivating resilience can help overcome obstacles and build confidence. Some strategies for cultivating resilience include:

1. Reframing negative thoughts: Practice challenging negative thoughts and replacing them with more positive or realistic ones. This can help shift perspective and build resilience in the face of adversity.

2. Practicing self-compassion: Be kind and gentle with yourself when facing challenges or setbacks. Treat yourself with the same compassion and understanding you would offer to a friend.

3. Seeking support: Reach out to your support network when facing challenges or feeling overwhelmed. Sharing your experiences and seeking guidance from others can help build resilience.

4. Setting realistic goals: Break down larger goals into smaller, achievable steps. Celebrate each small success along the way, building confidence and motivation.

Celebrating Neurodiversity: The Benefits of a Diverse World

Neurodiversity benefits society as a whole by bringing unique perspectives, skills, and talents to the table. Embracing neurodiversity fosters innovation, creativity, and inclusivity in various fields. By celebrating neurodiversity, we can create a more equitable and understanding world.

Neurodivergent individuals have made significant contributions in fields such as science, technology, art, and advocacy. Their unique perspectives and ways of thinking have led to groundbreaking discoveries and advancements. By embracing neurodiversity, we can tap into the full potential of all individuals and create a society that values and celebrates diversity.

Understanding and embracing neurodiversity is crucial for creating an inclusive and accepting society. Neurodivergent individuals have unique strengths and perspectives that should be celebrated and valued. By recognizing the challenges they face, providing support and accommodations, and fostering a sense of community, we can create a world that embraces neurodiversity and supports the well-being of all individuals. Let us strive to be more understanding, compassionate, and inclusive in our interactions with neurodivergent individuals, and work towards a future where everyone feels valued and accepted.

Chapter 8: From Procrastination to Productivity: How Behavioral Interventions Can Help You Achieve Your Goals

Procrastination is a common phenomenon that affects individuals across all walks of life. It is the act of delaying or postponing tasks or actions, often to the point of causing unnecessary stress and negative consequences. Procrastination can manifest in various ways, such as putting off important work assignments, avoiding household chores, or delaying personal goals and aspirations.

The prevalence of procrastination in society is significant. Research suggests that approximately 20% of adults identify themselves as chronic procrastinators, while up to 70% of individuals experience procrastination to some degree. This widespread issue can have detrimental effects on individuals' mental health, productivity, and overall well-being.

Addressing procrastination is crucial because it can hinder personal growth, limit opportunities, and lead to increased stress and anxiety. By understanding the underlying causes of procrastination and implementing effective strategies to overcome it, individuals can improve their productivity, achieve their goals, and lead more fulfilling lives.

The Science of Procrastination: Why We Delay Tasks

From an evolutionary perspective, procrastination can be seen as a survival mechanism. Our ancestors were more likely to prioritize immediate needs, such as finding food and shelter, over long-term goals. This tendency to prioritize short-term gratification over long-term benefits has been ingrained in our brains over time.

Psychological factors also contribute to procrastination. Fear of failure or success, perfectionism, low self-esteem, and lack of motivation are common psychological barriers that can lead to procrastination. Additionally, individuals may engage in procrastination as a form of self-sabotage or a way to avoid uncomfortable emotions associated with the task at hand.

Brain chemistry plays a role in procrastination as well. The prefrontal cortex, responsible for executive functions such as decision-making and impulse control, may be less active in chronic procrastinators. This can lead to difficulties in initiating and sustaining tasks, as well as poor time management skills.

Consequences of Procrastination: How It Affects Our Lives

Procrastination can have significant negative impacts on mental health. Chronic procrastinators often experience increased levels of stress, anxiety, and depression. The constant pressure of impending deadlines and the guilt associated with not completing tasks can take a toll on one's well-being. Moreover, the cycle of procrastination can lead to a decreased sense of self-worth and a lack of confidence in one's abilities.

In terms of productivity and performance, procrastination can be detrimental. Delaying tasks often leads to rushed and subpar work, as individuals are forced to complete assignments under time constraints. This can result in lower quality outcomes and missed opportunities for growth and advancement. Additionally, procrastination can lead to a backlog of unfinished tasks, causing individuals to feel overwhelmed and further perpetuating the cycle of procrastination.

Procrastination can also strain relationships and hinder personal development. When individuals consistently fail to meet their commitments or follow through on promises, it can erode trust and create tension in personal and professional relationships. Furthermore, procrastination can prevent individuals from pursuing their passions and achieving their goals, leading to a sense of unfulfillment and regret.

Behavioral Interventions: An Effective Way to Overcome Procrastination

Behavioral interventions are strategies and techniques that aim to modify behavior patterns and promote positive change. They have been proven effective in addressing procrastination by targeting the underlying causes and providing individuals with practical tools to overcome it.

One of the key benefits of using behavioral interventions is that they focus on changing behavior rather than solely relying on willpower or motivation. By implementing specific techniques and strategies, individuals can develop new habits and routines that promote productivity and goal achievement.

There are various examples of behavioral interventions that can help individuals overcome procrastination. These include setting goals, breaking down tasks, managing time effectively, using positive reinforcement, engaging in cognitive restructuring, and establishing accountability measures. By combining these interventions and tailoring them to individual needs and preferences, individuals can create a comprehensive approach to address their procrastination tendencies.

Goal Setting: The First Step Towards Productivity

Setting goals is an essential component of overcoming procrastination. Goals provide individuals with a clear direction and purpose, helping them prioritize tasks and allocate their time and energy effectively. Without clear goals, individuals may feel overwhelmed or unsure of where to start, leading to procrastination.

The SMART goal-setting framework is a useful tool for setting achievable goals. SMART stands for Specific, Measurable, Attainable, Relevant, and Time-bound. Specific goals are clear and well-defined, while measurable goals can be tracked and evaluated. Attainable goals are realistic and within reach, while relevant goals align with one's values and aspirations. Lastly, time-bound goals have a specific deadline or timeframe attached to them.

When setting goals, it is important to consider the individual's strengths, limitations, and priorities. By setting realistic and meaningful goals, individuals can increase their motivation and commitment to completing tasks in a timely manner.

Breaking Down Tasks: How to Make Them More Manageable

Breaking down tasks into smaller, more manageable steps is an effective strategy for overcoming procrastination. Large or complex tasks can often feel overwhelming, leading individuals to avoid or delay them. By breaking tasks down into smaller components, individuals can reduce feelings of overwhelm and increase their sense of progress and accomplishment.

There are various techniques for breaking down tasks. One approach is to create a task list or checklist that outlines all the necessary steps required to complete a task. This allows individuals to visualize the process and track their progress as they complete each step. Another technique is to use the Pomodoro Technique, which involves breaking work into 25-minute intervals with short breaks in between. This helps individuals stay focused and motivated while also providing regular opportunities for rest and rejuvenation.

By breaking down tasks, individuals can approach their work in a more systematic and organized manner, reducing the likelihood of procrastination and increasing productivity.

Time Management Techniques: Strategies to Maximize Your Time

Effective time management is crucial for overcoming procrastination. By managing time wisely, individuals can prioritize tasks, allocate resources efficiently, and create a structured routine that promotes productivity.

There are various techniques for managing time effectively. One popular approach is the Eisenhower Matrix, which involves categorizing tasks into four quadrants based on their urgency and importance. This helps individuals identify which tasks require immediate attention and which can be delegated or eliminated.

Another technique is the Pomodoro Technique, mentioned earlier in the context of task breakdown. By working in focused intervals with scheduled breaks, individuals can optimize their productivity while also preventing burnout.

Additionally, creating a daily or weekly schedule can help individuals allocate their time effectively and ensure that important tasks are given priority. By setting aside dedicated time blocks for specific activities, individuals can reduce the likelihood of procrastination and increase their overall efficiency.

Chapter 9: The Power of Positive Reinforcement: Rewarding Yourself for Accomplishments

Positive reinforcement is a powerful tool for overcoming procrastination. By rewarding oneself for completing tasks or achieving milestones, individuals can increase their motivation and reinforce positive behaviors.

Positive reinforcement can take various forms, depending on individual preferences and interests. It could be as simple as taking a short break to engage in a favorite hobby or treating oneself to a small indulgence. The key is to choose rewards that are meaningful and enjoyable, as this will increase motivation and make the process of completing tasks more enjoyable.

Examples of positive reinforcement include going for a walk in nature after completing a challenging work assignment, treating oneself to a favorite meal after finishing household chores, or taking a day off to relax after accomplishing a long-term goal. By incorporating positive reinforcement into one's routine, individuals can create a positive association with completing tasks and reduce the likelihood of procrastination.

Cognitive Restructuring: Changing Your Thoughts to Change Your Behavior

Cognitive restructuring is a technique that involves identifying and challenging negative or unhelpful thoughts and replacing them with more positive and constructive ones. By changing one's thoughts, individuals can change their behavior and overcome procrastination.

The first step in cognitive restructuring is to become aware of negative thoughts or beliefs that contribute to procrastination. These may include thoughts such as "I'm not good enough," "I'll never finish this on time," or "It's too overwhelming." Once these thoughts are identified, individuals can challenge them by examining the evidence for and against them. This helps to create a more balanced and realistic perspective.

After challenging negative thoughts, individuals can replace them with more positive and empowering ones. For example, instead of thinking "I'll never finish this on time," one could reframe it as "I have successfully completed similar tasks in the past, and I have the skills and resources to do it again."

By engaging in cognitive restructuring, individuals can shift their mindset from one of self-doubt and negativity to one of confidence and optimism. This can significantly reduce the likelihood of procrastination and increase motivation and productivity.

Accountability: How to Stay on Track with Your Goals

Accountability is a powerful tool for overcoming procrastination. By establishing external sources of accountability, individuals can increase their commitment to completing tasks and reduce the likelihood of procrastination.

There are various techniques for establishing accountability. One approach is to find an accountability partner or join a support group where individuals can share their goals, progress, and challenges. This provides a sense of community and support, as well as an opportunity for feedback and encouragement.

Another technique is to publicly commit to one's goals by sharing them with friends, family, or colleagues. By making one's goals known to others, individuals create a sense of social pressure and accountability, increasing their motivation to follow through.

Additionally, using technology tools such as productivity apps or habit trackers can help individuals stay accountable to their goals. These tools provide reminders, progress tracking, and visual representations of one's achievements, making it easier to stay on track and avoid procrastination.

Moving Forward with Behavioral Interventions

In conclusion, procrastination is a common problem that affects individuals in various aspects of their lives. By understanding the underlying causes of procrastination and implementing effective behavioral interventions, individuals can overcome this challenge and achieve their goals.

Behavioral interventions such as goal setting, task breakdown, time management, positive reinforcement, cognitive restructuring, and accountability can all contribute to overcoming procrastination. By combining these strategies and tailoring them to individual needs and preferences, individuals can create a comprehensive approach to address their procrastination tendencies.

Moving forward with behavioral interventions requires commitment, consistency, and self-reflection. It is important to recognize that overcoming procrastination is a journey that may involve setbacks and challenges along the way. However, by persevering and implementing these strategies consistently, individuals can break free from the cycle of procrastination and unlock their full potential.

Chapter 9: Breaking Down the Myths and Misconceptions of Neurodevelopmental Disorders

Neurodevelopmental disorders are a group of conditions that affect the development of the brain and nervous system. These disorders typically manifest in early childhood and can have a significant impact on an individual's cognitive, social, and emotional functioning. Examples of neurodevelopmental disorders include autism spectrum disorder (ASD), attention deficit hyperactivity disorder (ADHD), intellectual disability, and specific learning disorders.

Myth: Neurodevelopmental Disorders are caused by bad parenting

One common myth surrounding neurodevelopmental disorders is that they are caused by bad parenting. This myth suggests that if parents were more attentive or disciplined their children better, these disorders would not exist. However, this belief is not supported by scientific evidence.

Research has consistently shown that neurodevelopmental disorders have a strong genetic component. Studies have identified specific genes and genetic variations that are associated with an increased risk of developing these disorders. Additionally, neurodevelopmental disorders are often diagnosed in multiple members of the same family, further supporting the role of genetics.

Blaming parents for their child's neurodevelopmental disorder can lead to feelings of guilt and shame. It is important to recognize that these disorders are not caused by parenting style or behavior, but rather by complex interactions between genetic and environmental factors.

Myth: Neurodevelopmental Disorders are a result of poor nutrition

Another myth surrounding neurodevelopmental disorders is that they are a result of poor nutrition. This belief suggests that if individuals with these disorders had a better diet, their symptoms would improve or even disappear. However, there is no scientific evidence to support this claim.

While nutrition plays an important role in overall health and well-being, it does not directly cause or cure neurodevelopmental disorders. These disorders are primarily influenced by genetic and neurological factors. While a balanced diet can support overall brain health, it is not a cure for neurodevelopmental disorders.

It is important to approach the treatment of neurodevelopmental disorders with evidence-based interventions, such as therapy and medication, rather than relying solely on dietary changes.

Misconception: Neurodevelopmental Disorders are just a phase

A common misconception about neurodevelopmental disorders is that they are just a phase that individuals will eventually grow out of. This misconception can lead to delayed diagnosis and intervention, which can have long-term negative effects on individuals with these disorders.

Neurodevelopmental disorders are lifelong conditions that require ongoing support and management. While symptoms may change or improve over time, the underlying neurological differences that contribute to these disorders persist into adulthood.

Early intervention is crucial for individuals with neurodevelopmental disorders. Research has shown that early diagnosis and appropriate interventions can significantly improve outcomes and quality of life for individuals with these disorders.

Misconception: Neurodevelopmental Disorders only affect children

Another misconception about neurodevelopmental disorders is that they only affect children. While it is true that many neurodevelopmental disorders are diagnosed in childhood, they can continue to impact individuals throughout their lives.

For example, individuals with ADHD may struggle with executive functioning skills, such as organization and time management, well into adulthood. Similarly, individuals with autism spectrum disorder may experience challenges with social communication and sensory processing throughout their lives.

Recognizing and addressing neurodevelopmental disorders in adults is crucial for promoting their overall well-being and success. By providing appropriate support and accommodations, individuals with these disorders can thrive in various aspects of their lives, including education, employment, and relationships.

Myth: Neurodevelopmental Disorders can be cured

One myth surrounding neurodevelopmental disorders is that they can be cured. This belief suggests that if individuals receive the right treatment or therapy, their symptoms will completely disappear. However, neurodevelopmental disorders are lifelong conditions that cannot be cured.

While there is no cure for these disorders, there are evidence-based interventions and treatments that can help manage symptoms and improve quality of life. For example, behavioral therapy and medication can be effective in reducing the impact of symptoms associated with ADHD or autism spectrum disorder.

It is important to approach the treatment of neurodevelopmental disorders with realistic expectations. Instead of focusing on a cure, the goal should be to provide individuals with the tools and support they need to navigate their daily lives and reach their full potential.

Misconception: Neurodevelopmental Disorders are a sign of low intelligence

A common misconception about neurodevelopmental disorders is that they are a sign of low intelligence. This misconception stems from a misunderstanding of the cognitive differences associated with these disorders.

While individuals with neurodevelopmental disorders may have challenges in certain areas, such as social communication or executive functioning, it does not mean that they are less intelligent. In fact, many individuals with these disorders have unique strengths and abilities in areas such as visual thinking, problem-solving, or creativity.

It is important to recognize and celebrate the diverse talents and abilities of individuals with neurodevelopmental disorders. By focusing on their strengths and providing appropriate support, we can help them thrive and contribute to society in meaningful ways.

Myth: Neurodevelopmental Disorders are overdiagnosed

One myth surrounding neurodevelopmental disorders is that they are overdiagnosed. This belief suggests that these disorders are being diagnosed too frequently, leading to unnecessary labels and interventions. However, there is no evidence to support this claim.

In fact, research suggests that neurodevelopmental disorders are often underdiagnosed and undertreated. Many individuals with these disorders go undiagnosed until adulthood, leading to missed opportunities for early intervention and support.

Accurate diagnosis is crucial for individuals with neurodevelopmental disorders to access appropriate resources and interventions. By recognizing and addressing these disorders early on, we can provide individuals with the support they need to thrive.

Misconception: Neurodevelopmental Disorders are just an excuse for bad behavior

Another misconception about neurodevelopmental disorders is that they are just an excuse for bad behavior. This misconception stems from a lack of understanding of the underlying causes of behavior in individuals with these disorders.

Neurodevelopmental disorders can impact an individual's ability to regulate their emotions, control impulses, and understand social cues. This can result in behaviors that may be perceived as challenging or disruptive.

It is important to approach these behaviors with empathy and understanding, rather than judgment or blame. By recognizing the underlying causes of behavior and providing appropriate support and interventions, we can help individuals with neurodevelopmental disorders develop strategies to manage their behavior effectively.

Myth: Neurodevelopmental Disorders are not real

One of the most harmful myths surrounding neurodevelopmental disorders is that they are not real. This belief suggests that these disorders are simply made up or exaggerated, leading to stigma and discrimination against individuals with these conditions.

Neurodevelopmental disorders are recognized by reputable medical and psychiatric organizations, such as the American Psychiatric Association and the World Health Organization. These organizations have established diagnostic criteria and guidelines for the assessment and treatment of these disorders.

Furthermore, there is a wealth of scientific research that supports the existence and impact of neurodevelopmental disorders. Neuroimaging studies have shown differences in brain structure and function in individuals with these disorders, further validating their biological basis.

It is crucial to recognize the validity of neurodevelopmental disorders and to promote acceptance and support for individuals with these conditions.

Understanding and Accepting Neurodevelopmental Disorders

In conclusion, neurodevelopmental disorders are complex conditions that have a significant impact on individuals' lives. It is important to dispel myths and misconceptions surrounding these disorders in order to promote understanding, acceptance, and support for individuals with neurodevelopmental disorders.

By recognizing the genetic and neurological basis of these disorders, we can avoid blaming parents or attributing them to poor nutrition. Instead, we can focus on providing evidence-based interventions and support to individuals with these conditions.

It is crucial to understand that neurodevelopmental disorders are not just a phase or something that individuals will grow out of. Early intervention and ongoing support are essential for individuals with these disorders to reach their full potential.

Furthermore, it is important to recognize that neurodevelopmental disorders can affect individuals throughout their lives, not just in childhood. By providing appropriate support and accommodations, we can help individuals with these disorders thrive in various aspects of their lives.

Lastly, it is crucial to recognize the validity of neurodevelopmental disorders and to promote acceptance and support for individuals with these conditions. By educating ourselves and others, we can create a more inclusive and understanding society for individuals with neurodevelopmental disorders.

Chapter 10: Celebrating Neurodiversity: Embracing Differences in Autism Spectrum Disorder

Neurodiversity is a concept that recognizes and celebrates the natural variations in human brain function and behavior. It emphasizes the idea that neurological differences, such as autism, ADHD, and dyslexia, are simply variations of the human experience rather than disorders that need to be fixed or cured. In recent years, there has been a growing recognition of the importance of neurodiversity in society, as it promotes inclusivity, acceptance, and understanding for all individuals. This blog post will explore the concept of neurodiversity, its importance for society, and various topics related to embracing and supporting neurodiverse individuals.

What is neurodiversity and why is it important?

Neurodiversity refers to the idea that neurological differences are a natural part of human diversity, similar to variations in race, gender, or sexual orientation. It recognizes that individuals with conditions such as autism, ADHD, and dyslexia have unique strengths and perspectives that can contribute to society in meaningful ways. Neurodiversity challenges the notion that these differences are deficits or disorders that need to be fixed or normalized.

Embracing neurodiversity is important for society because it promotes inclusivity and acceptance for all individuals. By recognizing and valuing the strengths and talents of neurodiverse individuals, we can create a more inclusive society where everyone has equal opportunities to thrive. Additionally, neurodiversity encourages a shift in focus from trying to "fix" individuals to providing support and accommodations that allow them to reach their full potential. This approach benefits not only neurodiverse individuals but also society as a whole by harnessing the unique perspectives and abilities they bring.

Understanding the autism spectrum: a brief overview

The autism spectrum refers to a range of conditions characterized by challenges with social skills, repetitive behaviors, and communication difficulties. Autism is a lifelong developmental disorder that affects how individuals perceive and interact with the world around them. It is important to note that autism is a spectrum, meaning that individuals can have a wide range of abilities and challenges.

Common characteristics and traits of individuals with autism include difficulties with social interactions, such as understanding nonverbal cues and maintaining eye contact. They may also have restricted interests and repetitive behaviors, such as lining up objects or repeating certain phrases. Sensory sensitivities are also common, with individuals being either hypersensitive or hyposensitive to certain stimuli like noise or touch.

The benefits of embracing neurodiversity in society

Embracing neurodiversity in society has numerous benefits. Firstly, it promotes inclusivity and acceptance for all individuals, regardless of their neurological differences. This creates a more compassionate and understanding society where everyone feels valued and respected.

Secondly, neurodiversity encourages the recognition and utilization of the unique strengths and talents of neurodiverse individuals. For example, individuals with autism often have exceptional attention to detail, pattern recognition skills, and the ability to think outside the box. By embracing these strengths, society can benefit from their unique perspectives and contributions in various fields such as science, technology, and the arts.

Furthermore, embracing neurodiversity fosters innovation and creativity. Neurodiverse individuals often have different ways of thinking and problem-solving, which can lead to new ideas and approaches. By creating an inclusive environment that values diverse perspectives, society can tap into this potential for innovation.

Challenging stereotypes and misconceptions about autism

There are many stereotypes and misconceptions about autism that can be harmful and perpetuate stigma. One common misconception is that all individuals with autism are nonverbal or have intellectual disabilities. In reality, autism is a spectrum, and individuals can have a wide range of abilities. Many individuals with autism are highly intelligent and capable of leading fulfilling lives.

Another harmful stereotype is that individuals with autism lack empathy or social skills. While it is true that individuals with autism may struggle with social interactions, this does not mean they lack empathy. In fact, many individuals with autism have a deep sense of empathy and care deeply about others.

It is important to challenge these stereotypes and misconceptions because they can lead to discrimination and exclusion. By promoting accurate information and understanding, we can create a more inclusive society where individuals with autism are valued for their unique strengths and abilities.

The importance of inclusive education for neurodiverse learners

Inclusive education is crucial for neurodiverse learners as it ensures that all students have equal access to education and the opportunity to reach their full potential. Inclusive education involves providing appropriate accommodations and support to meet the diverse needs of students with disabilities, including those on the autism spectrum.

Inclusive education benefits neurodiverse learners by promoting their social and academic development. By being included in mainstream classrooms, students with autism have the opportunity to learn from their peers and develop important social skills. Inclusive education also allows neurodiverse learners to access the same curriculum as their peers, ensuring that they are not left behind academically.

Examples of inclusive education practices include providing individualized support, such as visual aids or assistive technology, to help students with autism understand and engage with the material. It also involves creating a supportive and accepting classroom environment where all students feel valued and included.

Celebrating the unique strengths and talents of individuals with autism

Individuals with autism have unique strengths and talents that should be celebrated and valued. One common strength among individuals with autism is attention to detail. They often have an exceptional ability to notice patterns and small details that others may overlook. This attention to detail can be valuable in fields such as science, engineering, or art.

Another strength of individuals with autism is their ability to think outside the box. They often have a unique perspective and can come up with innovative solutions to problems. This creativity and divergent thinking can be an asset in various fields, including technology and design.

Furthermore, individuals with autism often have a strong focus and dedication to their interests. They may develop deep knowledge and expertise in specific areas, such as trains, dinosaurs, or computers. This passion and dedication can lead to remarkable achievements and contributions in their chosen fields.

The role of advocacy and support for neurodiverse individuals and families

Advocacy and support are crucial for neurodiverse individuals and their families to ensure that they have access to the resources and accommodations they need. Advocacy involves speaking up for the rights and needs of neurodiverse individuals, while support provides practical assistance and guidance.

Advocacy organizations play a vital role in promoting the rights and well-being of neurodiverse individuals. They work to raise awareness, challenge discrimination, and advocate for policy changes that promote inclusivity and support. These organizations also provide resources and support for individuals and families navigating the challenges of living with autism.

Support services for neurodiverse individuals and families can include therapy, educational support, and assistance with daily living skills. These services aim to help individuals with autism develop their strengths, overcome challenges, and lead fulfilling lives. Support can also extend to families, providing them with information, guidance, and a network of support.

Overcoming barriers to employment for individuals with autism

Individuals with autism often face barriers to employment due to misconceptions, lack of understanding, and limited opportunities. However, there are successful employment programs that aim to overcome these barriers and provide meaningful employment opportunities for individuals with autism.

One barrier to employment is the lack of understanding about the strengths and abilities of individuals with autism. Many employers may not be aware of the unique skills that individuals with autism can bring to the workplace, such as attention to detail, reliability, and a strong work ethic. By educating employers and promoting the benefits of hiring neurodiverse individuals, these misconceptions can be challenged.

Another barrier is the lack of support and accommodations in the workplace. Many individuals with autism may require certain accommodations, such as a quiet workspace or clear instructions, to perform their best. By providing these accommodations and creating an inclusive work environment, employers can ensure that individuals with autism have equal opportunities to succeed.

Successful employment programs for individuals with autism often involve job training and support. These programs provide individuals with the skills they need to succeed in the workplace, such as communication skills, problem-solving abilities, and job-specific training. They also provide ongoing support and mentorship to help individuals navigate the challenges of employment.

Navigating relationships and social interactions with neurodiverse individuals

Navigating relationships and social interactions with neurodiverse individuals requires understanding, patience, and empathy. It is important to recognize that individuals with autism may have different social communication styles and may struggle with certain aspects of social interactions.

One key aspect of navigating relationships with neurodiverse individuals is to be patient and understanding. Individuals with autism may have difficulty understanding social cues or expressing themselves verbally. It is important to give them time to process information and communicate in their own way.

Another important aspect is to be accepting and inclusive. Neurodiverse individuals may have unique interests or ways of interacting that may seem different from the norm. By accepting and embracing these differences, we can create an inclusive environment where everyone feels valued and respected.

Successful social interaction programs for individuals with autism often involve teaching social skills in a structured and supportive environment. These programs focus on teaching skills such as making eye contact, initiating conversations, and understanding nonverbal cues. They also provide opportunities for practice and reinforcement of these skills in real-life situations.

The future of neurodiversity: promoting acceptance and understanding

The future of neurodiversity lies in promoting acceptance and understanding in all aspects of society. This includes education, employment, healthcare, and social interactions. By promoting acceptance and understanding, we can create a more inclusive society where neurodiverse individuals are valued for their unique strengths and abilities.

One way to promote acceptance and understanding is through education and awareness. By educating the public about neurodiversity and challenging stereotypes and misconceptions, we can create a more informed and accepting society. This can be done through school curricula, public awareness campaigns, and community events.

Another way to promote acceptance is through inclusive policies and practices. This includes creating inclusive education environments, providing reasonable accommodations in the workplace, and ensuring access to healthcare services that meet the needs of neurodiverse individuals. By implementing these policies and practices, we can create a more inclusive society where everyone has equal opportunities to thrive.

Resources and organizations for celebrating and supporting neurodiversity

There are numerous resources and organizations available for celebrating and supporting neurodiversity. These resources provide information, support, and advocacy for individuals with autism and their families.

Some notable organizations include the Autism Society, Autism Speaks, and the National Autistic Society. These organizations provide a wealth of information about autism, support services, advocacy efforts, and resources for individuals with autism and their families.

Additionally, there are online communities and forums where individuals with autism and their families can connect with others who share similar experiences. These communities provide a supportive space for sharing stories, seeking advice, and finding a sense of belonging.

In conclusion, neurodiversity is an important concept that recognizes the natural variations in human brain function and behavior. Embracing neurodiversity promotes inclusivity, acceptance, and understanding for all individuals. By recognizing the unique strengths and talents of neurodiverse individuals, we can create a more inclusive society where everyone has equal opportunities to thrive.

Throughout this blog post, we have explored various topics related to neurodiversity, including the autism spectrum, challenging stereotypes, inclusive education, celebrating strengths, advocacy and support, employment barriers, social interactions, and promoting acceptance and understanding. By promoting acceptance and understanding of neurodiversity in all aspects of society, we can create a more inclusive and compassionate world for all individuals.

Chapter 11: Celebrating Diversity: Embracing Community Acceptance in Today's World

In today's world, diversity and inclusion have become increasingly important topics of discussion. As societies become more interconnected and globalized, it is crucial to recognize and celebrate the diversity that exists within our communities. Diversity encompasses a wide range of characteristics, including race, ethnicity, gender, sexuality, religion, and more. By embracing diversity and promoting acceptance, we can create a stronger and more inclusive society.

Unfortunately, prejudice and discrimination still persist in many parts of the world. People are often judged or mistreated based on their differences, leading to social divisions and inequality. It is essential to challenge these biases and work towards a more inclusive society where everyone is valued and respected.

Understanding Diversity: What it Means and Why It Matters

Diversity refers to the variety of human differences that exist within a community or society. These differences can be visible, such as race or gender, or invisible, such as sexual orientation or religious beliefs. It is important to recognize that diversity goes beyond just physical characteristics; it also includes different perspectives, experiences, and backgrounds.

Diversity matters because it enriches our communities and broadens our horizons. When people from different backgrounds come together, they bring unique perspectives and ideas that can lead to innovation and creativity. By embracing diversity, we can foster a more inclusive society where everyone feels valued and included.

The Benefits of Embracing Diversity: A Stronger, More Resilient Community

Embracing diversity has numerous benefits for communities and society as a whole. Firstly, diversity promotes social cohesion by bringing people from different backgrounds together. When individuals interact with others who are different from them, they gain a better understanding of different cultures and perspectives. This leads to increased empathy and tolerance, which are essential for building strong and resilient communities.

Research has also shown that diverse communities are more innovative and economically prosperous. When people from different backgrounds come together, they bring a wide range of skills, knowledge, and experiences. This diversity of thought can lead to more creative problem-solving and better decision-making. Additionally, diverse communities are more attractive to businesses and investors, as they offer a broader customer base and a wider talent pool.

Overcoming Obstacles: Addressing Prejudice and Discrimination

Prejudice and discrimination continue to be significant obstacles to achieving a truly inclusive society. Prejudice refers to preconceived opinions or attitudes towards individuals or groups based on their perceived differences. Discrimination, on the other hand, involves treating people unfairly or unequally based on these differences.

To address prejudice and discrimination, it is important to raise awareness and educate people about the harmful effects of these biases. This can be done through community outreach programs, workshops, and educational campaigns. It is also crucial to challenge stereotypes and promote positive representations of diverse groups in the media and entertainment industry.

Additionally, individuals can play a role in addressing prejudice and discrimination by speaking out against injustice and standing up for those who are marginalized. By promoting empathy and understanding, we can create a more inclusive society where everyone feels valued and respected.

Celebrating Differences: The Role of Cultural Festivals and Events

Cultural festivals and events play a vital role in promoting diversity and acceptance. These events provide an opportunity for people from different backgrounds to come together and celebrate their unique cultures and traditions. They also allow individuals to learn about other cultures, fostering understanding and appreciation.

One example of a popular cultural festival is the Carnival in Rio de Janeiro, Brazil. This vibrant event showcases the rich cultural heritage of Brazil through music, dance, costumes, and parades. Another example is Diwali, the Festival of Lights celebrated by Hindus around the world. Diwali brings people together to celebrate the victory of light over darkness and good over evil.

By participating in cultural festivals and events, individuals can gain a deeper understanding of different cultures and traditions. This can help break down stereotypes and promote acceptance and inclusion.

Building Bridges: The Importance of Dialogue and Understanding

Dialogue and understanding are essential in promoting diversity and acceptance. By engaging in open and respectful conversations with people from different backgrounds, we can learn from one another and challenge our own biases.

To engage in productive dialogue, it is important to approach conversations with an open mind and a willingness to listen. It is also crucial to ask questions and seek clarification when necessary. By actively listening to others' perspectives, we can gain a better understanding of their experiences and challenges.

It is also important to be aware of our own biases and prejudices. By acknowledging our own limitations, we can work towards overcoming them and becoming more inclusive individuals.

Education and Awareness: Teaching Tolerance and Acceptance

Education plays a crucial role in promoting diversity and acceptance. By teaching tolerance and acceptance from a young age, we can help create a more inclusive society.

Schools can incorporate diversity education into their curriculum, teaching students about different cultures, religions, and perspectives. This can help break down stereotypes and promote empathy and understanding.

There are also numerous educational programs and initiatives that focus on promoting tolerance and acceptance. For example, the Anti-Defamation League offers educational resources for teachers to address issues of prejudice and discrimination in the classroom. The UNESCO Associated Schools Project Network promotes intercultural dialogue and understanding among students worldwide.

By investing in education and awareness programs, we can equip future generations with the knowledge and skills needed to create a more inclusive society.

The Power of Representation: Diversity in Media and Entertainment

Representation is crucial in promoting diversity and acceptance. When individuals see themselves represented positively in the media and entertainment industry, it helps validate their experiences and identities.

Unfortunately, representation has historically been lacking for many marginalized groups. However, there have been positive changes in recent years, with more diverse voices being heard and represented in the media.

For example, the movie "Black Panther" was celebrated for its positive representation of African culture and its predominantly black cast. The television show "Pose" has been praised for its authentic portrayal of the LGBTQ+ community, particularly transgender individuals of color.

By promoting diverse representation in the media and entertainment industry, we can challenge stereotypes and promote acceptance and inclusion.

Diversity in the Workplace: Creating Inclusive Environments

Diversity is not only important in society but also in the workplace. By creating inclusive work environments, businesses can benefit from a wide range of perspectives and experiences.

To create an inclusive workplace, it is important to implement policies and practices that promote diversity and prevent discrimination. This can include diversity training programs, mentorship opportunities for underrepresented groups, and flexible work arrangements to accommodate different needs.

It is also crucial to foster a culture of inclusion where everyone feels valued and respected. This can be achieved by promoting open communication, recognizing and celebrating individual differences, and providing equal opportunities for career advancement.

By embracing diversity in the workplace, businesses can attract top talent, improve employee satisfaction and productivity, and better serve their diverse customer base.

Celebrating Diversity in Everyday Life: Small Acts of Kindness and Acceptance

While large-scale events and initiatives are important in promoting diversity and acceptance, small acts of kindness and acceptance in everyday life can also make a big difference.

Simple acts such as smiling at a stranger, offering a helping hand to someone in need, or engaging in a friendly conversation with someone from a different background can help break down barriers and promote understanding.

It is also important to challenge our own biases and assumptions. By actively seeking out diverse perspectives and experiences, we can broaden our own understanding of the world.

By celebrating diversity in our everyday lives, we can create a ripple effect that promotes acceptance and inclusion in our communities.

Moving Forward with a Commitment to Diversity and Community Acceptance

In conclusion, celebrating diversity and promoting acceptance is crucial in today's world. By recognizing and valuing the differences that exist within our communities, we can create a stronger and more inclusive society.

Understanding diversity and its importance is the first step towards promoting acceptance. By embracing diversity, we can benefit from a wide range of perspectives and experiences that lead to innovation and creativity.

Overcoming obstacles such as prejudice and discrimination requires education, awareness, and dialogue. By engaging in open and respectful conversations with people from different backgrounds, we can challenge our own biases and promote understanding.

Cultural festivals and events play a vital role in promoting diversity and acceptance by bringing people from different backgrounds together to celebrate their unique cultures and traditions.

Education plays a crucial role in promoting diversity and acceptance by teaching tolerance and acceptance from a young age. By investing in education and awareness programs, we can equip future generations with the knowledge and skills needed to create a more inclusive society.

Representation is crucial in promoting diversity and acceptance. By promoting diverse representation in the media and entertainment industry, we can challenge stereotypes and promote acceptance.

Diversity is not only important in society but also in the workplace. By creating inclusive work environments, businesses can benefit from a wide range of perspectives and experiences.

Small acts of kindness and acceptance in everyday life can also make a big difference in promoting diversity and acceptance. By celebrating diversity in our everyday lives, we can create a ripple effect that promotes acceptance and inclusion in our communities.

Moving forward, it is important for individuals to commit to promoting diversity and acceptance in their own lives and communities. By embracing diversity, challenging biases, and promoting understanding, we can create a more inclusive society where everyone feels valued and respected.

Chapter 12: The Future is Accessible: Advancements in Technology for All

In today's digital age, technology plays a crucial role in our daily lives. From communication to education, entertainment to employment, technology has become an integral part of how we navigate the world. However, for the millions of people with disabilities worldwide, accessing and using technology can be a significant challenge. This is where accessible technology comes in.

Accessible technology refers to devices, software, and applications that are designed to be usable by individuals with disabilities. It aims to remove barriers and provide equal access to information and opportunities for people with disabilities. According to the World Health Organization (WHO), there are over 1 billion people worldwide living with some form of disability. This represents a significant portion of the global population that can benefit from accessible technology.

Assistive Technology: A Game Changer for People with Disabilities

Assistive technology is a subset of accessible technology that specifically focuses on devices and software designed to assist individuals with disabilities in performing tasks that they may otherwise have difficulty with. These technologies can range from simple tools like magnifiers and hearing aids to more complex software and devices like screen readers and prosthetic limbs.

One example of assistive technology is screen reading software, which converts text on a computer screen into synthesized speech or braille output for individuals with visual impairments. Another example is the use of prosthetic limbs, which can greatly enhance mobility and independence for individuals with limb loss or limb difference.

The benefits of assistive technology for people with disabilities are immense. It can help individuals overcome barriers and participate fully in various aspects of life, including education, employment, and social interactions. Assistive technology can also improve quality of life by promoting independence, increasing access to information, and enhancing communication abilities.

The Role of Artificial Intelligence in Accessibility

Artificial intelligence (AI) refers to the simulation of human intelligence in machines that are programmed to think and learn like humans. AI has the potential to revolutionize accessibility by providing intelligent solutions to address the specific needs of individuals with disabilities.

One example of AI-powered accessibility features is voice recognition technology, which allows individuals with mobility impairments to control devices and perform tasks using voice commands. AI can also be used to develop personalized learning platforms that adapt to the unique learning needs of individuals with cognitive disabilities.

The benefits of AI in accessibility are numerous. It can provide personalized and adaptive solutions that cater to the specific needs of individuals with disabilities. AI-powered technologies can also learn and improve over time, making them more effective and efficient in assisting individuals with disabilities.

Virtual Reality: A Tool for Empathy and Inclusion

Virtual reality (VR) refers to a computer-generated simulation of a three-dimensional environment that can be interacted with in a seemingly real or physical way. VR has gained popularity in recent years for its immersive and interactive nature, but it also has great potential in promoting empathy and inclusion for individuals with disabilities.

One example of VR applications for accessibility is the use of virtual environments to simulate real-world scenarios for individuals with mobility impairments. This allows them to experience and navigate inaccessible spaces virtually, providing them with a better understanding of the challenges faced by people with disabilities.

The benefits of VR in promoting empathy and inclusion are significant. It can help raise awareness and understanding of the barriers faced by individuals with disabilities, leading to increased empathy and support. VR can also provide opportunities for individuals with disabilities to participate in activities and experiences that may otherwise be inaccessible to them.

Wearable Technology: Enhancing Accessibility on the Go

Wearable technology refers to devices that can be worn on the body, typically as accessories or clothing, that incorporate advanced electronic technologies. These devices are designed to enhance accessibility by providing real-time information, communication, and assistance for individuals with disabilities.

One example of wearable technology for accessibility is smartwatches that can provide notifications and alerts for individuals with hearing impairments. These devices can vibrate or display visual cues to alert the wearer of incoming calls, messages, or alarms.

The benefits of wearable technology for people with disabilities are significant. It can provide real-time assistance and support, allowing individuals to navigate their environment more easily and independently. Wearable technology can also enhance communication and social interactions, improving the overall quality of life for individuals with disabilities.

The Internet of Things: A More Accessible Future for All

The Internet of Things (IoT) refers to the network of physical devices, vehicles, appliances, and other objects embedded with sensors, software, and connectivity that enables them to connect and exchange data. IoT has the potential to greatly enhance accessibility by creating a more connected and inclusive environment.

One example of IoT devices for accessibility is smart home technology that allows individuals with disabilities to control various aspects of their home environment using voice commands or mobile applications. This can include adjusting lighting, temperature, and security systems.

The benefits of IoT in promoting accessibility are significant. It can create a more connected and inclusive environment that adapts to the specific needs of individuals with disabilities. IoT devices can also provide real-time data and information that can assist individuals in making informed decisions and navigating their environment more effectively.

Accessible Design: Creating Inclusive Products and Services

Accessible design refers to the process of designing products, services, and environments that can be used by individuals with disabilities. It involves considering the specific needs and abilities of individuals with disabilities throughout the design process to ensure equal access and usability.

Examples of accessible design principles include providing alternative formats for information (e.g., braille or audio), ensuring clear and intuitive navigation, and incorporating universal design principles that benefit all users, regardless of ability.

The benefits of accessible design for people with disabilities are immense. It can remove barriers and provide equal access to information, products, and services. Accessible design can also enhance usability and user experience for all individuals, leading to increased customer satisfaction and loyalty.

The Importance of User Testing and Feedback in Accessible Design

User testing and feedback refer to the process of gathering input and insights from individuals with disabilities throughout the design process. This involves conducting usability tests, surveys, and interviews to understand the specific needs and challenges faced by individuals with disabilities.

Examples of user testing and feedback in accessible design include conducting focus groups with individuals with disabilities to gather insights on product usability, conducting accessibility audits to identify barriers, and incorporating user feedback into the design process.

The benefits of user testing and feedback in promoting accessibility are significant. It ensures that products and services are designed with the specific needs of individuals with disabilities in mind, leading to improved usability and user experience. User testing and feedback also promote inclusivity by involving individuals with disabilities in the design process, giving them a voice and empowering them to shape the technologies they use.

Government Policies and Regulations: Promoting Accessibility in Technology

Government policies and regulations play a crucial role in promoting accessibility in technology. They set standards and guidelines that businesses and organizations must adhere to, ensuring equal access and opportunities for individuals with disabilities.

Examples of government initiatives promoting accessibility include the Americans with Disabilities Act (ADA) in the United States, which prohibits discrimination against individuals with disabilities in various areas, including employment, public accommodations, and telecommunications. The European Accessibility Act (EAA) is another example, which aims to harmonize accessibility requirements for certain products and services across the European Union.

The benefits of government policies and regulations in promoting accessibility are significant. They provide a legal framework that ensures equal access and opportunities for individuals with disabilities. Government initiatives also raise awareness about the importance of accessibility and encourage businesses and organizations to prioritize inclusive design.

The Business Case for Accessibility: Why Inclusive Design is Good for Business

Inclusive design is not only beneficial for individuals with disabilities but also for businesses. There is a strong business case for accessibility, as it can lead to increased customer satisfaction, loyalty, and market share.

Companies that prioritize inclusive design can tap into a large and growing market of individuals with disabilities. According to the World Bank, people with disabilities represent a trillion-dollar market segment. By designing products and services that are accessible and inclusive, businesses can attract and retain customers with disabilities, gaining a competitive advantage in the market.

Examples of companies that have benefited from inclusive design include Microsoft, which has made significant strides in developing accessible technology and has seen increased customer satisfaction and loyalty as a result. Apple is another example, with its commitment to accessibility features in its products, which has garnered praise from individuals with disabilities and advocacy groups.

The benefits of inclusive design for businesses and their customers are significant. It can lead to increased customer satisfaction and loyalty, improved brand reputation, and expanded market share. Inclusive design also promotes innovation and creativity by considering the diverse needs and abilities of all users.

The Future of Accessible Technology and the Power of Inclusion

In conclusion, accessible technology has the power to transform the lives of individuals with disabilities by removing barriers and providing equal access to information, opportunities, and experiences. Assistive technology, artificial intelligence, virtual reality, wearable technology, the Internet of Things, accessible design, user testing and feedback, government policies and regulations, and inclusive design all play crucial roles in promoting accessibility.

The future of accessible technology holds great promise. As technology continues to advance, there will be even more opportunities to develop innovative solutions that cater to the specific needs of individuals with disabilities. The power of inclusion cannot be underestimated. By prioritizing accessibility and inclusive design, businesses and individuals can create a more equitable and inclusive society where everyone has equal access to information, opportunities, and experiences.

It is essential for businesses to recognize the business case for accessibility and prioritize inclusive design. By doing so, they can tap into a large and growing market of individuals with disabilities, gain a competitive advantage, and contribute to a more inclusive society. Individuals also have a role to play by advocating for accessibility and inclusion, supporting businesses that prioritize accessibility, and demanding equal access and opportunities for all. Together, we can create a future where accessible technology is the norm, and everyone has the opportunity to thrive.

Chapter 13: Mapping Your Future: A Guide to Successful Career Planning

Career planning is a crucial aspect of achieving professional success. It involves setting clear goals, assessing one's skills and interests, researching different career paths and industries, networking, gaining relevant experience and education, crafting a strong resume and cover letter, navigating the job search process, interviewing with confidence, negotiating salary and benefits, and continuously reevaluating and adjusting one's career plan. By engaging in career planning, individuals can increase their job satisfaction, achieve a better work-life balance, and enhance their earnings potential.

Understanding the Importance of Career Planning

Career planning is the process of setting goals and creating a roadmap to achieve those goals in one's professional life. It is essential because it provides individuals with direction and purpose in their careers. Without a plan, individuals may find themselves stuck in unfulfilling jobs or unable to progress in their chosen field. Career planning allows individuals to identify their strengths and weaknesses, explore different career options, and make informed decisions about their professional development.

One of the key benefits of career planning is increased job satisfaction. When individuals have a clear understanding of their career goals and are actively working towards them, they are more likely to feel fulfilled in their work. They can align their skills and interests with their job responsibilities, leading to a greater sense of purpose and engagement. Additionally, career planning can help individuals achieve a better work-life balance by identifying opportunities for growth and advancement that align with their personal values and priorities.

Another significant benefit of career planning is higher earnings potential. By setting clear goals and taking steps to develop the necessary skills and qualifications, individuals can position themselves for higher-paying jobs or promotions within their current organization. Career planning also allows individuals to identify industries or sectors that offer better financial opportunities and make strategic decisions about their career path.

Assessing Your Skills and Interests

Self-assessment is a critical component of career planning as it helps individuals gain a better understanding of their skills, interests, and values. By assessing oneself, individuals can identify their strengths and weaknesses, which can guide their career choices and development.

There are several ways to assess one's skills and interests. One effective method is taking personality tests or career assessments. These tests can provide insights into one's personality traits, interests, and work preferences. They can help individuals identify potential career paths that align with their strengths and passions.

Another way to assess skills and interests is by evaluating past experiences. Reflecting on previous jobs, internships, or volunteer work can help individuals identify tasks or responsibilities they enjoyed or excelled at. This self-reflection can provide valuable insights into one's skills and interests and guide future career decisions.

Identifying Your Career Goals

Setting clear and achievable career goals is crucial in career planning. Without goals, individuals may lack direction and motivation in their professional lives. By identifying specific goals, individuals can create a roadmap to guide their career development.

Career goals can vary depending on individual aspirations and circumstances. Some common examples of career goals include getting a promotion within a certain timeframe, changing industries to pursue a passion, starting a business, or becoming an industry expert in a particular field. It is important to set goals that are realistic and achievable, taking into account one's skills, interests, and current circumstances.

When setting career goals, it is helpful to break them down into smaller milestones or objectives. This allows individuals to track their progress and make adjustments along the way. By setting achievable goals, individuals can stay motivated and focused on their professional development.

Researching Career Paths and Industries

Researching different career paths and industries is an essential step in career planning. It allows individuals to gather information about potential job opportunities, industry trends, required qualifications, and salary ranges. This research helps individuals make informed decisions about their career choices and identify the best path to achieve their goals.

There are several ways to research career paths and industries. Online resources such as job search websites, industry-specific websites, and professional networking platforms can provide valuable information about different careers and industries. Attending career fairs and industry conferences can also provide opportunities to learn more about specific industries and connect with professionals in the field. Additionally, conducting informational interviews with professionals working in desired industries can provide insights into the day-to-day responsibilities, challenges, and opportunities in a particular career.

By conducting thorough research, individuals can gain a better understanding of the skills and qualifications required for their desired career path. This knowledge can guide their decisions about gaining relevant experience and education.

Networking and Building Professional Relationships

Networking and building professional relationships are crucial aspects of career planning. By connecting with professionals in their field of interest, individuals can gain valuable insights, access job opportunities, and build a strong professional network.

Networking can take various forms, including attending industry events, joining professional organizations, participating in online forums or groups, and reaching out to professionals for informational interviews. It is important to approach networking with a genuine interest in building relationships rather than solely focusing on personal gain. Building authentic connections with professionals can lead to mentorship opportunities, referrals for job openings, and access to valuable resources.

Networking also provides individuals with the opportunity to learn from others' experiences and gain insights into different career paths. By connecting with professionals who have achieved success in their desired field, individuals can gain valuable advice and guidance on how to navigate their own career paths.

Gaining Relevant Experience and Education

Gaining relevant experience and education is crucial in achieving career goals. Employers often look for candidates who have practical experience in their field of interest or possess the necessary qualifications for the job.

There are several ways to gain relevant experience and education. Volunteering or interning in a related field can provide hands-on experience and help individuals develop the skills necessary for their desired career path. Taking courses or pursuing certifications can also enhance one's knowledge and qualifications. Online courses, workshops, and industry-specific certifications are widely available and can be completed at one's own pace.

It is important to continuously seek opportunities to gain relevant experience and education throughout one's career. By staying updated on industry trends and acquiring new skills, individuals can position themselves for growth and advancement.

Crafting a Strong Resume and Cover Letter

Having a strong resume and cover letter is essential in the job search process. These documents serve as the first impression for potential employers and can significantly impact one's chances of securing an interview.

When crafting a resume, it is important to tailor it to the specific job description and highlight relevant skills and experiences. Including quantifiable achievements and measurable results can also make a resume stand out. Additionally, using action verbs and concise language can make a resume more impactful.

A cover letter should complement the resume by providing additional context and highlighting why one is a good fit for the position. It is important to customize the cover letter for each job application and address it to the hiring manager or recruiter by name if possible. The cover letter should showcase one's enthusiasm for the role and demonstrate how one's skills and experiences align with the job requirements.

Navigating the Job Search Process

Having a strategic approach to the job search process is crucial in finding the right opportunities. It involves using various resources, leveraging personal connections, and being proactive in seeking out job openings.

Job search engines such as Indeed, LinkedIn, and Glassdoor can be valuable tools in finding job openings. These platforms allow individuals to search for jobs based on specific criteria such as location, industry, or job title. Additionally, networking with professionals in one's field of interest can provide access to hidden job opportunities that may not be advertised publicly.

It is important to customize each job application to match the requirements of the position. Tailoring the resume and cover letter to highlight relevant skills and experiences can significantly increase the chances of getting noticed by employers. Following up with a thank-you email or note after an interview can also leave a positive impression on potential employers.

Interviewing with Confidence

Preparing for job interviews and presenting oneself confidently is crucial in the job search process. Employers often look for candidates who can effectively communicate their skills, experiences, and qualifications.

Before an interview, it is important to research the company and understand its mission, values, and culture. This knowledge can help individuals tailor their responses to align with the company's goals and demonstrate their interest in the position.

Practicing common interview questions and preparing thoughtful responses can also boost confidence during an interview. It is important to showcase one's skills and experiences by providing specific examples and quantifiable achievements. Additionally, dressing professionally, maintaining good eye contact, and displaying positive body language can leave a lasting impression on interviewers.

Negotiating Salary and Benefits

Negotiating salary and benefits is an important aspect of the job offer process. By advocating for oneself and negotiating effectively, individuals can secure a compensation package that aligns with their skills and experiences.

Before entering into salary negotiations, it is important to research industry standards and salary ranges for similar positions. This knowledge can provide a benchmark for negotiations and help individuals make informed decisions about their worth.

During negotiations, it is important to be prepared to make a counteroffer if the initial offer does not meet one's expectations. It is also important to consider other aspects of the compensation package such as benefits, vacation time, and opportunities for growth and advancement.

Continuously Reevaluating and Adjusting Your Career Plan

Continuously reevaluating and adjusting one's career plan is crucial in staying on track towards achieving professional goals. As individuals gain new experiences, acquire new skills, or encounter new opportunities, it is important to reassess their goals and make adjustments as necessary.

Seeking feedback from mentors, supervisors, or trusted colleagues can provide valuable insights into one's strengths and areas for improvement. This feedback can guide individuals in making informed decisions about their career development.

Being open to new opportunities and being willing to take calculated risks can also lead to unexpected career advancements. By staying adaptable and embracing change, individuals can position themselves for growth and seize new opportunities as they arise.

Career planning is a crucial aspect of achieving professional success. By setting clear goals, assessing one's skills and interests, researching different career paths and industries, networking, gaining relevant experience and education, crafting a strong resume and cover letter, navigating the job search process, interviewing with confidence, negotiating salary and benefits, and continuously reevaluating and adjusting one's career plan, individuals can increase their job satisfaction, achieve a better work-life balance, and enhance their earnings potential. By investing time and effort into career planning, individuals can take control of their professional lives and achieve their long-term goals.

Chapter 14: Hidden Gems on Campus: 5 Underrated Resources You Need to Know About

Introduction: Uncovering the Hidden Gems on Your Campus

When it comes to college life, many students focus solely on attending classes and completing assignments. However, there is so much more to the college experience than just academics. One of the most valuable aspects of being a college student is the access to a wide range of campus resources. These resources are designed to support and enhance your education, personal growth, and overall well-being. By taking advantage of these hidden gems on your campus, you can make the most of your college experience and set yourself up for success in the future.

Overview of the different resources available

College campuses are often filled with a plethora of resources that are available to students. These resources are designed to provide support in various areas of student life, including academics, career development, mental health, physical health, technology, and extracurricular activities. Some of the most common campus resources include the library, career services, writing centers, counseling services, campus recreation centers, tech centers, student organizations, health centers, and study abroad programs.

Each of these resources offers unique benefits and opportunities for students. By utilizing these resources, you can enhance your academic performance, develop important skills for your future career, take care of your mental and physical health, explore new interests and hobbies, and broaden your horizons through international experiences. It is important to familiarize yourself with these resources and take advantage of them throughout your college journey.

The Library: More Than Just Books

When most people think of a library, they envision rows upon rows of books. While this is certainly true for college libraries as well, they offer so much more than just a collection of books. College libraries are often equipped with state-of-the-art research materials that can greatly enhance your academic pursuits. From online databases to scholarly journals and archives, the library provides access to a wealth of information that can support your research papers and projects.

In addition to research materials, college libraries also offer study spaces and resources. These spaces are designed to provide a quiet and focused environment for students to study and work on assignments. Many libraries also offer group study rooms, computer labs, and printing services. Librarians are available to assist students with finding resources, navigating databases, and conducting research. They can also provide guidance on citation styles and help with formatting papers.

Another hidden gem within the library is the specialized collections and archives. Many college libraries have unique collections that focus on specific subjects or themes. These collections often include rare books, manuscripts, photographs, and other historical artifacts. By exploring these collections, you can gain a deeper understanding of your field of study and engage in research that goes beyond the standard curriculum.

Career Services: Your Path to Professional Success

One of the main goals of attending college is to prepare for a successful career. This is where career services come in. Career services offices are dedicated to helping students navigate the job market and develop the skills necessary for professional success. They offer a wide range of resources and services that can support you throughout your college journey and beyond.

One of the most valuable resources offered by career services is assistance with resumes and cover letters. These documents are essential when applying for internships, jobs, or graduate school programs. Career services professionals can help you craft a compelling resume and cover letter that highlights your skills, experiences, and accomplishments. They can also provide feedback on your existing resume and cover letter to ensure they are polished and professional.

In addition to resume and cover letter assistance, career services offices provide job and internship search resources. They often have job boards or online platforms where employers post opportunities specifically for students. Career services professionals can help you navigate these resources, search for relevant positions, and provide guidance on how to tailor your application materials to specific opportunities.

Networking is another important aspect of career development, and career services offices often provide networking opportunities for students. They may host career fairs, employer panels, or networking events where you can connect with professionals in your field of interest. These events can be invaluable for making connections, learning about potential career paths, and gaining insight into the job market.

The Writing Center: Improving Your Writing Skills

Strong writing skills are essential for success in college and beyond. The writing center is a valuable resource that can help you improve your writing skills and become a more effective communicator. Writing centers offer one-on-one tutoring sessions where you can receive personalized feedback and guidance on your writing assignments.

During these tutoring sessions, writing center tutors can help you with all aspects of the writing process, from brainstorming and outlining to revising and editing. They can provide feedback on your organization, clarity, grammar, and style. They can also help you develop strategies for overcoming writer's block and managing your time effectively.

In addition to one-on-one tutoring sessions, writing centers often offer workshops and writing groups. These workshops cover various topics related to writing, such as thesis statements, research strategies, and citation styles. Writing groups provide a supportive environment where you can share your work with peers and receive feedback.

Whether you are struggling with a specific assignment or looking to improve your overall writing skills, the writing center is a valuable resource that can help you become a more confident and proficient writer.

Counseling Services: Taking Care of Your Mental Health

College can be an exciting and transformative time in your life, but it can also be challenging and stressful. It is important to prioritize your mental health and seek support when needed. Counseling services on campus provide confidential counseling sessions where you can talk to a trained professional about any concerns or issues you may be facing.

Counselors are equipped to help students navigate a wide range of challenges, including stress, anxiety, depression, relationship issues, academic difficulties, and more. They provide a safe and nonjudgmental space for you to express your thoughts and feelings and work through any challenges you may be experiencing.

In addition to individual counseling sessions, counseling services often offer support groups and workshops. Support groups provide an opportunity to connect with peers who may be facing similar challenges. They can provide a sense of community and support as you navigate college life. Workshops cover various topics related to mental health and well-being, such as stress management, mindfulness, and self-care.

Counseling services can also provide referrals to outside resources if needed. If you require more specialized or long-term support, counselors can help connect you with off-campus therapists or mental health professionals who can provide the appropriate care.

Campus Recreation: Staying Active and Healthy

Maintaining a healthy lifestyle is important for overall well-being and academic success. Campus recreation centers offer a wide range of resources and opportunities for students to stay active and prioritize their physical health.

Fitness classes and facilities are often available at campus recreation centers. These classes can include yoga, Zumba, spin, weightlifting, and more. They provide a fun and engaging way to stay active and improve your fitness levels. Fitness facilities are equipped with state-of-the-art equipment that can be used by students at their convenience.

Intramural sports and clubs are another popular option for staying active on campus. These sports leagues and clubs allow students to participate in friendly competition and engage in physical activity with their peers. Whether you enjoy team sports like soccer or basketball or prefer individual activities like running or swimming, there is likely an intramural sport or club that suits your interests.

Outdoor recreation opportunities are also available on many college campuses. These opportunities can include hiking trails, bike paths, rock climbing walls, and more. Taking advantage of these outdoor spaces can provide a break from the demands of academic life and allow you to connect with nature.

The Tech Center: Access to Cutting-Edge Technology

Technology plays a crucial role in college life, and the tech center on campus provides access to cutting-edge technology and resources. Computer labs are often available for students to use, equipped with the latest software and hardware. These labs provide a quiet and focused environment for completing assignments, conducting research, or working on group projects.

Equipment rental services are another valuable resource offered by tech centers. Students can often rent laptops, cameras, video equipment, and other technology for a specified period of time. This can be particularly useful if you need access to specialized equipment for a specific project or assignment.

Technical support and training are also provided by tech centers. If you encounter any issues with your personal devices or need assistance with software or applications, technical support staff are available to help. They can troubleshoot problems, provide guidance on using specific software, and offer training sessions to help you develop your technical skills.

Student Organizations: Finding Your Community

College is not just about academics; it is also about finding your community and exploring your interests. Student organizations provide a platform for students to connect with others who share similar interests or passions. There are typically a wide range of clubs and organizations available on campus, covering various topics such as academic disciplines, hobbies, cultural groups, social justice issues, and more.

Joining a student organization can provide numerous benefits. It allows you to meet new people, make friends, and develop a sense of belonging on campus. It also provides opportunities for leadership and volunteerism, which can enhance your resume and help you develop important skills such as teamwork, communication, and organization.

Student organizations often host networking events, guest speakers, workshops, and social events that allow you to further engage with your interests and connect with professionals in your field of interest. These events can provide valuable opportunities for learning, personal growth, and professional development.

The Health Center: Taking Care of Your Physical Health

Taking care of your physical health is essential for overall well-being and academic success. The health center on campus provides a wide range of services and resources to support your physical health needs.

Medical and dental services are often available at the health center. These services can include routine check-ups, vaccinations, treatment for minor illnesses and injuries, and dental cleanings. Having access to these services on campus can save you time and money compared to seeking medical care off-campus.

Health education and prevention programs are another valuable resource offered by the health center. These programs provide information and resources on various topics such as nutrition, sexual health, stress management, and more. They can help you make informed decisions about your health and develop healthy habits that will benefit you throughout your life.

Counseling and support services are also available at the health center. If you are struggling with mental health issues or need support in managing stress or other challenges, counselors can provide guidance and assistance. They can help you develop coping strategies, connect you with additional resources if needed, and provide a safe space for you to discuss any concerns or issues you may be facing.

Study Abroad Programs: Broadening Your Horizons

Studying abroad is an incredible opportunity to broaden your horizons, immerse yourself in a different culture, and gain a global perspective. Many colleges offer study abroad programs that allow students to spend a semester or year studying in a different country.

These programs provide opportunities for cultural immersion and language learning. By living and studying in a different country, you can gain a deeper understanding of different cultures, customs, and perspectives. You can also develop language skills and enhance your intercultural communication abilities.

Study abroad programs often offer academic credit transfer options. This means that the courses you take while studying abroad can count towards your degree requirements. This allows you to continue making progress towards your degree while also experiencing a different educational system and learning from international faculty.

Studying abroad can be a transformative experience that allows you to develop important skills such as adaptability, independence, and cross-cultural communication. It can also provide a unique and valuable addition to your resume, demonstrating your ability to navigate new environments and work with diverse groups of people.

Conclusion: Making the Most of Your Campus Resources

College is a time of growth, exploration, and learning. By utilizing the hidden gems on your campus, you can enhance your college experience and set yourself up for success in the future. From the library to career services, writing centers to counseling services, campus recreation to tech centers, student organizations to health centers, and study abroad programs, there are a wide range of resources available to support your academic, personal, and professional development.

It is important to take the time to familiarize yourself with these resources and make use of them throughout your college journey. They are included in your tuition and fees, so it is in your best interest to take full advantage of them. Whether you need assistance with research, career development, writing skills, mental health support, physical fitness, technology access, community engagement, physical health care, or international experiences, there is likely a campus resource that can meet your needs.

By utilizing these resources, you can enhance your academic performance, develop important skills for your future career, take care of your mental and physical health, explore new interests and hobbies, and broaden your horizons through international experiences. Don't miss out on the hidden gems on your campus - they are there to support you and help you make the most of your college experience.

Chapter 15: From Yoga to Mindfulness: Effective Ways to Combat Stress in Your Daily Life

Stress has become an inevitable part of our lives. Whether it's due to work pressures, relationship issues, or financial concerns, stress can have a significant impact on our overall health and well-being. It is important to manage stress effectively in order to maintain a healthy lifestyle and prevent the negative consequences that chronic stress can have on our bodies and minds.

Understanding the Impact of Stress on Your Body and Mind

Stress can have both physical and mental effects on our bodies. When we experience stress, our bodies release hormones such as cortisol and adrenaline, which can increase heart rate, blood pressure, and muscle tension. These physical responses are part of the body's natural "fight or flight" response to stress. However, when stress becomes chronic, these physical responses can take a toll on our bodies, leading to a weakened immune system, digestive problems, and an increased risk of developing chronic illnesses such as heart disease and diabetes.

In addition to the physical effects, stress can also have a significant impact on our mental health. Chronic stress can lead to symptoms of anxiety and depression, as well as difficulty concentrating and making decisions. It can also affect our sleep patterns, leading to insomnia or disrupted sleep. The long-term consequences of chronic stress can be detrimental to our overall well-being and quality of life.

The Connection Between Yoga and Stress Reduction

Yoga has been practiced for thousands of years and is known for its ability to promote relaxation and reduce stress. The combination of physical postures, breathing exercises, and meditation in yoga helps to calm the mind and relax the body. By focusing on the present moment and connecting with the breath, yoga helps to shift our attention away from stressful thoughts and worries.

Scientific research has shown that yoga can have a positive impact on stress reduction. A study published in the Journal of Clinical Psychology found that practicing yoga for just 25 minutes a day for eight weeks significantly reduced symptoms of anxiety and depression. Another study published in the Journal of Alternative and Complementary Medicine found that yoga was effective in reducing stress and improving overall well-being in individuals with chronic stress.

Mindfulness: A Powerful Tool for Managing Stress

Mindfulness is the practice of paying attention to the present moment without judgment. It involves bringing our awareness to our thoughts, feelings, and bodily sensations in a non-reactive way. By practicing mindfulness, we can become more aware of our stress triggers and learn to respond to them in a more calm and balanced way.

The benefits of mindfulness for stress management are well-documented. Research has shown that mindfulness can reduce symptoms of anxiety and depression, improve attention and focus, and increase feelings of well-being. A study published in the Journal of Consulting and Clinical Psychology found that mindfulness-based stress reduction (MBSR) was effective in reducing stress and improving overall quality of life in individuals with chronic stress.

To practice mindfulness in daily life, you can start by setting aside a few minutes each day to sit quietly and focus on your breath. As thoughts arise, simply observe them without judgment and gently bring your attention back to your breath. You can also incorporate mindfulness into everyday activities such as eating, walking, or washing dishes by bringing your full attention to the present moment.

Incorporating Meditation into Your Daily Routine

Meditation is another powerful tool for managing stress. It involves sitting quietly and focusing your attention on a specific object or mantra, or simply observing your thoughts and feelings without judgment. By practicing meditation regularly, you can train your mind to become more calm and focused, which can help reduce stress and anxiety.

The benefits of meditation for stress relief have been widely studied. Research has shown that meditation can reduce symptoms of anxiety and depression, improve attention and concentration, and increase feelings of well-being. A study published in the Journal of Psychosomatic Medicine found that meditation was effective in reducing stress and improving overall quality of life in individuals with chronic stress.

To start a meditation practice, find a quiet and comfortable place where you can sit for a few minutes each day. Close your eyes and focus your attention on your breath, or choose a mantra to repeat silently to yourself. As thoughts arise, simply observe them without judgment and gently bring your attention back to your breath or mantra. Start with just a few minutes a day and gradually increase the duration as you become more comfortable with the practice.

The Benefits of Deep Breathing for Stress Relief

Deep breathing is a simple yet effective technique for reducing stress and anxiety. When we are stressed, our breathing tends to become shallow and rapid. By practicing deep breathing, we can activate the body's relaxation response and promote a sense of calm and relaxation.

Deep breathing involves taking slow, deep breaths in through the nose, filling the lungs completely, and then exhaling slowly through the mouth. This type of breathing stimulates the vagus nerve, which helps to activate the body's relaxation response. It also helps to increase oxygen flow to the brain, which can improve focus and concentration.

To practice deep breathing, find a quiet and comfortable place where you can sit or lie down. Close your eyes and take a deep breath in through your nose, allowing your belly to rise as you fill your lungs with air. Hold the breath for a moment, and then exhale slowly through your mouth, allowing your belly to fall as you release the air. Repeat this process several times, focusing on the sensation of the breath as it enters and leaves your body.

How Exercise Can Help You Manage Stress

Exercise is not only beneficial for physical health but also plays a crucial role in managing stress. When we engage in physical activity, our bodies release endorphins, which are natural mood-boosting chemicals that help reduce stress and improve overall well-being. Exercise also helps to reduce levels of stress hormones such as cortisol and adrenaline, and promotes better sleep, which can further reduce stress levels.

Various types of exercise can be effective for stress management. Aerobic exercises such as running, swimming, or cycling can help release tension and increase feelings of relaxation. Yoga and Pilates combine physical movement with mindfulness and deep breathing, making them particularly effective for stress reduction. Strength training exercises such as weightlifting or resistance training can also help reduce stress by promoting a sense of empowerment and confidence.

To incorporate exercise into your daily routine, find activities that you enjoy and that fit into your schedule. Aim for at least 30 minutes of moderate-intensity exercise most days of the week. If you're new to exercise, start slowly and gradually increase the duration and intensity as you build strength and endurance. Remember to listen to your body and choose activities that feel good for you.

The Importance of Getting Enough Sleep for Stress Management

Sleep plays a crucial role in managing stress. When we are sleep-deprived, our bodies produce more stress hormones such as cortisol, which can increase feelings of anxiety and tension. Lack of sleep can also affect our mood, concentration, and overall well-being.

To improve sleep quality, it is important to establish a regular sleep routine. Try to go to bed and wake up at the same time every day, even on weekends. Create a relaxing bedtime routine that includes activities such as reading, taking a warm bath, or practicing relaxation techniques. Make your bedroom a comfortable and sleep-friendly environment by keeping it cool, dark, and quiet. Avoid stimulating activities such as watching TV or using electronic devices before bed, as the blue light emitted by these devices can interfere with sleep.

Eating a Healthy Diet to Reduce Stress Levels

The food we eat can have a significant impact on our stress levels. Certain foods can help reduce stress and anxiety, while others can exacerbate these symptoms. A healthy diet that includes a variety of nutrient-rich foods can help support our bodies and minds during times of stress.

Foods that can help reduce stress and anxiety include those rich in omega-3 fatty acids, such as fatty fish, walnuts, and flaxseeds. These healthy fats have been shown to reduce inflammation in the body and promote brain health. Foods rich in magnesium, such as leafy green vegetables, nuts, and whole grains, can also help reduce stress by promoting relaxation and better sleep. Other stress-reducing foods include those high in antioxidants, such as berries, dark chocolate, and green tea.

On the other hand, certain foods can increase stress levels. Foods high in sugar and refined carbohydrates can cause blood sugar spikes and crashes, leading to mood swings and increased feelings of stress.

Caffeine and alcohol can also exacerbate symptoms of anxiety and disrupt sleep patterns. It is important to be mindful of your diet and choose foods that nourish your body and support your overall well-being.

The Role of Social Support in Coping with Stress

Social connections play a crucial role in managing stress. Having a strong support network of family, friends, or colleagues can provide emotional support, practical assistance, and a sense of belonging. Research has shown that individuals with strong social support are better able to cope with stress and have lower levels of anxiety and depression.

To build and maintain a support network, it is important to prioritize your relationships and make time for social activities. Reach out to friends or family members regularly to check in and offer support. Join clubs or organizations that align with your interests or hobbies to meet like-minded individuals. Consider seeking professional help if you are struggling with chronic stress or anxiety, as therapists or counselors can provide guidance and support.

Finding Time for Self-Care in Your Busy Schedule

Self-care is an essential component of stress management. Taking time for yourself and engaging in activities that bring you joy and relaxation can help reduce stress and improve overall well-being.

However, in our busy lives, it can be challenging to find time for self-care.

To make self-care a priority, it is important to set boundaries and establish a routine that includes regular self-care activities. Start by identifying activities that you enjoy and that help you relax, such as reading, taking a bath, practicing yoga, or spending time in nature. Schedule these activities into your daily or weekly routine and treat them as non-negotiable appointments with yourself. Remember that self-care is not selfish but rather a necessary part of maintaining your physical and mental health.

Seeking Professional Help for Chronic Stress and Anxiety

While self-help techniques can be effective for managing stress, there may be times when professional help is needed. If you are experiencing chronic stress or anxiety that is interfering with your daily life, it is important to seek help from a healthcare professional.

There are various treatment options available for chronic stress and anxiety, including therapy, medication, and alternative therapies such as acupuncture or massage. Cognitive-behavioral therapy (CBT) is a common form of therapy that focuses on identifying and changing negative thought patterns and behaviors that contribute to stress and anxiety. Medications such as antidepressants or anti-anxiety medications may be prescribed in certain cases. It is important to work with a healthcare professional to determine the best treatment plan for your individual needs.

In conclusion, managing stress is crucial for our overall health and well-being. Stress can have a significant impact on our bodies and minds, leading to physical and mental health problems if left unaddressed. By incorporating various techniques such as yoga, mindfulness, meditation, deep breathing, exercise, sleep hygiene, healthy eating, social support, and self-care into our daily lives, we can effectively manage stress and improve our quality of life. It is important to try different techniques and seek professional help if needed, as everyone's journey to stress management is unique. Remember that taking care of yourself is not selfish but rather a necessary part of living a healthy and fulfilling life.

Chapter 16: From Student to Mentor: How Peer Mentoring Can Help You Grow Personally and Professionally

Peer mentoring is a powerful tool for personal and professional growth. It involves a mutually beneficial relationship between individuals of similar backgrounds or experiences, where one person provides guidance, support, and knowledge to another. This form of mentoring is particularly effective because it allows individuals to learn from someone who has faced similar challenges and can provide relevant advice and insights.

Personal and professional growth is essential for success in today's fast-paced and competitive world. It is important to continuously develop our skills, knowledge, and abilities in order to stay relevant and achieve our goals. Peer mentoring offers a unique opportunity to learn from others who have already walked the path we are on or are currently on. By engaging in peer mentoring relationships, we can gain valuable insights, expand our networks, and enhance our personal and professional development.

What is Peer Mentoring and How Does it Work?

Peer mentoring is a form of mentoring where individuals of similar backgrounds or experiences support and guide each other. It is a collaborative relationship where both parties benefit from the exchange of knowledge, skills, and experiences. Unlike traditional mentoring relationships where there is a clear power dynamic between the mentor and mentee, peer mentoring is based on equality and mutual respect.

In a peer mentoring relationship, both individuals have the opportunity to learn from each other's experiences, share resources, provide emotional support, and offer guidance. The mentor acts as a role model and provides advice based on their own experiences, while the mentee benefits from the mentor's knowledge and expertise.

There are different types of peer mentoring programs, including formal programs offered by educational institutions or organizations, as well as informal programs that individuals establish on their own. Formal programs often have structured guidelines and objectives, while informal programs allow for more flexibility and customization based on the needs of the participants.

The Benefits of Peer Mentoring for Students and Young Professionals

Peer mentoring offers numerous benefits for students and young professionals in their personal and professional lives.

Academically, peer mentoring can provide valuable support and guidance to help students succeed in their studies. Mentors can share study tips, provide feedback on assignments, and offer guidance on navigating the academic system. This can lead to improved grades, increased confidence, and a better understanding of the subject matter.

In terms of career development, peer mentoring can be instrumental in helping young professionals navigate their chosen field. Mentors can provide insights into the industry, offer advice on career paths, and help mentees develop the skills and knowledge needed to succeed. This can lead to increased job opportunities, professional growth, and a stronger network of contacts.

On a personal level, peer mentoring can provide emotional support and a sense of belonging. Mentors can offer guidance on personal challenges, provide a listening ear, and help mentees develop resilience and coping strategies. This can lead to increased self-confidence, improved mental health, and a greater sense of purpose.

Socially, peer mentoring can help individuals build strong relationships and expand their networks. Mentors can introduce mentees to new people, provide opportunities for networking, and help mentees develop social skills. This can lead to increased social capital, improved communication skills, and a broader support system.

How Peer Mentoring Can Help You Develop Leadership Skills

Leadership skills are essential for success in any field or endeavor. They involve the ability to inspire and motivate others, make decisions, communicate effectively, and take initiative. Peer mentoring can be a powerful tool for developing these skills.

By engaging in peer mentoring relationships, individuals have the opportunity to practice and develop their leadership skills in a supportive environment. Mentors can provide guidance on leadership principles and strategies, offer feedback on leadership behaviors, and help mentees identify areas for improvement.

Examples of leadership skills that can be developed through peer mentoring include:

1. Communication: Peer mentoring requires effective communication between the mentor and mentee. This includes active listening, asking questions, and providing feedback. By practicing these skills in a mentoring relationship, individuals can

improve their overall communication skills, which are essential for effective leadership.

2. Decision-making: Mentors often provide guidance and advice to mentees, helping them make informed decisions. By observing and learning from their mentor's decision-making process, mentees can develop their own decision-making skills and become more confident in their ability to make sound judgments.

3. Emotional intelligence: Peer mentoring involves building strong relationships and providing emotional support. This requires empathy, self-awareness, and the ability to understand and manage emotions. By engaging in peer mentoring relationships, individuals can develop their emotional intelligence, which is a key component of effective leadership.

4. Problem-solving: Mentors often help mentees navigate challenges and obstacles. This requires problem-solving skills, such as critical thinking, creativity, and the ability to analyze situations from different perspectives. By working through problems with their mentor, mentees can develop their problem-solving skills and become more effective leaders.

Building Strong Relationships Through Peer Mentoring

Building strong relationships is essential for personal and professional success. Strong relationships provide support, guidance, and a sense of belonging. Peer mentoring can be a powerful tool for building these relationships.

In a peer mentoring relationship, individuals have the opportunity to develop a deep connection based on shared experiences and mutual support. Mentors can provide guidance, advice, and encouragement, while mentees can offer fresh perspectives, enthusiasm, and a willingness to learn.

Through regular meetings and open communication, peer mentoring relationships can grow into strong friendships that extend beyond the mentoring program. These relationships can provide ongoing support and guidance throughout one's personal and professional journey.

Examples of strong relationships built through peer mentoring include:

1. Lifelong friendships: Many peer mentoring relationships evolve into lifelong friendships. The shared experiences and mutual support create a strong bond that extends beyond the mentoring program.

2. Professional networks: Peer mentoring relationships often lead to the expansion of professional networks. Mentors can introduce mentees to their contacts, provide recommendations, and help mentees establish connections in their chosen field.

3. Collaborative partnerships: Peer mentoring relationships can also lead to collaborative partnerships. Mentors and mentees may discover shared interests or complementary skills, leading to joint projects or business ventures.

Overcoming Challenges and Obstacles with Peer Mentoring Support

Challenges and obstacles are a natural part of life and can often hinder personal and professional growth. Peer mentoring can provide valuable support and guidance in overcoming these challenges.

Common challenges and obstacles that individuals may face include:

1. Lack of confidence: Many individuals struggle with self-doubt and lack of confidence, which can hinder their ability to take risks or pursue their goals. Peer mentors can provide encouragement, reassurance, and guidance to help mentees build confidence and overcome self-limiting beliefs.

2. Time management: Balancing personal and professional responsibilities can be challenging, especially for students and young professionals. Peer mentors can offer strategies, tips, and advice on effective time management, helping mentees prioritize tasks and achieve a better work-life balance.

3. Career transitions: Changing careers or pursuing new opportunities can be daunting. Peer mentors who have gone through similar transitions can provide guidance, advice, and support to help mentees navigate these changes.

4. Work-life balance: Achieving a healthy work-life balance is essential for overall well-being. Peer mentors can share strategies for managing stress, setting boundaries, and prioritizing self-care.

Peer mentoring relationships provide a safe space for individuals to discuss their challenges and obstacles openly. Mentors can offer guidance based on their own experiences, provide emotional support, and help mentees develop strategies for overcoming these challenges.

Examples of challenges and obstacles overcome through peer mentoring include:

1. Overcoming imposter syndrome: Many individuals struggle with imposter syndrome, feeling like they don't belong or aren't qualified for their roles. Peer mentors can share their own experiences with imposter syndrome and provide strategies for overcoming it.

2. Navigating workplace politics: Workplace politics can be complex and challenging to navigate. Peer mentors who have experience in the same industry or organization can provide guidance on how to navigate these dynamics and build positive relationships with colleagues.

3. Overcoming fear of failure: Fear of failure can hold individuals back from taking risks or pursuing their goals. Peer mentors can share their own experiences with failure and provide encouragement and support to help mentees overcome this fear.

The Role of Communication in Peer Mentoring Relationships

Effective communication is essential for successful peer mentoring relationships. It involves active listening, asking questions, providing feedback, and expressing thoughts and feelings clearly and respectfully.

In a peer mentoring relationship, communication plays a crucial role in building trust, understanding each other's needs and expectations, and resolving conflicts. By practicing effective communication skills in a mentoring relationship, individuals can improve their overall communication skills, which are essential for personal and professional success.

Peer mentoring can improve communication skills in several ways:

1. Active listening: Peer mentors must actively listen to their mentees in order to understand their needs, concerns, and goals. By practicing active listening skills, individuals can become better listeners in all areas of their lives.

2. Asking questions: Peer mentors often ask probing questions to help mentees reflect on their experiences and gain new insights.

By observing their mentor's questioning techniques, mentees can learn how to ask thoughtful questions that promote deeper understanding.

3. Providing feedback: Peer mentors provide feedback to help mentees improve their skills and achieve their goals. By receiving feedback from their mentor, mentees can learn how to give constructive feedback in a respectful and helpful manner.

4. Expressing thoughts and feelings: Peer mentoring relationships provide a safe space for individuals to express their thoughts and feelings openly. By practicing self-expression in a mentoring relationship, individuals can become more comfortable expressing themselves in other areas of their lives.

Examples of effective communication in peer mentoring relationships include:

1. Active listening: The mentor listens attentively to the mentee's concerns and asks clarifying questions to ensure understanding.

2. Asking open-ended questions: The mentor asks open-ended questions that encourage the mentee to reflect on their experiences and gain new insights.

3. Providing constructive feedback: The mentor provides feedback that is specific, actionable, and focused on helping the mentee improve their skills or achieve their goals.

4. Expressing empathy: The mentor expresses empathy and understanding towards the mentee's challenges and offers support and encouragement.

Setting Goals and Achieving Success with Peer Mentoring

Setting goals is essential for personal and professional growth. Goals provide direction, motivation, and a sense of purpose. Peer mentoring can be instrumental in helping individuals set and achieve their goals.

In a peer mentoring relationship, mentors can help mentees clarify their goals, break them down into actionable steps, and hold them accountable for their progress. Mentors can also provide guidance on overcoming obstacles, staying motivated, and celebrating achievements.

Peer mentoring can help individuals set and achieve goals in several ways:

1. Clarifying goals: Mentors can help mentees clarify their goals by asking probing questions, challenging assumptions, and encouraging reflection. By discussing their goals with a mentor, individuals can gain clarity and focus on what they truly want to achieve.

2. Breaking down goals: Mentors can help mentees break down their goals into smaller, manageable steps. By breaking down goals into actionable tasks, individuals can make progress towards their goals more effectively.

3. Providing accountability: Peer mentors can hold mentees accountable for their progress by checking in regularly, providing feedback, and offering support. This accountability can help individuals stay motivated and on track towards their goals.

4. Celebrating achievements: Mentors can help mentees celebrate their achievements, no matter how small. By acknowledging and celebrating progress, individuals can stay motivated and maintain a positive mindset.

Examples of goals achieved through peer mentoring include:

1. Academic success: Mentees who set goals to improve their grades or excel in their studies can work with their mentor to develop effective study strategies, manage their time effectively, and stay motivated.

2. Career advancement: Mentees who set goals to advance in their careers can work with their mentor to develop a career plan, improve their skills, and expand their professional network.

3. Personal growth: Mentees who set goals for personal growth, such as improving their communication skills or developing a healthier lifestyle, can work with their mentor to develop action plans and hold themselves accountable.

The Importance of Accountability in Peer Mentoring

Accountability is essential for personal and professional growth. It involves taking responsibility for one's actions, commitments, and goals. Peer mentoring can help individuals improve their accountability by providing support, guidance, and feedback.

In a peer mentoring relationship, mentors can hold mentees accountable for their progress by checking in regularly, providing feedback on their actions, and offering support when needed. This accountability can help individuals stay motivated, overcome obstacles, and achieve their goals.

Peer mentoring can improve accountability in several ways:

1. Regular check-ins: Mentors can schedule regular check-ins with mentees to review progress towards goals, discuss challenges or obstacles, and provide feedback. These check-ins provide an opportunity for mentees to reflect on their actions and make adjustments if necessary.

2. Goal setting: Mentors can help mentees set specific, measurable, achievable, relevant, and time-bound (SMART) goals. By setting clear goals, individuals are more likely to hold themselves accountable for their actions.

3. Feedback and support: Mentors can provide feedback on mentees' actions and offer support when needed. This feedback and support can help mentees stay motivated, overcome obstacles, and make necessary adjustments to achieve their goals.

Examples of accountability in peer mentoring relationships include:

1. Regular progress updates: Mentees provide regular progress updates to their mentor, sharing their achievements, challenges, and next steps.

2. Action plans: Mentees develop action plans with their mentor, outlining the specific steps they will take to achieve their goals. These action plans serve as a roadmap and help individuals stay focused and accountable.

3. Feedback and reflection: Mentors provide feedback on mentees' actions and encourage reflection on their progress. This feedback and reflection help individuals assess their performance and make necessary adjustments.

How to Find the Right Peer Mentoring Program for You

Finding the right peer mentoring program is essential for a successful mentoring experience. There are several factors to consider when choosing a program that aligns with your needs and goals.

1. Objectives: Consider the objectives of the peer mentoring program. Does it align with your personal or professional goals? Look for programs that have clear objectives and a structured approach to mentoring.

2. Format: Consider the format of the program. Is it a formal program offered by an educational institution or organization? Or

is it an informal program established by individuals? Decide which format suits your needs and preferences.

3. Compatibility: Consider the compatibility between mentors and mentees in the program. Are there opportunities to connect with individuals who have similar backgrounds or experiences? Look for programs that prioritize compatibility to ensure a meaningful mentoring relationship. This can be achieved by matching mentors and mentees based on shared interests, goals, or industry experience. Compatibility is crucial as it allows for a stronger connection and understanding between the mentor and mentee, leading to more effective guidance and support. Additionally, compatibility can foster a sense of trust and rapport, making it easier for mentees to open up and seek advice from their mentors. Ultimately, a program that prioritizes compatibility will enhance the overall mentoring experience and increase the likelihood of achieving desired outcomes for both mentors and mentees.

Chapter 17: Breaking the 9-5 Mold: How Flexible Scheduling Can Revolutionize Your Career

The traditional 9-5 workday has long been the standard for many industries, but it is not without its limitations. This rigid schedule can often be restrictive and does not always align with the needs and preferences of employees. However, there is a solution that offers more flexibility and can address these limitations - flexible scheduling.

What is Flexible Scheduling?

Flexible scheduling refers to a variety of arrangements that allow employees to have more control over when and where they work. This can include options such as telecommuting, compressed workweeks, and job sharing. Unlike the traditional 9-5 workday, flexible scheduling allows employees to have more autonomy and freedom in managing their work-life balance.

Telecommuting, also known as remote work or working from home, allows employees to work from a location outside of the office. This can be especially beneficial for those who have long commutes or prefer to work in a more comfortable environment. Compressed workweeks involve working longer hours on fewer days, such as working four 10-hour days instead of five 8-hour days. Job sharing involves two or more employees sharing the responsibilities of one full-time position.

The Benefits of Flexible Scheduling for Employees

Flexible scheduling offers numerous benefits for employees. One of the most significant advantages is the improvement in work-life balance. With the ability to choose when and where they work, employees can better manage their personal responsibilities and commitments. This can lead to reduced stress and improved mental health, as employees have more time for self-care and relaxation.

Furthermore, flexible scheduling has been shown to increase job satisfaction and employee engagement. When employees have more control over their schedules, they are more likely to feel valued and trusted by their employers. This can result in higher levels of motivation and productivity, as well as a stronger sense of loyalty towards the company.

Increased Productivity and Employee Engagement

Flexible scheduling has been proven to increase productivity and employee engagement. When employees have the freedom to work during their most productive hours, they are more likely to produce high-quality work. Additionally, flexible scheduling allows employees to work in environments that are conducive to their individual work styles, which can further enhance productivity.

Companies such as Microsoft and Dell have seen success with flexible scheduling. Microsoft implemented a flexible work policy that allowed employees to choose when and where they worked. As a result, they saw a 40% increase in productivity. Dell also experienced positive outcomes with flexible scheduling, reporting a 12% increase in employee engagement.

Reduced Stress and Improved Work-Life Balance

One of the most significant benefits of flexible scheduling is the reduction in stress and burnout. The traditional 9-5 workday can often lead to long commutes and limited time for personal activities. With flexible scheduling, employees have the opportunity to create a better work-life balance, allowing for more time with family and hobbies.

Studies have shown that flexible scheduling can lead to reduced stress levels. A study conducted by the University of Minnesota found that employees who had control over their schedules reported lower levels of stress and higher levels of job satisfaction. Another study by the American Psychological Association found that employees who had access to flexible scheduling reported lower levels of burnout.

The Benefits of Flexible Scheduling for Employers

Flexible scheduling is not only beneficial for employees but also for employers. One of the advantages is the ability to attract and retain top talent. In today's competitive job market, offering flexible scheduling can be a significant advantage in attracting highly skilled individuals who value work-life balance.

Additionally, flexible scheduling can lead to cost savings for employers. With telecommuting options, companies can reduce overhead costs associated with office space and utilities.

Furthermore, increased employee engagement and productivity can result in higher efficiency and ultimately lead to cost savings.

Companies such as Google and Amazon have successfully implemented flexible scheduling and have seen positive outcomes. Google offers a variety of flexible work options, including telecommuting and flexible hours. This has allowed them to attract top talent and maintain a high level of employee satisfaction. Amazon also offers flexible scheduling options, which has contributed to their reputation as an employer of choice.

Attracting and Retaining Top Talent

Flexible scheduling can be a competitive advantage in attracting and retaining top talent. In today's workforce, employees are increasingly seeking work-life balance and flexibility in their schedules. By offering flexible scheduling options, employers can differentiate themselves from their competitors and attract highly skilled individuals who value these benefits.

Furthermore, flexible scheduling can improve diversity and inclusion in the workplace. By accommodating different schedules and preferences, companies can create a more inclusive environment that caters to the needs of a diverse workforce. This can lead to increased employee satisfaction and a stronger sense of belonging.

Companies such as Netflix and Salesforce have successfully used flexible scheduling to attract and retain employees. Netflix offers unlimited vacation time and allows employees to set their own schedules. This has contributed to their reputation as a company that values work-life balance and has helped them attract top talent. Salesforce also offers flexible scheduling options, which has resulted in high employee satisfaction rates.

Cost Savings and Increased Efficiency

Flexible scheduling can lead to cost savings for employers. With telecommuting options, companies can reduce expenses associated with office space, utilities, and other overhead costs. Additionally, increased employee engagement and productivity can result in higher efficiency, which can lead to cost savings.

Companies such as IBM and Best Buy have seen cost savings and increased efficiency with flexible scheduling. IBM implemented a telecommuting program that allowed employees to work remotely. This resulted in significant cost savings, with the company reducing its office space by 78 million square feet and saving $100 million annually. Best Buy also experienced positive outcomes with flexible scheduling, reporting a 35% increase in productivity.

Challenges and Solutions for Implementing Flexible Scheduling

While flexible scheduling offers numerous benefits, there can be challenges in implementing it. One common challenge is resistance from managers and supervisors who may be hesitant to change the traditional work structure. To overcome this, it is important to educate managers about the benefits of flexible scheduling and provide training on how to effectively manage remote teams.

Another challenge is ensuring effective communication and collaboration between employees who may be working different schedules or locations. This can be addressed by implementing technology tools that facilitate communication, such as video conferencing and project management software. Additionally, setting clear expectations and guidelines for remote work can help ensure that employees are accountable and productive.

Best Practices for Successful Flexible Scheduling

To successfully implement flexible scheduling, it is important to follow best practices. One of the key factors is setting clear expectations and guidelines for employees. This includes defining core working hours, establishing communication protocols, and outlining performance expectations.

Flexibility and adaptability are also crucial for successful flexible scheduling. Employers should be open to adjusting schedules and arrangements based on the needs of employees and the business. This can help create a positive work environment where employees feel supported and valued.

Furthermore, regular communication and feedback are essential for successful flexible scheduling. Employers should regularly check in with employees to ensure that they have the resources they need and are meeting their goals. This can help address any challenges or concerns that may arise and ensure that employees feel supported.

Embracing the Future of Work with Flexible Scheduling

In conclusion, the traditional 9-5 workday has its limitations, but flexible scheduling offers a solution that can benefit both employees and employers. By allowing employees to have more control over when and where they work, flexible scheduling can improve work-life balance, reduce stress, increase productivity, and attract top talent.

Employers should embrace flexible scheduling as a solution for the limitations of the traditional workday. By adapting to the changing needs and expectations of the modern workforce, companies can create a more inclusive and productive work environment. With clear expectations, effective communication, and a focus on flexibility and adaptability, employers can successfully implement flexible scheduling and reap the benefits it offers.

Chapter 18: Creating a Safe Haven: How Sensory-Friendly Spaces Benefit Everyone

Sensory-friendly spaces are designed to accommodate individuals with sensory processing disorders, providing them with a safe and comfortable environment. These spaces are specifically designed to minimize sensory overload and create a calming atmosphere. They are equipped with features such as soft lighting, quiet areas, and sensory tools to help individuals regulate their sensory input.

Creating sensory-friendly spaces is crucial because it allows individuals with sensory processing disorders to participate fully in various activities and engage with their surroundings without feeling overwhelmed. These spaces provide a sense of inclusion and acceptance, allowing individuals to feel more comfortable and supported in their daily lives.

The Importance of Creating Safe Havens

Sensory-friendly spaces serve as safe havens for individuals with sensory processing disorders. These individuals often experience sensory overload, which occurs when their senses are overwhelmed by stimuli in their environment. This can lead to feelings of anxiety, stress, and even physical discomfort.

By creating sensory-friendly spaces, individuals with sensory processing disorders have a place where they can retreat to when they feel overwhelmed. These spaces are designed to minimize sensory input and provide a calming environment, allowing individuals to regulate their senses and find relief from sensory overload.

Who Benefits from Sensory-Friendly Spaces?

Sensory-friendly spaces are not only beneficial for individuals with sensory processing disorders but also for those with anxiety disorders, autism spectrum disorder (ASD), and attention deficit hyperactivity disorder (ADHD).

Individuals with anxiety disorders often experience heightened sensitivity to their surroundings, leading to increased anxiety levels. Sensory-friendly spaces provide a calming environment that helps reduce anxiety and promote relaxation.

Similarly, individuals with ASD often have difficulty processing sensory information, which can lead to sensory overload. Sensory-friendly spaces provide a safe and accommodating environment where individuals with ASD can feel more comfortable and engaged.

Individuals with ADHD may also benefit from sensory-friendly spaces as they often struggle with focus and attention. These spaces can help create a more structured and organized environment, reducing distractions and promoting better concentration.

Sensory-Friendly Spaces in Public Places

Many public places have recognized the importance of creating sensory-friendly spaces to accommodate individuals with sensory processing disorders. Examples of sensory-friendly spaces in public places include sensory rooms in airports, museums, and shopping centers.

These spaces are designed to provide a quiet and calming environment away from the hustle and bustle of public areas. They often include features such as dim lighting, comfortable seating, and sensory tools like weighted blankets or fidget toys. These spaces allow individuals with sensory processing disorders to take a break from overwhelming stimuli and recharge before continuing with their activities.

The benefits of sensory-friendly spaces in public places are significant. They promote inclusivity and accessibility, allowing individuals with sensory processing disorders to participate fully in public activities. These spaces also raise awareness about sensory processing disorders and help create a more understanding and accepting society.

Designing Sensory-Friendly Spaces at Home

Creating sensory-friendly spaces at home is equally important as it provides individuals with a safe and comfortable environment where they can relax and engage with their surroundings. Here are some tips for designing sensory-friendly spaces at home:

1. Choose calming colors: Use soft, neutral colors on the walls and furniture to create a soothing atmosphere.

2. Control lighting: Install dimmer switches or use soft lighting options to create a calming ambiance.

3. Provide comfortable seating: Choose furniture that is comfortable and supportive, such as bean bags or cushioned chairs.

4. Create quiet areas: Designate specific areas in the home where individuals can retreat to when they need a break from sensory input.

5. Incorporate sensory tools: Include items like weighted blankets, fidget toys, or noise-canceling headphones to help individuals regulate their senses.

Sensory-friendly spaces at home provide individuals with a safe haven where they can relax and recharge. These spaces promote a sense of calm and well-being, allowing individuals to better manage their sensory processing needs.

The Role of Sensory-Friendly Spaces in Education

Sensory-friendly spaces play a crucial role in supporting learning in the classroom. These spaces provide a calm and structured environment where students with sensory processing disorders can focus and engage with their studies.

Sensory-friendly classrooms often include features such as flexible seating options, visual schedules, and quiet areas. These spaces are designed to minimize distractions and provide students with the tools they need to regulate their sensory input.

Examples of sensory-friendly classrooms include classrooms with adjustable lighting, noise-reducing materials, and designated sensory breaks. These classrooms create an inclusive learning environment where all students can thrive.

Sensory-Friendly Spaces in the Workplace

Sensory-friendly spaces are not limited to public places or educational settings; they also have a place in the workplace. Many companies are recognizing the benefits of creating sensory-friendly spaces to support their employees' well-being and productivity.

Sensory-friendly workplaces often include features such as quiet rooms, adjustable lighting, and designated break areas. These spaces allow employees to take a break from sensory input and recharge before returning to their work tasks.

Examples of sensory-friendly workplaces include companies that provide noise-canceling headphones, flexible workspaces, and natural lighting options. These workplaces prioritize the well-being of their employees and create an inclusive environment where everyone can thrive.

How Sensory-Friendly Spaces Support Mental Health

Sensory-friendly spaces have a significant impact on mental health. For individuals with sensory processing disorders or other mental health conditions, these spaces provide a sense of safety and comfort, reducing anxiety levels and promoting overall well-being.

Sensory-friendly spaces help individuals regulate their sensory input, which can have a positive effect on their mental health. By creating an environment that minimizes sensory overload, these spaces allow individuals to feel more in control of their surroundings and reduce feelings of stress and overwhelm.

Additionally, sensory-friendly spaces promote a sense of acceptance and inclusivity, which can have a profound impact on individuals' self-esteem and mental well-being. These spaces create a supportive environment where individuals feel understood and valued, leading to improved mental health outcomes.

Overcoming Common Challenges in Creating Sensory-Friendly Spaces

Creating sensory-friendly spaces can come with its challenges. Some common challenges include limited resources, lack of awareness or understanding, and the need for collaboration among various stakeholders.

Limited resources can make it difficult to create fully equipped sensory-friendly spaces. However, by prioritizing the most essential elements, such as comfortable seating and calming lighting, it is possible to create effective sensory-friendly spaces even with limited resources.

Lack of awareness or understanding about sensory processing disorders can also be a challenge. Educating the community about the importance of sensory-friendly spaces and raising awareness about the needs of individuals with sensory processing disorders can help overcome this challenge.

Collaboration among various stakeholders is crucial in creating effective sensory-friendly spaces. This includes collaboration between architects, designers, educators, and individuals with sensory processing disorders themselves. By involving all stakeholders in the design process, it ensures that the space meets the specific needs of the individuals who will be using it.

Best Practices for Creating Effective Sensory-Friendly Spaces

Creating effective sensory-friendly spaces requires careful planning and consideration. Here are some best practices to keep in mind:

1. Prioritize comfort: Choose furniture and materials that are comfortable and supportive to create a relaxing environment.

2. Minimize sensory input: Use soft lighting, soundproofing materials, and calming colors to minimize sensory overload.

3. Provide sensory tools: Include items like weighted blankets, fidget toys, or noise-canceling headphones to help individuals regulate their senses.

4. Designate quiet areas: Create designated quiet areas where individuals can retreat to when they need a break from sensory input.

5. Seek feedback: Regularly seek feedback from individuals using the space to ensure that it meets their specific needs and preferences.

Collaboration and feedback are key to creating effective sensory-friendly spaces. By involving individuals with sensory processing disorders in the design process and seeking their input, it ensures that the space is truly accommodating and supportive.

The Impact of Sensory-Friendly Spaces on Our Lives

Sensory-friendly spaces have a profound impact on the lives of individuals with sensory processing disorders and other related conditions. These spaces provide a safe haven where individuals can regulate their sensory input, reduce anxiety levels, and feel more comfortable and supported.

Creating more sensory-friendly spaces in our communities is crucial to promote inclusivity and accessibility. By raising awareness about sensory processing disorders and the importance of sensory-friendly spaces, we can create a more understanding and accepting society.

Sensory-friendly spaces are not limited to public places; they also have a place in our homes, schools, and workplaces. By incorporating sensory-friendly design principles into these environments, we can support the well-being and success of individuals with sensory processing disorders and other related conditions.

In conclusion, sensory-friendly spaces play a vital role in creating a more inclusive and supportive society. By prioritizing the needs of individuals with sensory processing disorders, we can create environments that promote well-being, reduce anxiety levels, and allow everyone to thrive.

Chapter 19: The Power of Prioritization: How to Manage Your Time Like a Pro

Time is a valuable resource that needs to be managed effectively. In today's fast-paced world, it's easy to feel overwhelmed and like there's never enough time to get everything done. That's why prioritization is a key component of time management. The ability to prioritize tasks can help you achieve your goals and increase productivity.

When you prioritize tasks, you are essentially identifying the most important ones and focusing on them first. This allows you to make the most of your time and avoid wasting it on unimportant tasks. By prioritizing, you can ensure that you are spending your time and energy on the things that will have the biggest impact on your goals.

Understanding the Concept of Prioritization

Prioritization involves evaluating tasks based on their importance and urgency. It requires you to determine which tasks are most crucial to your goals and focus on those first. By doing so, you can ensure that you are making progress on the things that matter most.

One effective tool for prioritizing tasks is the Eisenhower Matrix. This matrix categorizes tasks into four quadrants based on their importance and urgency. Tasks that are both important and urgent should be done immediately, while tasks that are important but not urgent should be scheduled for later. Tasks that are urgent but not important can be delegated or eliminated, and tasks that are neither urgent nor important can be eliminated altogether.

Another method for prioritizing tasks is the ABCDE Method. With this method, you assign each task a letter from A to E based on its level of importance. A tasks are the most important and should be done first, while E tasks are the least important and can be eliminated if necessary.

The Pareto Principle is another useful concept in prioritization. This principle states that 80% of your results come from 20% of your efforts. By focusing on the tasks that will have the biggest impact, you can maximize your productivity and achieve more in less time.

Techniques for Prioritizing Your Tasks

There are several techniques you can use to prioritize your tasks effectively. One of the most popular methods is the Eisenhower Matrix, as mentioned earlier. This matrix helps you categorize tasks based on their importance and urgency, allowing you to focus on the most critical tasks first.

Another technique is the ABCDE Method. With this method, you assign each task a letter from A to E based on its level of importance. A tasks are the most important and should be done first, while E tasks are the least important and can be eliminated if necessary. This method helps you prioritize tasks based on their impact on your goals and priorities.

The Pareto Principle is another useful concept in prioritization. This principle states that 80% of your results come from 20% of your efforts. By focusing on the tasks that will have the biggest impact, you can maximize your productivity and achieve more in less time.

The Benefits of Prioritizing Your Time

Prioritizing your time has numerous benefits. First and foremost, it increases productivity and efficiency. By focusing on the most important tasks, you can make progress on your goals and achieve more in less time. This allows you to be more productive and accomplish more throughout the day.

In addition to increased productivity, prioritization also reduces stress and overwhelm. When you have a clear plan for what needs to be done and when, it's easier to stay focused and avoid feeling overwhelmed by the sheer number of tasks on your plate. Prioritization helps you break down tasks into manageable steps, making them feel less daunting.

Prioritizing your time also improves your overall time management skills. By practicing prioritization regularly, you become better at identifying what needs to be done first and how to allocate your time effectively. This skill becomes invaluable as you navigate through your personal and professional life.

Finally, prioritization gives you a greater sense of accomplishment and satisfaction. When you prioritize your tasks and focus on the most important ones, you can see tangible progress towards your goals. This sense of accomplishment boosts your motivation and confidence, driving you to continue prioritizing and achieving even more.

How to Identify Your Most Important Tasks

To effectively prioritize your tasks, it's important to first determine your goals and priorities. What are the most important things you want to achieve? What tasks will have the biggest impact on those goals? By identifying your goals and priorities, you can better evaluate tasks based on their importance.

When evaluating tasks, consider their impact on your goals. Will completing a particular task bring you closer to achieving your goals? If so, it should be prioritized. On the other hand, if a task doesn't align with your goals or won't have a significant impact, it can be deprioritized or eliminated altogether.

It's also important to consider the consequences of not completing a task. Will not completing a task have negative consequences or hinder your progress towards your goals? If so, it should be prioritized. However, if the consequences are minimal or non-existent, the task can be deprioritized.

By evaluating tasks based on their impact on your goals and the consequences of not completing them, you can identify your most important tasks and prioritize them accordingly.

Tips for Creating a Daily To-Do List

Creating a daily to-do list is an effective way to prioritize your tasks and stay organized. Here are some tips for creating a daily to-do list:

1. Start with your most important tasks: Begin your list by identifying the tasks that are most crucial to your goals. These should be the tasks that will have the biggest impact on your progress.

2. Break down larger tasks into smaller, manageable steps: If you have larger tasks that seem overwhelming, break them down into smaller, more manageable steps. This makes them feel less daunting and allows you to make progress on them more easily.

3. Be realistic about what you can accomplish in a day: It's important to be realistic about what you can actually accomplish in a day. Don't overload your to-do list with too many tasks, as this can

lead to feeling overwhelmed and discouraged. Instead, focus on a few key tasks that you know you can realistically complete.

By following these tips, you can create a daily to-do list that helps you prioritize your tasks and stay organized.

The Role of Time Blocking in Prioritization

Time blocking is a technique that involves scheduling specific blocks of time for tasks. This technique helps you stay focused and avoid distractions, as you have dedicated time set aside for each task. By allocating specific time slots for your most important tasks, you ensure that they receive the attention they deserve.

Time blocking also helps you identify gaps in your schedule and make the most of your time. By visually seeing how your time is allocated throughout the day, you can identify areas where you may have extra time or where tasks are overlapping. This allows you to make adjustments and optimize your schedule for maximum productivity.

To implement time blocking, start by identifying your most important tasks and allocating dedicated time slots for them. Be sure to also schedule breaks and downtime to prevent burnout and maintain a healthy work-life balance. Experiment with different time blocks and adjust as needed to find a system that works best for you.

Overcoming Procrastination through Prioritization

Procrastination is a common challenge when it comes to managing time effectively. It often stems from feeling overwhelmed or unsure of where to start. However, prioritization can help overcome procrastination by breaking down tasks and focusing on the most important ones.

When faced with a daunting task, start by breaking it down into smaller, more manageable steps. This makes the task feel less overwhelming and allows you to make progress on it more easily. By focusing on the most important steps, you can prioritize your efforts and avoid getting stuck in a cycle of procrastination.

Setting deadlines and using accountability can also help overcome procrastination. By setting specific deadlines for tasks, you create a sense of urgency and motivation to get them done. Additionally, sharing your goals and progress with others can provide a sense of accountability, making it more likely that you will follow through on your commitments.

The Art of Saying No: Prioritizing Your Commitments

Learning to say no is an important skill for effective time management. Saying no to non-essential commitments allows you to prioritize your time and focus on the things that matter most. It's important to evaluate commitments based on their impact on your goals and priorities.

When faced with a new commitment or request, consider how it aligns with your goals and priorities. Will taking on this commitment bring you closer to achieving your goals? If not, it may be necessary to decline or find an alternative solution.

Saying no can be difficult, especially if you're used to saying yes to everything. However, it's important to remember that by saying no to non-essential commitments, you are creating space for the things that truly matter. Prioritizing your time in this way allows you to focus on what's most important and achieve greater results.

Prioritizing Self-Care: Making Time for Yourself

Prioritizing self-care is essential for overall well-being and productivity. It's important to schedule time for activities that recharge and energize you, such as exercise, hobbies, or spending time with loved ones. By making self-care a priority, you can prevent burnout and improve your mental health.

When creating your daily to-do list or time blocking schedule, be sure to include dedicated time for self-care activities. Treat these activities as non-negotiable commitments, just like any other task on your list. By prioritizing self-care, you are investing in your overall well-being and ensuring that you have the energy and motivation to tackle your other tasks.

Mastering the Power of Prioritization for Maximum Productivity

In conclusion, prioritization is a key component of effective time management. By identifying your most important tasks and focusing on them first, you can increase productivity and achieve your goals. Prioritization requires practice and discipline, but the benefits are well worth the effort.

By understanding the concept of prioritization and utilizing techniques such as the Eisenhower Matrix, ABCDE Method, and Pareto Principle, you can effectively prioritize your tasks and make the most of your time. Additionally, by learning to say no to non-essential commitments and prioritizing self-care, you can create a balanced and fulfilling life.

Remember, time is a valuable resource that cannot be replenished. By mastering the power of prioritization, you can make the most of your time and achieve greater results in all areas of your life. So start prioritizing today and watch your productivity soar!

Chapter 20: From Procrastination to Productivity: How to Improve Your Study Habits

Effective study habits are crucial for academic success. Whether you are a student in school or a professional looking to enhance your knowledge and skills, developing effective study habits can help you retain information, improve your understanding of the subject matter, and ultimately achieve your goals. In this article, we will explore various strategies and techniques that can help you develop effective study habits. From understanding procrastination to setting realistic goals, creating a study schedule, prioritizing tasks, eliminating distractions, developing a positive mindset, taking effective notes, engaging with study material, utilizing group study, managing time effectively, and overcoming procrastination, we will cover all aspects of effective studying.

Understanding Procrastination: What Causes It and How to Overcome It

Procrastination is the act of delaying or postponing tasks that need to be accomplished. It is a common problem that many students and professionals face when it comes to studying. Procrastination can have negative effects on studying as it leads to poor time management, increased stress levels, and decreased productivity.

There are several common causes of procrastination. One of the main causes is a lack of motivation or interest in the subject matter. When students or professionals do not find the topic engaging or relevant to their goals, they tend to put off studying. Another cause of procrastination is poor time management skills. When individuals do not allocate enough time for studying or fail to prioritize their tasks effectively, they often find themselves rushing to complete assignments at the last minute.

To overcome procrastination, it is important to first identify the underlying causes. If lack of motivation is the issue, try finding ways to make the subject matter more interesting or relevant to your goals. For example, if you are studying history and find it boring, try relating it to current events or finding real-life examples that demonstrate its importance. If poor time management is the issue, create a study schedule and stick to it. Break down your tasks into smaller, manageable chunks and set deadlines for each task. By taking small steps and staying organized, you can overcome procrastination and develop effective study habits.

The Importance of Setting Realistic Goals for Effective Study Habits

Setting goals is an essential part of effective studying. Goals provide direction and motivation, helping you stay focused and on track. When setting goals for studying, it is important to be realistic and achievable. Setting unrealistic goals can lead to frustration and demotivation, while setting achievable goals can boost your confidence and keep you motivated.

To set realistic goals, start by assessing your current knowledge and skills in the subject matter. Identify areas that need improvement and set specific goals to address those areas. For example, if you are studying math and struggling with algebra, set a goal to improve your understanding of algebra by practicing a certain number of problems each day.

It is also important to set measurable goals. Instead of setting a vague goal like "improve my math skills," set a specific goal like "score at least 90% on my next math test." This allows you to track your progress and evaluate whether you have achieved your goal.

Lastly, set time-bound goals. Give yourself a deadline to complete each goal. This helps create a sense of urgency and prevents procrastination. For example, if you have a math test in two weeks, set a goal to complete all the practice problems by the end of the first week.

By setting realistic and achievable goals, you can stay motivated and make the most of your study time.

Creating a Study Schedule: Tips and Tricks to Stay on Track

Having a study schedule is essential for effective studying. It helps you allocate time for studying, ensures that you cover all the necessary material, and prevents procrastination. Here are some tips for creating a study schedule that works for you:

1. Assess your current commitments: Before creating a study schedule, take into account your other commitments such as work, extracurricular activities, and personal responsibilities. This will help you determine how much time you can realistically dedicate to studying.

2. Prioritize your tasks: Identify the most important tasks that need to be completed and allocate more time to those tasks. This will ensure that you focus on what matters most and avoid wasting time on less important tasks.

3. Break down your tasks: Break down your study material into smaller, manageable chunks. This will make it easier to allocate time for each topic and prevent overwhelm. For example, if you have a

history exam coming up, break down the material by chapters or topics and allocate specific time slots for each.

4. Be flexible: While having a study schedule is important, it is also important to be flexible. Life happens, and unexpected events or emergencies may arise. Allow some flexibility in your schedule to accommodate for these situations.

5. Take breaks: It is important to take regular breaks while studying to prevent burnout and maintain focus. Schedule short breaks every hour or so to rest and recharge.

Once you have created your study schedule, it is important to stick to it. Treat your study schedule as a commitment and prioritize it just like any other important task in your life.

The Power of Prioritization: How to Focus on What Matters Most

When it comes to studying, prioritization is key. It helps you focus on what matters most and ensures that you allocate your time and energy effectively. Here are some tips for prioritizing tasks effectively:

1. Identify urgent vs. important tasks: Urgent tasks are those that require immediate attention, while important tasks are those that contribute to your long-term goals. Prioritize tasks that are both urgent and important first, as they have the highest impact on your success.

2. Use the Eisenhower Matrix: The Eisenhower Matrix is a tool that helps you categorize tasks based on their urgency and importance. It consists of four quadrants: urgent and important, important but not urgent, urgent but not important, and neither urgent nor important. Prioritize tasks in the first quadrant, then move on to the second quadrant, and so on.

3. Consider deadlines: Take into account any deadlines or due dates for your tasks. Prioritize tasks that have imminent deadlines to ensure that you complete them on time.

4. Evaluate the impact: Consider the impact that each task will have on your overall goals. Prioritize tasks that have a higher impact or contribute directly to your success.

By prioritizing tasks effectively, you can focus on what matters most and make the most of your study time.

Eliminating Distractions: Strategies for Staying Focused While Studying

Distractions can hinder effective studying and prevent you from achieving your goals. Common distractions include social media, smartphones, noise, and other people. Here are some strategies for eliminating distractions and staying focused while studying:

1. Create a distraction-free study environment: Find a quiet and comfortable place to study where you can minimize distractions. This could be a library, a coffee shop, or a dedicated study space at home. Remove any potential distractions from your study area, such as your smartphone or other electronic devices.

2. Use technology wisely: While technology can be a distraction, it can also be a useful tool for studying. Use apps or software that help you stay focused and block distracting websites or notifications.

3. Set boundaries with others: Let your family, friends, or roommates know when you are studying and ask them to respect your study time. Minimize interruptions by closing the door or using noise-canceling headphones.

4. Take regular breaks: Taking regular breaks can actually improve focus and productivity. Use breaks to relax and recharge, but be mindful of the time to avoid getting carried away.

5. Practice mindfulness: Mindfulness techniques, such as deep breathing or meditation, can help you stay present and focused. Take a few minutes before starting your study session to clear your mind and set your intentions.

By eliminating distractions and creating a focused study environment, you can maximize your productivity and make the most of your study time.

Developing a Positive Mindset: How to Stay Motivated Throughout the Study Process

Having a positive mindset is crucial for staying motivated throughout the study process. It helps you overcome challenges, stay focused, and maintain a sense of optimism. Here are some tips for developing a positive mindset:

1. Set realistic expectations: Avoid setting unrealistic expectations for yourself, as this can lead to disappointment and demotivation. Instead, set achievable goals and celebrate small victories along the way.

2. Focus on progress, not perfection: Instead of striving for perfection, focus on making progress. Recognize that learning is a journey and that it is okay to make mistakes or encounter setbacks along the way.

3. Surround yourself with positive influences: Surround yourself with people who support and encourage your goals. Avoid negative influences or individuals who bring you down.

4. Practice self-care: Take care of your physical and mental well-being by getting enough sleep, eating nutritious meals, exercising regularly, and engaging in activities that bring you joy.

5. Stay inspired: Find ways to stay inspired and motivated. This could be through reading books or articles related to your field of study, watching motivational videos or TED talks, or listening to podcasts or audiobooks.

By developing a positive mindset, you can stay motivated and overcome challenges throughout the study process.

Effective Note-Taking Techniques: How to Maximize Your Learning Potential

Taking effective notes is an essential part of studying. It helps you retain information, organize your thoughts, and maximize your learning potential. Here are some tips for taking effective notes:

1. Be organized: Use a structured format for your notes, such as bullet points, headings, or mind maps. This will help you organize your thoughts and make it easier to review your notes later.

2. Be selective: Avoid writing down every single word or sentence. Instead, focus on key concepts, main ideas, and supporting details. This will help you stay engaged and prevent you from getting overwhelmed.

3. Use abbreviations and symbols: Develop your own system of abbreviations and symbols to save time and space. For example, use arrows to indicate cause and effect relationships or asterisks to highlight important points.

4. Review and revise: Regularly review and revise your notes to reinforce your understanding of the material. This can be done by

summarizing your notes, creating flashcards, or teaching the material to someone else.

5. Use technology: Consider using note-taking apps or software that allow you to take digital notes, highlight text, or add annotations. This can make it easier to organize and search for information.

By taking effective notes, you can enhance your understanding of the material and improve your overall learning experience.

Active Learning Strategies: How to Engage with Your Study Material

Active learning is a powerful strategy that involves engaging with the study material rather than passively consuming it. It helps you retain information, improve your understanding, and apply what you have learned in real-life situations. Here are some tips for engaging with your study material:

1. Ask questions: As you read or study, ask yourself questions about the material. This helps you actively process the information and identify any gaps in your understanding.

2. Discuss with others: Engage in discussions with classmates, study groups, or online forums to exchange ideas and perspectives. This can help deepen your understanding of the material and provide different insights.

3. Teach someone else: One of the most effective ways to learn is by teaching someone else. Explain the material to a friend, family member, or even a stuffed animal. This forces you to articulate your thoughts and solidify your understanding.

4. Use visual aids: Visual aids, such as diagrams, charts, or graphs, can help you visualize complex concepts and make connections

between different ideas. Create your own visual aids or use online resources to enhance your learning experience.

5. Practice problem-solving: For subjects that involve problem-solving, such as math or science, actively practice solving problems. This helps you apply the concepts you have learned and reinforces your understanding.

By actively engaging with your study material, you can deepen your understanding and improve your ability to apply what you have learned.

The Benefits of Group Study: How to Collaborate with Peers for Better Results

Group study can be a highly effective way to enhance your learning experience. It allows you to collaborate with peers, exchange ideas, and gain different perspectives. Here are some benefits of group study:

1. Enhanced understanding: Group study provides an opportunity to discuss complex concepts and clarify any misunderstandings. Explaining concepts to others can deepen your own understanding and fill in any gaps in knowledge.

2. Different perspectives: Studying with peers from diverse backgrounds or with different learning styles can provide different perspectives on the material. This can help you see things from different angles and gain new insights.

3. Accountability: Studying in a group can help keep you accountable and motivated. Knowing that others are relying on you can provide a sense of responsibility and encourage you to stay on track.

4. Division of labor: Group study allows you to divide the workload and share the responsibilities. Each member can focus on a specific topic or area of expertise and then teach it to the rest of the group.

5. Peer support: Studying with peers provides a support system where you can ask questions, seek clarification, and receive feedback. This can boost your confidence and provide emotional support during challenging times.

While group study can be highly beneficial, it is important to approach it with the right mindset and establish clear goals and expectations. Set specific objectives for each study session, allocate time for individual study, and ensure that the group remains focused and productive.

Effective Time Management: How to Make the Most of Your Study Time

Effective time management is crucial for making the most of your study time. It helps you allocate your time effectively, prioritize tasks, and avoid wasting time on unproductive activities. Here are some tips for effective time management:

1. Set goals and priorities: Start by setting clear goals and priorities for your study sessions. Identify the most important tasks that need to be completed and allocate more time to those tasks.

2. Break down tasks: Break down larger tasks into smaller, manageable chunks. This makes it easier to allocate time for each task and prevents overwhelm.

3. Use a planner or calendar: Use a planner or calendar to schedule your study sessions and allocate specific time slots for each

task. This helps you stay organized and ensures that you have enough time for all your commitments.

4. Avoid multitasking: Multitasking can actually decrease productivity and lead to poor quality work. Instead, focus on one task at a time and give it your full attention.

5. Take breaks: Taking regular breaks is important for maintaining focus and preventing burnout. Schedule short breaks every hour or so to rest and recharge.

6. Avoid time-wasting activities: Identify any activities that are not productive or do not contribute to your goals, and eliminate them from your routine. This could include excessive social media scrolling, watching too much television, or engaging in gossip. Instead, focus on activities that align with your priorities and bring you closer to achieving your objectives. By being mindful of how you spend your time, you can maximize productivity and make progress towards your goals more efficiently.

Chapter 21: The Power of Connection: Finding Support for Your Mental Health

Connection is a fundamental aspect of human existence. It is through connection that we form relationships, build support networks, and find a sense of belonging. In the realm of mental health, connection plays a crucial role in our overall well-being. It has been shown to have a profound impact on our mental health, helping to reduce feelings of loneliness, isolation, and depression. In this article, we will explore the importance of connection for mental health and discuss various ways to cultivate and maintain strong connections in our lives.

The Importance of Connection for Mental Health

Connection is essential for our mental health because it provides us with a sense of belonging and support. When we feel connected to others, we are more likely to experience positive emotions, have higher self-esteem, and feel a greater sense of purpose in life. On the other hand, when we lack connection, we may feel isolated, lonely, and disconnected from the world around us.

Research has consistently shown that social isolation and loneliness can have detrimental effects on our mental health. Studies have found that individuals who are socially isolated are at a higher risk of developing mental health disorders such as depression and anxiety. Additionally, loneliness has been linked to increased rates of suicide and substance abuse.

Building a Support Network: Where to Start

Building a support network is an important step in cultivating connection and improving our mental health. A support network consists of individuals who provide emotional support, encouragement, and practical assistance when needed. Here are some tips for building a support network:

1. Identify supportive people in your life: Start by identifying the people in your life who are supportive and understanding. These may be family members, friends, or colleagues who you feel comfortable talking to about your thoughts and feelings.

2. Seek out new connections: If you feel like you don't have many supportive people in your life, consider seeking out new connections. This can be done through joining clubs or organizations that align with your interests, attending community events, or volunteering for a cause you care about.

3. Be open and vulnerable: Building connections requires vulnerability. Be open and honest with the people in your life about your struggles and needs. This will help foster deeper connections and create a safe space for support.

The Benefits of Peer Support Groups

Peer support groups are a valuable resource for individuals seeking connection and support. These groups consist of individuals who share similar experiences or challenges and come together to provide mutual support and understanding. Here are some benefits of peer support groups:

1. Shared experiences: Peer support groups provide a space where individuals can share their experiences, challenges, and successes with others who can relate. This can help reduce feelings of isolation and provide a sense of validation and understanding.

2. Emotional support: Peer support groups offer emotional support from individuals who have been through similar experiences. This can be particularly helpful for individuals dealing with mental health issues, as they can find comfort in knowing they are not alone.

3. Practical advice and coping strategies: Peer support groups often provide practical advice and coping strategies for dealing with specific challenges. Members can share their own strategies for managing symptoms or overcoming obstacles, providing valuable insights and tools for others in the group.

The Role of Therapy in Creating Connection

Therapy can play a crucial role in helping individuals create and maintain connections in their lives. Therapists provide a safe and non-judgmental space where individuals can explore their thoughts, feelings, and relationships. Here are some ways therapy can help with connection:

1. Building self-awareness: Therapy helps individuals develop self-awareness, which is essential for building healthy connections. By understanding our own thoughts, emotions, and behaviors, we can better navigate our relationships with others.

2. Improving communication skills: Therapy can help individuals improve their communication skills, which are vital for

building strong connections. Therapists can teach effective communication techniques and provide guidance on how to express needs, set boundaries, and resolve conflicts.

3. Addressing past traumas: Past traumas can often hinder our ability to form and maintain connections. Therapy provides a safe space to address and heal from these traumas, allowing individuals to move forward and build healthier relationships.

The Power of Family and Friends in Mental Health

Family and friends play a significant role in our mental health. They are often our primary sources of support, love, and understanding. Here are some reasons why family and friends are important for our mental health:

1. Emotional support: Family and friends provide emotional support during challenging times. They offer a listening ear, a shoulder to cry on, and words of encouragement when we need them most.

2. Sense of belonging: Our family and friends provide us with a sense of belonging and acceptance. They are the people who know us best and love us unconditionally, which can be incredibly comforting and reassuring.

3. Social connection: Spending time with loved ones helps us feel connected to the world around us. It provides opportunities for laughter, shared experiences, and meaningful connections that contribute to our overall well-being.

The Impact of Isolation on Mental Health

Isolation can have severe negative effects on our mental health. When we are isolated, we lack the social connections that are essential for our well-being. Here are some ways isolation can impact mental health:

1. Increased risk of depression: Studies have shown that individuals who are socially isolated are at a higher risk of developing depression. The lack of social interaction and support can contribute to feelings of sadness, hopelessness, and despair.

2. Heightened anxiety: Isolation can also lead to increased levels of anxiety. Without the support and reassurance of others, individuals may feel more vulnerable and anxious about their safety or ability to cope with challenges.

3. Decreased self-esteem: Isolation can negatively impact our self-esteem and self-worth. Without the validation and support of others, we may question our value and feel a sense of worthlessness.

Online Communities: Finding Connection in the Digital Age

In today's digital age, online communities have become a valuable resource for individuals seeking connection and support. Online communities provide a platform for individuals to connect with others who share similar interests, experiences, or challenges. Here are some benefits of online communities for mental health:

1. Accessibility: Online communities are accessible to individuals regardless of their location or physical abilities. This makes it easier for individuals who may be unable to attend in-person support groups or events to find connection and support.

2. Anonymity: Online communities often allow individuals to remain anonymous if they choose to do so. This can be particularly helpful for individuals who may feel more comfortable sharing their thoughts and feelings without revealing their identity.

3. Niche communities: Online communities cater to a wide range of interests and challenges, allowing individuals to find specific communities that align with their needs. This can provide a sense of belonging and understanding that may be difficult to find in offline settings.

Overcoming Stigma: Sharing Your Mental Health Journey

Overcoming stigma is an important step in creating connection and finding support for our mental health journey. Stigma refers to the negative attitudes, beliefs, and stereotypes that surround mental health issues. Here are some tips for overcoming stigma:

1. Educate yourself: Educate yourself about mental health issues so that you can better understand your own experiences and challenge any misconceptions or stereotypes you may encounter.

2. Share your story: Sharing your mental health journey can help break down stigma and encourage others to do the same. By sharing your experiences, you may inspire others to seek help and create a more supportive environment.

3. Seek support from like-minded individuals: Surround yourself with individuals who are supportive and understanding of mental health issues. This can help create a safe space where you can be open and honest about your experiences without fear of judgment or stigma.

The Connection Between Physical and Mental Health

There is a strong connection between physical and mental health. Taking care of our physical health can have a positive impact on our mental well-being, and vice versa. Here are some tips for improving physical health to improve mental health:

1. Exercise regularly: Regular exercise has been shown to have numerous benefits for mental health. It can help reduce symptoms of depression and anxiety, improve mood, and increase overall well-being.

2. Get enough sleep: Sleep plays a crucial role in our mental health. Aim for 7-9 hours of quality sleep each night to ensure your brain and body have time to rest and recharge.

3. Eat a balanced diet: A healthy diet is essential for both physical and mental well-being. Focus on consuming a variety of fruits, vegetables, whole grains, lean proteins, and healthy fats to nourish your body and mind.

Cultivating Resilience Through Connection

Connection can help cultivate resilience, which is the ability to bounce back from adversity and cope with life's challenges. Here are some tips for cultivating resilience through connection:

1. Seek support during difficult times: Reach out to your support network during challenging times. Share your thoughts and feelings with trusted individuals who can provide emotional support and guidance.

2. Practice self-care: Self-care is an important aspect of resilience. Take time to engage in activities that bring you joy, relaxation, and rejuvenation.

3. Foster positive relationships: Surround yourself with positive, supportive individuals who uplift you and encourage your growth. These relationships can provide a strong foundation for resilience.

The Long-Term Benefits of Maintaining Strong Connections

Maintaining strong connections in our lives has numerous long-term benefits for our mental health. Here are some reasons why it is important to prioritize connection:

1. Improved mental well-being: Strong connections provide a sense of belonging, support, and understanding, which can significantly improve our mental well-being.

2. Increased resilience: Building and maintaining connections can help cultivate resilience, allowing us to better cope with life's challenges and bounce back from adversity.

3. Enhanced overall health: Research has shown that individuals with strong social connections have better overall health outcomes. They are less likely to develop chronic diseases and have a higher life expectancy.

In conclusion, connection is vital for our mental health and overall well-being. It provides us with a sense of belonging, support, and purpose in life. Building and maintaining strong connections can have a profound impact on our mental health, helping to reduce feelings of loneliness, isolation, and depression. Whether through building a support network, joining peer support groups, seeking therapy, or fostering relationships with family and friends, there are numerous ways to cultivate connection in our lives. By prioritizing connection and making it a daily practice, we can improve our mental health and create a more fulfilling and meaningful life.

Chapter 22: The Power of Connection: Finding Support for Your Mental Health

Connection is a fundamental aspect of human existence. It is through connection that we form relationships, build support networks, and find a sense of belonging. In the realm of mental health, connection plays a crucial role in our overall well-being. It has been shown to have a profound impact on our mental health, helping to reduce feelings of loneliness, isolation, and depression. In this article, we will explore the importance of connection for mental health and discuss various ways to cultivate and maintain strong connections in our lives.

The Importance of Connection for Mental Health

Connection is essential for our mental health because it provides us with a sense of belonging and support. When we feel connected to others, we are more likely to experience positive emotions, have higher self-esteem, and feel a greater sense of purpose in life. On the other hand, when we lack connection, we may feel isolated, lonely, and disconnected from the world around us.

Research has consistently shown that social isolation and loneliness can have detrimental effects on our mental health. Studies have found that individuals who are socially isolated are at a higher risk of developing mental health disorders such as depression and anxiety. Additionally, loneliness has been linked to increased rates of suicide and substance abuse.

Building a Support Network: Where to Start

Building a support network is an important step in cultivating connection and improving our mental health. A support network consists of individuals who provide emotional support, encouragement, and practical assistance when needed. Here are some tips for building a support network:

1. Identify supportive people in your life: Start by identifying the people in your life who are supportive and understanding. These may be family members, friends, or colleagues who you feel comfortable talking to about your thoughts and feelings.

2. Seek out new connections: If you feel like you don't have many supportive people in your life, consider seeking out new connections. This can be done through joining clubs or organizations that align with your interests, attending community events, or volunteering for a cause you care about.

3. Be open and vulnerable: Building connections requires vulnerability. Be open and honest with the people in your life about your struggles and needs. This will help foster deeper connections and create a safe space for support.

The Benefits of Peer Support Groups

Peer support groups are a valuable resource for individuals seeking connection and support. These groups consist of individuals who share similar experiences or challenges and come together to provide mutual support and understanding. Here are some benefits of peer support groups:

1. Shared experiences: Peer support groups provide a space where individuals can share their experiences, challenges, and successes with others who can relate. This can help reduce feelings of isolation and provide a sense of validation and understanding.

2. Emotional support: Peer support groups offer emotional support from individuals who have been through similar experiences. This can be particularly helpful for individuals dealing with mental health issues, as they can find comfort in knowing they are not alone.

3. Practical advice and coping strategies: Peer support groups often provide practical advice and coping strategies for dealing with specific challenges. Members can share their own strategies for managing symptoms or overcoming obstacles, providing valuable insights and tools for others in the group.

The Role of Therapy in Creating Connection

Therapy can play a crucial role in helping individuals create and maintain connections in their lives. Therapists provide a safe and non-judgmental space where individuals can explore their thoughts, feelings, and relationships. Here are some ways therapy can help with connection:

1. Building self-awareness: Therapy helps individuals develop self-awareness, which is essential for building healthy connections. By understanding our own thoughts, emotions, and behaviors, we can better navigate our relationships with others.

2. Improving communication skills: Therapy can help individuals improve their communication skills, which are vital for

building strong connections. Therapists can teach effective communication techniques and provide guidance on how to express needs, set boundaries, and resolve conflicts.

3. Addressing past traumas: Past traumas can often hinder our ability to form and maintain connections. Therapy provides a safe space to address and heal from these traumas, allowing individuals to move forward and build healthier relationships.

The Power of Family and Friends in Mental Health

Family and friends play a significant role in our mental health. They are often our primary sources of support, love, and understanding. Here are some reasons why family and friends are important for our mental health:

1. Emotional support: Family and friends provide emotional support during challenging times. They offer a listening ear, a shoulder to cry on, and words of encouragement when we need them most.

2. Sense of belonging: Our family and friends provide us with a sense of belonging and acceptance. They are the people who know us best and love us unconditionally, which can be incredibly comforting and reassuring.

3. Social connection: Spending time with loved ones helps us feel connected to the world around us. It provides opportunities for laughter, shared experiences, and meaningful connections that contribute to our overall well-being.

The Impact of Isolation on Mental Health

Isolation can have severe negative effects on our mental health. When we are isolated, we lack the social connections that are essential for our well-being. Here are some ways isolation can impact mental health:

1. Increased risk of depression: Studies have shown that individuals who are socially isolated are at a higher risk of developing depression. The lack of social interaction and support can contribute to feelings of sadness, hopelessness, and despair.

2. Heightened anxiety: Isolation can also lead to increased levels of anxiety. Without the support and reassurance of others, individuals may feel more vulnerable and anxious about their safety or ability to cope with challenges.

3. Decreased self-esteem: Isolation can negatively impact our self-esteem and self-worth. Without the validation and support of others, we may question our value and feel a sense of worthlessness.

Online Communities: Finding Connection in the Digital Age

In today's digital age, online communities have become a valuable resource for individuals seeking connection and support. Online communities provide a platform for individuals to connect with others who share similar interests, experiences, or challenges. Here are some benefits of online communities for mental health:

1. Accessibility: Online communities are accessible to individuals regardless of their location or physical abilities. This makes it easier for individuals who may be unable to attend in-person support groups or events to find connection and support.

2. Anonymity: Online communities often allow individuals to remain anonymous if they choose to do so. This can be particularly helpful for individuals who may feel more comfortable sharing their thoughts and feelings without revealing their identity.

3. Niche communities: Online communities cater to a wide range of interests and challenges, allowing individuals to find specific communities that align with their needs. This can provide a sense of belonging and understanding that may be difficult to find in offline settings.

Overcoming Stigma: Sharing Your Mental Health Journey

Overcoming stigma is an important step in creating connection and finding support for our mental health journey. Stigma refers to the negative attitudes, beliefs, and stereotypes that surround mental health issues. Here are some tips for overcoming stigma:

1. Educate yourself: Educate yourself about mental health issues so that you can better understand your own experiences and challenge any misconceptions or stereotypes you may encounter.

2. Share your story: Sharing your mental health journey can help break down stigma and encourage others to do the same. By sharing your experiences, you may inspire others to seek help and create a more supportive environment.

3. Seek support from like-minded individuals: Surround yourself with individuals who are supportive and understanding of mental health issues. This can help create a safe space where you can be open and honest about your experiences without fear of judgment or stigma.

The Connection Between Physical and Mental Health

There is a strong connection between physical and mental health. Taking care of our physical health can have a positive impact on our mental well-being, and vice versa. Here are some tips for improving physical health to improve mental health:

1. Exercise regularly: Regular exercise has been shown to have numerous benefits for mental health. It can help reduce symptoms of depression and anxiety, improve mood, and increase overall well-being.

2. Get enough sleep: Sleep plays a crucial role in our mental health. Aim for 7-9 hours of quality sleep each night to ensure your brain and body have time to rest and recharge.

3. Eat a balanced diet: A healthy diet is essential for both physical and mental well-being. Focus on consuming a variety of fruits, vegetables, whole grains, lean proteins, and healthy fats to nourish your body and mind.

Cultivating Resilience Through Connection

Connection can help cultivate resilience, which is the ability to bounce back from adversity and cope with life's challenges. Here are some tips for cultivating resilience through connection:

1. Seek support during difficult times: Reach out to your support network during challenging times. Share your thoughts and feelings with trusted individuals who can provide emotional support and guidance.

2. Practice self-care: Self-care is an important aspect of resilience. Take time to engage in activities that bring you joy, relaxation, and rejuvenation.

3. Foster positive relationships: Surround yourself with positive, supportive individuals who uplift you and encourage your growth. These relationships can provide a strong foundation for resilience.

The Long-Term Benefits of Maintaining Strong Connections

Maintaining strong connections in our lives has numerous long-term benefits for our mental health. Here are some reasons why it is important to prioritize connection:

1. Improved mental well-being: Strong connections provide a sense of belonging, support, and understanding, which can significantly improve our mental well-being.

2. Increased resilience: Building and maintaining connections can help cultivate resilience, allowing us to better cope with life's challenges and bounce back from adversity.

3. Enhanced overall health: Research has shown that individuals with strong social connections have better overall health outcomes. They are less likely to develop chronic diseases and have a higher life expectancy.

In conclusion, connection is vital for our mental health and overall well-being. It provides us with a sense of belonging, support, and purpose in life. Building and maintaining strong connections can have a profound impact on our mental health, helping to reduce feelings of loneliness, isolation, and depression. Whether through building a support network, joining peer support groups, seeking therapy, or fostering relationships with family and friends, there are numerous ways to cultivate connection in our lives. By prioritizing connection and making it a daily practice, we can improve our mental health and create a more fulfilling and meaningful life.

Chapter 23: Breaking Down Barriers: How to Foster Inclusivity in Your Community

Inclusivity is the practice of creating an environment where everyone feels valued, respected, and included. It is about recognizing and embracing the diversity of individuals and ensuring that everyone has equal opportunities to participate and contribute. Inclusivity is not just a buzzword; it is a fundamental aspect of a healthy and thriving society.

The importance of inclusivity in society cannot be overstated. When individuals from different backgrounds, cultures, and perspectives come together, it leads to a richer and more vibrant community. Inclusivity fosters creativity, innovation, and problem-solving by bringing together diverse ideas and experiences. It also promotes social cohesion and harmony by reducing discrimination, prejudice, and inequality.

There are numerous benefits to fostering inclusivity in society. Firstly, it promotes social justice by ensuring that everyone has equal access to resources, opportunities, and rights. Inclusivity also leads to better decision-making as diverse perspectives help to challenge assumptions and biases. Additionally, inclusivity improves productivity and performance in various settings such as workplaces, schools, and communities. When individuals feel included and valued, they are more motivated to contribute their best.

Identifying Barriers: Recognizing What Prevents Inclusivity

Despite the importance of inclusivity, there are several barriers that prevent its realization in society. One common barrier is prejudice and discrimination based on factors such as race, gender, religion, sexual orientation, or disability. These biases can lead to exclusion, marginalization, and unequal treatment of certain groups.

Another barrier to inclusivity is lack of awareness and understanding. Many people may not be aware of their own biases or the experiences of others. This lack of awareness can perpetuate stereotypes and prevent meaningful connections from forming.

In addition, structural barriers such as policies, practices, and systems that favor certain groups over others can hinder inclusivity. For example, inaccessible physical environments can exclude individuals with disabilities, while discriminatory hiring practices can limit opportunities for certain racial or ethnic groups.

Education and Awareness: The First Step to Fostering Inclusivity

Education and awareness are crucial in breaking down barriers and fostering inclusivity. It is important for individuals to educate themselves about different cultures, perspectives, and experiences. This can be done through reading books, attending workshops or seminars, or engaging in conversations with people from diverse backgrounds.

Educating others about inclusivity is equally important. This can be done through formal education programs, awareness campaigns, or simply having open and honest conversations with friends, family, and colleagues. By sharing knowledge and experiences, individuals can challenge stereotypes, dispel myths, and promote understanding.

Encouraging Diversity: Embracing Differences in Your Community

Diversity is a key component of inclusivity. It is about recognizing and embracing the differences that exist among individuals. Diversity encompasses various aspects such as race, ethnicity, gender, age, sexual orientation, religion, socioeconomic status, and more.

Promoting diversity in different settings is essential for fostering inclusivity. In workplaces, for example, organizations can implement diversity hiring practices to ensure that their workforce reflects the diversity of the community they serve. Schools can incorporate diverse perspectives into their curriculum to expose students to different cultures and experiences. Communities can celebrate diversity through events and festivals that showcase various traditions and customs.

Embracing diversity not only creates a more inclusive environment but also brings numerous benefits. It leads to increased creativity and innovation as individuals with different backgrounds bring unique perspectives and ideas to the table. It also enhances problem-solving by encouraging critical thinking and challenging assumptions.

Creating Safe Spaces: Promoting a Welcoming Environment

Creating safe spaces is essential for fostering inclusivity. A safe space is an environment where individuals feel comfortable expressing themselves without fear of judgment or discrimination. It is a place where everyone's voice is heard and respected.

To create safe spaces, it is important to establish clear guidelines and expectations for behavior. This can be done through the development of codes of conduct or policies that promote respect and inclusivity. It is also important to actively address any instances of discrimination or harassment that may occur within the space.

In addition, creating physical spaces that are accessible and inclusive is crucial. This can involve providing ramps or elevators for individuals with mobility impairments, gender-neutral restrooms for transgender individuals, or sensory-friendly spaces for individuals with autism.

Building Relationships: Connecting with Others to Break Down Barriers

Building relationships with people from different backgrounds is a powerful way to break down barriers and foster inclusivity. By connecting with others, individuals can gain a deeper understanding of different perspectives and experiences.

One strategy for building relationships is to actively seek out opportunities to engage with diverse communities. This can involve attending cultural events, volunteering for organizations that serve marginalized groups, or joining community groups that promote inclusivity.

It is also important to approach these relationships with an open mind and a willingness to listen and learn. By actively listening to others' experiences and perspectives, individuals can challenge their own biases and broaden their understanding of the world.

Empowering Voices: Amplifying Underrepresented Groups

Amplifying the voices of underrepresented groups is crucial for fostering inclusivity. Many marginalized communities have been historically silenced or ignored, and it is important to create platforms and opportunities for them to be heard.

One strategy for empowering underrepresented groups is to provide them with leadership roles and decision-making positions. This can be done in workplaces, schools, or community organizations. By giving individuals from underrepresented groups a seat at the table, their perspectives and experiences can shape policies and practices.

Another strategy is to actively seek out and promote the work of individuals from underrepresented groups. This can involve featuring their stories in media outlets, showcasing their art or music in cultural events, or inviting them to speak at conferences or panels.

Addressing Bias: Confronting Prejudices and Stereotypes

Addressing bias is a crucial step in fostering inclusivity. Bias refers to the preconceived notions or stereotypes that individuals hold about certain groups of people. These biases can lead to discrimination, exclusion, and unequal treatment.

One strategy for addressing bias is to engage in self-reflection and introspection. Individuals can examine their own beliefs, attitudes, and behaviors to identify any biases they may hold. This can involve questioning assumptions, challenging stereotypes, and actively seeking out diverse perspectives.

It is also important to confront biases when they arise in others. This can involve speaking up when witnessing discriminatory behavior or challenging stereotypes when they are perpetuated. By addressing bias, individuals can create a more inclusive environment where everyone feels valued and respected.

Taking Action: Implementing Inclusive Policies and Practices

Taking action is essential for turning inclusivity into a reality. It is not enough to simply talk about inclusivity; concrete steps must be taken to implement inclusive policies and practices.

In workplaces, this can involve implementing diversity hiring practices, providing diversity and inclusion training for employees, and creating mentorship programs for underrepresented groups. In schools, it can involve incorporating diverse perspectives into the curriculum, implementing anti-bullying policies, and providing support services for marginalized students.

Communities can take action by advocating for inclusive policies at the local level, supporting organizations that promote inclusivity, and creating spaces that are accessible and welcoming to all.

Measuring Progress: Evaluating the Impact of Inclusivity Efforts

Measuring progress is important for evaluating the impact of inclusivity efforts and identifying areas for improvement. It allows individuals and organizations to assess whether their actions are having the desired effect and make adjustments as needed.

One strategy for measuring progress is to collect data on diversity and inclusion metrics. This can involve tracking the representation of different groups in workplaces, schools, or community organizations. It can also involve conducting surveys or focus groups to gather feedback from individuals about their experiences of inclusivity.

Another strategy is to set goals and benchmarks for inclusivity and regularly assess progress towards these goals. This can involve developing action plans, implementing strategies, and monitoring outcomes.

The Benefits of Inclusivity and the Importance of Continuing the Work

Inclusivity is not a one-time effort; it is an ongoing process that requires continuous work and commitment. The benefits of inclusivity are numerous and far-reaching. It leads to a more vibrant and harmonious society, promotes social justice, enhances creativity and innovation, and improves decision-making.

To foster inclusivity, it is important to identify and address barriers, educate oneself and others, promote diversity, create safe spaces, build relationships, empower underrepresented groups, address bias, take action, and measure progress. By taking these steps, individuals and communities can create a more inclusive world where everyone feels valued, respected, and included.

Chapter 24: The Power of Disclosure: Why Honesty is Always the Best Policy

Honesty is a fundamental value that is essential for building trust and strong relationships. In today's world, where fake news and misinformation are rampant, honesty is more important than ever. It is the foundation upon which we build our interactions with others, and without it, our relationships and society as a whole can quickly crumble.

In a society where trust is often eroded by deception and dishonesty, being honest becomes a powerful act of rebellion. It is a way to stand up against the falsehoods and manipulations that surround us. Honesty allows us to navigate through the complexities of life with integrity and authenticity.

The Psychological Benefits of Disclosure: How Honesty Can Improve Mental Health

Research shows that being honest and open about our thoughts and feelings can improve our mental health. When we are honest with ourselves and others, we are able to express our true emotions and experiences. This can help us reduce stress, anxiety, and depression, as well as improve our self-esteem.

Honesty allows us to release the burden of carrying secrets and hiding our true selves. When we are honest, we no longer have to pretend or put on a facade. We can be authentic and genuine in our interactions with others, which leads to deeper connections and a greater sense of well-being.

The Role of Trust in Relationships: Why Honesty is Essential for Building Strong Bonds

Trust is the foundation of any healthy relationship. Without trust, relationships cannot thrive or grow. Honesty is essential for building trust, and without it, relationships can quickly break down.

When we are honest with others, we show them that we respect and value their feelings and opinions. We demonstrate that we can be relied upon to tell the truth, even when it may be difficult or uncomfortable. This builds trust and allows for open communication and vulnerability within the relationship.

The Ethics of Disclosure: The Moral Imperative to Tell the Truth

Honesty is not just a personal value, but a moral imperative. We have a responsibility to tell the truth, even when it's difficult or uncomfortable. Honesty is the foundation of ethical behavior and is essential for maintaining the integrity of our actions and decisions.

When we are honest, we uphold our own values and principles. We show respect for ourselves and others by being truthful and transparent. Honesty allows us to live with integrity and to be accountable for our actions.

The Consequences of Dishonesty: How Lying Can Damage Your Reputation

Dishonesty can have serious consequences, both personally and professionally. Lying can damage your reputation, erode trust, and lead to negative consequences. When we are caught in a lie, it can be difficult to regain the trust of others.

In personal relationships, dishonesty can lead to broken trust and damaged relationships. It can create a sense of betrayal and hurt that is difficult to repair. In professional settings, dishonesty can lead to loss of credibility and opportunities.

The Importance of Transparency in Business: Why Honesty is Key to Success

In business, honesty and transparency are essential for building trust with customers and stakeholders. Companies that prioritize honesty and transparency are more likely to succeed in the long run. When customers feel that they can trust a company, they are more likely to be loyal and recommend it to others.

Transparency in business also allows for better decision-making and problem-solving. When information is shared openly and honestly, it allows for collaboration and innovation. It creates an environment where employees feel valued and empowered.

The Power of Vulnerability: How Honesty Can Help You Connect with Others

Being honest and vulnerable can help us connect with others on a deeper level. When we share our struggles and challenges with others, it allows them to see us as human and relatable. It creates a sense of empathy and understanding.

When we are honest about our own vulnerabilities, it gives others permission to do the same. It creates a safe space for open and honest communication, which can lead to stronger and more meaningful relationships.

Overcoming Fear of Disclosure: Tips for Being Honest Even When It's Hard

Being honest can be scary, especially when we fear judgment or rejection. However, there are strategies we can use to overcome our fear of disclosure and be more honest in our relationships.

One strategy is to start small. Begin by being honest with yourself about your own thoughts and feelings. Practice self-reflection and self-awareness. This will help build confidence in your ability to be honest with others.

Another strategy is to choose the right time and place for disclosure. Find a safe and supportive environment where you feel comfortable sharing your thoughts and feelings. This could be with a trusted friend, family member, or therapist.

The Healing Power of Disclosure: How Honesty Can Help You Move On from Trauma

Honesty can be a powerful tool for healing from trauma and emotional pain. When we share our experiences with others, it allows us to process our emotions and move forward. It can provide a sense of validation and support.

Sharing our truth with others can also help us gain perspective and insight into our own experiences. It allows us to see that we are not alone in our struggles and that others have faced similar challenges.

The Benefits of Self-Disclosure: How Sharing Your Truth Can Help You Grow

Being honest with ourselves and others can help us grow and develop as individuals. Self-disclosure allows us to gain insight into our own thoughts and feelings. It helps us understand ourselves better and make more informed decisions.

Sharing our truth with others also allows for deeper connections and stronger relationships. When we are open and honest with others, it creates a sense of trust and authenticity. It allows others to see us for who we truly are, and it encourages them to do the same.

The Power of Honesty and the Importance of Living with Integrity

Honesty is a powerful value that can improve our mental health, relationships, and overall well-being. It is the foundation upon which trust is built, and it is essential for living a fulfilling and meaningful life.

Living with integrity means being honest with ourselves and others. It means being true to our values and principles, even when it may be difficult or uncomfortable. By embracing honesty, we can create a world where trust and authenticity are valued above all else.

Chapter 25: The Power of Disclosure: Why Honesty is Always the Best Policy

Honesty is a fundamental value that is essential for building trust and strong relationships. In today's world, where fake news and misinformation are rampant, honesty is more important than ever. It is the foundation upon which we build our interactions with others, and without it, our relationships and society as a whole can quickly crumble.

In a society where trust is often eroded by deception and dishonesty, being honest becomes a powerful act of rebellion. It is a way to stand up against the falsehoods and manipulations that surround us. Honesty allows us to navigate through the complexities of life with integrity and authenticity.

The Psychological Benefits of Disclosure: How Honesty Can Improve Mental Health

Research shows that being honest and open about our thoughts and feelings can improve our mental health. When we are honest with ourselves and others, we are able to express our true emotions and experiences. This can help us reduce stress, anxiety, and depression, as well as improve our self-esteem.

Honesty allows us to release the burden of carrying secrets and hiding our true selves. When we are honest, we no longer have to pretend or put on a facade. We can be authentic and genuine in our interactions with others, which leads to deeper connections and a greater sense of well-being.

The Role of Trust in Relationships: Why Honesty is Essential for Building Strong Bonds

Trust is the foundation of any healthy relationship. Without trust, relationships cannot thrive or grow. Honesty is essential for building trust, and without it, relationships can quickly break down.

When we are honest with others, we show them that we respect and value their feelings and opinions. We demonstrate that we can be relied upon to tell the truth, even when it may be difficult or uncomfortable. This builds trust and allows for open communication and vulnerability within the relationship.

The Ethics of Disclosure: The Moral Imperative to Tell the Truth

Honesty is not just a personal value, but a moral imperative. We have a responsibility to tell the truth, even when it's difficult or uncomfortable. Honesty is the foundation of ethical behavior and is essential for maintaining the integrity of our actions and decisions.

When we are honest, we uphold our own values and principles. We show respect for ourselves and others by being truthful and transparent. Honesty allows us to live with integrity and to be accountable for our actions.

The Consequences of Dishonesty: How Lying Can Damage Your Reputation

Dishonesty can have serious consequences, both personally and professionally. Lying can damage your reputation, erode trust, and lead to negative consequences. When we are caught in a lie, it can be difficult to regain the trust of others.

In personal relationships, dishonesty can lead to broken trust and damaged relationships. It can create a sense of betrayal and hurt that is difficult to repair. In professional settings, dishonesty can lead to loss of credibility and opportunities.

The Importance of Transparency in Business: Why Honesty is Key to Success

In business, honesty and transparency are essential for building trust with customers and stakeholders. Companies that prioritize honesty and transparency are more likely to succeed in the long run. When customers feel that they can trust a company, they are more likely to be loyal and recommend it to others.

Transparency in business also allows for better decision-making and problem-solving. When information is shared openly and honestly, it allows for collaboration and innovation. It creates an environment where employees feel valued and empowered.

The Power of Vulnerability: How Honesty Can Help You Connect with Others

Being honest and vulnerable can help us connect with others on a deeper level. When we share our struggles and challenges with others, it allows them to see us as human and relatable. It creates a sense of empathy and understanding.

When we are honest about our own vulnerabilities, it gives others permission to do the same. It creates a safe space for open and honest communication, which can lead to stronger and more meaningful relationships.

Overcoming Fear of Disclosure: Tips for Being Honest Even When It's Hard

Being honest can be scary, especially when we fear judgment or rejection. However, there are strategies we can use to overcome our fear of disclosure and be more honest in our relationships.

One strategy is to start small. Begin by being honest with yourself about your own thoughts and feelings. Practice self-reflection and self-awareness. This will help build confidence in your ability to be honest with others.

Another strategy is to choose the right time and place for disclosure. Find a safe and supportive environment where you feel comfortable sharing your thoughts and feelings. This could be with a trusted friend, family member, or therapist.

The Healing Power of Disclosure: How Honesty Can Help You Move On from Trauma

Honesty can be a powerful tool for healing from trauma and emotional pain. When we share our experiences with others, it allows us to process our emotions and move forward. It can provide a sense of validation and support.

Sharing our truth with others can also help us gain perspective and insight into our own experiences. It allows us to see that we are not alone in our struggles and that others have faced similar challenges.

The Benefits of Self-Disclosure: How Sharing Your Truth Can Help You Grow

Being honest with ourselves and others can help us grow and develop as individuals. Self-disclosure allows us to gain insight into our own thoughts and feelings. It helps us understand ourselves better and make more informed decisions.

Sharing our truth with others also allows for deeper connections and stronger relationships. When we are open and honest with others, it creates a sense of trust and authenticity. It allows others to see us for who we truly are, and it encourages them to do the same.

The Power of Honesty and the Importance of Living with Integrity

Honesty is a powerful value that can improve our mental health, relationships, and overall well-being. It is the foundation upon which trust is built, and it is essential for living a fulfilling and meaningful life.

Living with integrity means being honest with ourselves and others. It means being true to our values and principles, even when it may be difficult or uncomfortable. By embracing honesty, we can create a world where trust and authenticity are valued above all else.

Chapter 26: Empowering Yourself Through Self-Advocacy: Tips and Strategies

Self-advocacy is the ability to speak up for oneself and take action to meet one's needs and goals. It is an essential skill that empowers individuals to have control over their own lives and make informed decisions. Self-advocacy is particularly important for marginalized groups who may face systemic barriers and discrimination. By advocating for themselves, individuals can assert their rights, access resources, and create positive change in their lives and communities.

Understanding the Importance of Self-Advocacy

Self-advocacy is the ability to assert one's needs, rights, and interests effectively. It involves understanding one's own strengths and weaknesses, identifying what one needs or wants, and taking action to achieve those goals. Self-advocacy is important because it allows individuals to have control over their own lives and make decisions that align with their values and aspirations.

In many situations, self-advocacy is necessary to ensure that one's needs are met and rights are respected. For example, in healthcare settings, self-advocacy can help individuals communicate their symptoms, concerns, and treatment preferences to healthcare providers. In educational settings, self-advocacy can help students with disabilities access appropriate accommodations and support services. In the workplace, self-advocacy can help employees assert their rights, negotiate for fair treatment, and advance in their careers.

Identifying Your Needs and Goals

To practice self-advocacy effectively, it is important to first identify your needs and goals. This involves reflecting on what is important to you and what you want to achieve. It can be helpful to write down your needs and goals in a specific and realistic manner.

Being specific about your needs and goals helps you communicate them clearly to others. For example, instead of saying "I need help," you can say "I need assistance with transportation to medical appointments twice a week." Being realistic about your needs and goals helps you set achievable targets and avoid disappointment. For example, instead of setting a goal to become a professional athlete overnight, you can set a goal to improve your fitness level and participate in local sports events.

Examples of needs and goals can vary widely depending on individual circumstances. Some common examples include the need for accessible housing, the goal of completing a degree or certification program, the need for mental health support, or the goal of finding meaningful employment.

Building Confidence in Your Abilities

Building confidence in yourself is crucial for effective self-advocacy. When you believe in your abilities and worth, you are more likely to assert your needs and rights with conviction. Building confidence involves recognizing your strengths, challenging self-doubt, and taking steps to develop new skills.

One way to build confidence is to reflect on past successes and accomplishments. Remind yourself of times when you have overcome challenges or achieved something meaningful. Celebrate these successes and use them as evidence that you are capable of achieving your goals.

Another way to build confidence is to engage in activities that challenge you and help you develop new skills. This could involve taking on new responsibilities at work, participating in public speaking or leadership training, or pursuing hobbies that push you out of your comfort zone.

Developing Effective Communication Skills

Effective communication is essential for self-advocacy. It involves expressing yourself clearly, listening actively, and understanding others' perspectives. Improving your communication skills can help you articulate your needs and goals more effectively, negotiate with others, and build positive relationships.

One tip for improving communication skills is to practice active listening. This involves giving your full attention to the person speaking, asking clarifying questions, and summarizing what you have heard to ensure understanding. Active listening shows respect for others' perspectives and helps build rapport.

Another tip for improving communication skills is to use "I" statements when expressing your needs or concerns. For example, instead of saying "You never listen to me," you can say "I feel frustrated when I don't feel heard." Using "I" statements helps you take ownership of your feelings and avoids blaming or accusing others.

Examples of effective communication in self-advocacy include speaking up in meetings to share your ideas, asking for clarification when you don't understand something, and expressing your needs and concerns to healthcare providers or educators.

Setting Boundaries and Saying No

Setting boundaries and saying no are important aspects of self-advocacy. It involves recognizing your limits, asserting your needs, and protecting your well-being. Setting boundaries and saying no effectively can help you avoid burnout, maintain healthy relationships, and prioritize your own needs.

To set boundaries effectively, it is important to be clear about what is acceptable and unacceptable to you. Communicate your boundaries assertively and respectfully, using "I" statements to express your needs. For example, instead of saying "You always interrupt me," you can say "I would appreciate it if you could let me finish speaking before responding."

Saying no effectively involves being firm and assertive while still being respectful of others' feelings. It is okay to prioritize your own needs and decline requests that are not aligned with your goals or values. Practice saying no in a calm and confident manner, without feeling the need to justify or apologize for your decision.

Examples of situations where setting boundaries and saying no is necessary include declining additional work assignments when you are already overwhelmed, refusing to engage in activities that compromise your values or beliefs, and asserting your right to privacy or personal space.

Seeking Support and Resources

Seeking support and resources is an important part of self-advocacy. It involves reaching out to others for assistance, guidance, or information that can help you achieve your goals. Seeking support can provide valuable insights, connections, and resources that can enhance your self-advocacy efforts.

Support and resources can be found in various places, depending on your needs and goals. For example, if you are seeking support for mental health, you can reach out to therapists, support groups, or helplines. If you are seeking resources for education or employment, you can contact career centers, vocational rehabilitation agencies, or community organizations.

Examples of support and resources available include disability rights organizations, legal aid clinics, community centers, social service agencies, and online forums or communities. It is important to research and explore different options to find the support and resources that best meet your needs.

Overcoming Barriers and Obstacles

Self-advocacy can be challenging due to various barriers and obstacles. These can include systemic discrimination, lack of knowledge or awareness about rights and resources, fear of judgment or rejection, or internalized self-doubt. Overcoming these barriers requires resilience, persistence, and a willingness to challenge the status quo.

One way to overcome barriers is to educate yourself about your rights and available resources. This can involve researching laws and policies that protect your rights, attending workshops or trainings on self-advocacy, or seeking guidance from experts in the field.

Another way to overcome barriers is to build a support network of like-minded individuals who can provide encouragement, advice, and assistance. This can involve joining advocacy groups or organizations that focus on issues relevant to your needs and goals.

Examples of barriers and obstacles to self-advocacy include lack of accessible transportation for individuals with disabilities, discrimination in hiring practices for marginalized groups, or stigma surrounding mental health issues. Overcoming these barriers may involve advocating for policy changes, raising awareness through public campaigns, or challenging discriminatory practices through legal means.

Negotiating for Your Rights and Needs

Negotiation is an important skill in self-advocacy. It involves finding common ground, exploring options, and reaching agreements that meet your needs and goals. Effective negotiation can help you assert your rights, resolve conflicts, and create win-win situations.

To negotiate effectively, it is important to prepare in advance by identifying your needs and goals, understanding the other party's perspective, and considering possible compromises or alternatives. During the negotiation process, listen actively, ask questions, and express your needs and concerns clearly and respectfully.

One tip for effective negotiation is to focus on interests rather than positions. Instead of getting stuck on specific demands or solutions, try to understand the underlying needs and motivations of all parties involved. This can help you find creative solutions that address everyone's concerns.

Examples of negotiation in action include advocating for reasonable accommodations in the workplace, negotiating for fair compensation or benefits, or resolving conflicts with landlords or neighbors.

Self-Care Practices for Empowerment

Self-care is an essential practice for empowerment in self-advocacy. It involves taking care of your physical, emotional, and mental well-being to ensure that you have the energy and resilience to advocate for yourself effectively. Self-care practices can vary widely depending on individual preferences and needs.

Examples of self-care practices include engaging in regular exercise or physical activity, practicing mindfulness or meditation, seeking therapy or counseling, spending time with loved ones, pursuing hobbies or interests that bring joy, setting aside time for relaxation or self-reflection, and prioritizing sleep and nutrition.

Self-care is not selfish; it is necessary for maintaining balance and well-being. By taking care of yourself, you are better able to show up fully in your advocacy efforts and make a positive impact.

Celebrating Your Successes and Progress

Celebrating successes and progress is an important part of self-advocacy. It involves acknowledging your achievements, no matter how small, and recognizing the progress you have made towards your goals. Celebrating successes boosts confidence, motivation, and resilience.

To celebrate successes and progress, it is important to set milestones or benchmarks along the way. This allows you to track your progress and celebrate each step towards your larger goals. Celebrations can take many forms, such as treating yourself to something special, sharing your achievements with loved ones, or simply taking a moment to reflect on your accomplishments.

Examples of successes and progress to celebrate include completing a challenging project at work, advocating for a change in policy that benefits others, overcoming a fear or obstacle, or achieving a personal goal such as running a marathon or learning a new skill.

Continuously Improving Your Self-Advocacy Skills

Self-advocacy is a lifelong journey that requires continuous improvement. As you grow and evolve, your needs and goals may change, and new challenges may arise. It is important to be open to learning, seeking feedback, and adapting your approach as needed.

One way to continuously improve your self-advocacy skills is to reflect on your experiences and identify areas for growth. Consider what worked well in previous situations and what could be improved. Seek feedback from trusted individuals who can provide constructive criticism and suggestions for improvement.

Another way to continuously improve is to seek out opportunities for learning and skill development. This can involve attending workshops or trainings on self-advocacy, reading books or articles on related topics, or participating in support groups or mentoring programs.

Examples of how to continuously improve include seeking out new challenges that push you out of your comfort zone, practicing new communication techniques, or seeking additional education or training to enhance your knowledge and skills.

Self-advocacy is an essential skill that empowers individuals to have control over their own lives and make informed decisions. By advocating for themselves, individuals can assert their rights, access resources, and create positive change in their lives and communities. Understanding the importance of self-advocacy, identifying needs and goals, building confidence, developing effective communication skills, setting boundaries, seeking support, overcoming barriers, negotiating for rights and needs, practicing self-care, celebrating successes, and continuously improving are all key aspects of effective self-advocacy. By practicing these skills, individuals can become more empowered and create positive change in their lives and communities.

Chapter 27: From Passion to Action: The Importance of Advocacy in Creating Change

Advocacy is a powerful tool for creating change in society. It involves speaking up, raising awareness, and taking action to address issues and promote positive social change. Advocacy can take many forms, from grassroots movements to lobbying efforts, and it plays a crucial role in shaping public opinion, influencing policy decisions, and driving social progress.

In today's complex and interconnected world, advocacy has become more important than ever. It allows individuals and communities to voice their concerns, challenge the status quo, and work towards a more just and equitable society. By advocating for their rights and the rights of others, people can bring attention to important issues, mobilize support, and ultimately create lasting change.

Defining Advocacy: What it Means and Why it Matters

Advocacy can be defined as the act of supporting or promoting a cause or issue. It involves speaking out on behalf of oneself or others who may not have a voice, and working towards positive change. Advocacy can take many different forms, from writing letters to elected officials, to organizing protests or rallies, to using social media to raise awareness.

Advocacy is important because it gives individuals and communities the power to make their voices heard and influence decision-making processes. It allows people to address issues that are important to them, whether it's advocating for better healthcare, fighting for environmental protection, or promoting equality and social justice. By advocating for change, individuals can bring attention to important issues, challenge existing systems and structures, and work towards creating a more just and equitable society.

The Role of Passion in Advocacy: Why it is a Driving Force for Change

Passion plays a crucial role in advocacy. It is the driving force that motivates individuals to take action, speak out, and work towards creating change. When people are passionate about an issue, they are more likely to dedicate their time, energy, and resources to advocating for it.

Passion can drive change in several ways. First, it fuels determination and perseverance. Advocacy can be a long and challenging process, and it requires individuals to stay committed and focused on their goals. Passion gives people the strength and resilience to overcome obstacles, push through setbacks, and continue fighting for what they believe in.

Second, passion inspires others. When people see someone who is truly passionate about a cause, it can ignite their own passion and motivate them to get involved. Passion is contagious, and it can create a ripple effect, inspiring others to take action and join the advocacy movement.

Finally, passion brings authenticity and credibility to advocacy efforts. When individuals are truly passionate about an issue, it shines through in their words and actions. This authenticity helps to build trust and credibility with others, making it more likely that their message will be heard and taken seriously.

Advocacy in Action: Real-life Examples of Successful Advocacy Campaigns

There have been many successful advocacy campaigns throughout history that have had a significant impact on society. These campaigns have brought attention to important issues, mobilized support, and ultimately led to positive change.

One example of a successful advocacy campaign is the civil rights movement in the United States. Through nonviolent protests, marches, and acts of civil disobedience, activists fought for racial equality and an end to segregation. Their advocacy efforts led to landmark legislation such as the Civil Rights Act of 1964 and the Voting Rights Act of 1965, which outlawed discrimination based on race and ensured equal voting rights for all citizens.

Another example is the environmental movement. Advocacy groups such as Greenpeace and the Sierra Club have been instrumental in raising awareness about environmental issues such as climate change, deforestation, and pollution. Their advocacy efforts have led to increased public awareness, changes in government policies, and a greater emphasis on sustainability and conservation.

Additionally, the LGBTQ+ rights movement has made significant progress through advocacy. Activists and advocacy organizations have worked tirelessly to challenge discriminatory laws and attitudes, leading to the legalization of same-sex marriage in many countries and increased protections for LGBTQ+ individuals.

These examples demonstrate the power of advocacy in creating change. By raising awareness, mobilizing support, and putting pressure on decision-makers, advocacy campaigns can bring about significant social progress.

The Importance of Collaboration in Advocacy: Working Together for Greater Impact

Collaboration is essential in advocacy because it allows individuals and organizations to pool their resources, expertise, and networks to achieve a common goal. By working together, advocates can amplify their efforts, reach a wider audience, and have a greater impact.

Collaboration in advocacy can take many forms. It can involve partnering with other organizations or individuals who share similar goals and values. It can also involve forming coalitions or alliances with diverse stakeholders who may have different perspectives but are united by a common cause.

Collaboration is important because it brings together different perspectives, skills, and resources. It allows advocates to leverage their collective strengths and overcome individual limitations. By working together, advocates can share knowledge and best practices, coordinate their efforts, and maximize their impact.

Furthermore, collaboration can help to build a broader base of support for advocacy campaigns. By partnering with other organizations or individuals, advocates can tap into existing networks and reach new audiences. This can help to raise awareness about important issues, mobilize support, and create a groundswell of public opinion that puts pressure on decision-makers to take action.

Advocacy for Social Justice: How Advocacy Can Address Systemic Injustice

Advocacy plays a crucial role in promoting social justice. It allows individuals and communities to challenge systemic injustice, address inequalities, and work towards a more equitable society.

Systemic injustice refers to the ways in which social, economic, and political systems perpetuate inequality and discrimination. It can manifest in various forms, such as racism, sexism, ableism, and classism. Advocacy for social justice seeks to dismantle these systems of oppression and create a more just and equitable society for all.

Advocacy for social justice can take many forms. It can involve advocating for policy changes that address systemic inequalities, such as advocating for affordable housing, equal pay, or criminal justice reform. It can also involve raising awareness about the experiences and struggles of marginalized communities, challenging stereotypes and biases, and promoting inclusivity and diversity.

Advocacy for social justice is important because it gives a voice to those who are marginalized and oppressed. It allows individuals and communities to challenge the status quo, demand accountability from those in power, and work towards creating a society that values and respects the rights and dignity of all its members.

The Impact of Advocacy on Policy Change: How Advocacy Can Influence Laws and Regulations

Advocacy has a significant impact on policy change. By raising awareness, mobilizing support, and putting pressure on decision-makers, advocates can influence laws and regulations that address important issues and promote positive social change.

Advocacy can influence policy change in several ways. First, it can shape public opinion. By raising awareness about an issue, advocates can educate the public, challenge existing narratives, and change public attitudes and perceptions. This can create a groundswell of public support that puts pressure on decision-makers to take action.

Second, advocacy can influence the political agenda. By mobilizing support, organizing campaigns, and engaging with elected officials, advocates can bring attention to important issues and push them onto the political agenda. This can lead to policy debates, legislative action, and ultimately changes in laws and regulations.

Third, advocacy can influence the decision-making process. By providing evidence-based research, expert testimony, and compelling arguments, advocates can influence the decision-making process and shape policy outcomes. This can involve engaging with policymakers, participating in public consultations, and providing input into policy development processes.

Overall, advocacy has a powerful impact on policy change. By raising awareness, mobilizing support, and engaging with decision-makers, advocates can shape public opinion, influence the political agenda, and ultimately bring about changes in laws and regulations that address important issues and promote positive social change.

The Role of Technology in Advocacy: How Digital Tools Can Amplify Advocacy Efforts

Technology plays a crucial role in advocacy. It has revolutionized the way advocates communicate, organize, and mobilize support. Digital tools have made it easier than ever for individuals and organizations to raise awareness, engage with supporters, and amplify their advocacy efforts.

One way technology has transformed advocacy is through social media. Platforms such as Facebook, Twitter, and Instagram have become powerful tools for raising awareness about important issues, mobilizing support, and connecting with like-minded individuals. Social media allows advocates to reach a wide audience, share information and resources, and engage in real-time conversations about important issues.

Another way technology has impacted advocacy is through online organizing and mobilization. Platforms such as Change.org and Avaaz allow individuals to start online petitions and gather signatures in support of a cause. This can help to raise awareness, demonstrate public support, and put pressure on decision-makers to take action.

Additionally, technology has made it easier for advocates to collect and analyze data. This can help to inform advocacy strategies, measure impact, and make evidence-based arguments. Technology has also made it easier for advocates to collaborate and share resources. Online platforms such as Google Drive and Slack allow advocates to work together remotely, share documents and information, and coordinate their efforts.

Overall, technology has revolutionized advocacy by making it easier than ever for individuals and organizations to raise awareness, mobilize support, and amplify their efforts. By harnessing the power of digital tools, advocates can reach a wider audience, engage with supporters, and create a greater impact.

Overcoming Challenges in Advocacy: Strategies for Overcoming Resistance and Pushback

Advocacy can be challenging and often faces resistance and pushback from those who are opposed to change. However, there are strategies that advocates can use to overcome these challenges and continue their efforts.

One strategy is to build coalitions and alliances. By partnering with other organizations or individuals who share similar goals and values, advocates can leverage their collective strength and overcome individual limitations. This can help to amplify their efforts, reach a wider audience, and have a greater impact.

Another strategy is to engage with decision-makers and policymakers. By building relationships, providing evidence-based research, and making compelling arguments, advocates can influence the decision-making process and shape policy outcomes. This can involve participating in public consultations, meeting with elected officials, and providing input into policy development processes.

Additionally, advocates can use storytelling as a powerful tool for change. By sharing personal stories and experiences, advocates can humanize the issues they are advocating for and create empathy and understanding. This can help to challenge existing narratives, change public attitudes, and mobilize support.

Furthermore, advocates can use media and public relations strategies to raise awareness about important issues. By working with journalists, writing op-eds or press releases, and using social media platforms, advocates can reach a wider audience and generate media coverage that puts pressure on decision-makers to take action.

Overall, advocacy faces challenges but there are strategies that advocates can use to overcome resistance and pushback. By building coalitions, engaging with decision-makers, using storytelling techniques, and leveraging media and public relations strategies, advocates can continue their efforts and create lasting change.

Advocacy for the Future: How Advocacy Can Create a Better World for Generations to Come

Advocacy plays a crucial role in creating a better future for generations to come. By addressing important issues, challenging existing systems and structures, and promoting positive social change, advocates can create a more just, equitable, and sustainable world.

Advocacy for the future involves looking beyond the present and envisioning a better world. It involves advocating for policies and practices that promote social, economic, and environmental justice. It also involves empowering future generations to become advocates themselves, ensuring that the work of advocacy continues into the future.

Advocacy for the future can take many forms. It can involve advocating for policies that address climate change and promote sustainability. It can also involve advocating for education reforms that empower young people and prepare them for the challenges of the future. Additionally, it can involve advocating for policies that promote equality and social justice, ensuring that future generations have equal opportunities and access to resources.

By advocating for the future, individuals and communities can create a better world for generations to come. They can ensure that important issues are addressed, that systemic injustices are challenged, and that policies and practices are in place to promote a more just, equitable, and sustainable society.

The Power of Advocacy in Creating Lasting Change and Making a Difference

Advocacy is a powerful tool for creating lasting change and making a difference in society. It allows individuals and communities to address important issues, challenge existing systems and structures, and work towards a more just and equitable world.

Through advocacy, individuals can raise awareness about important issues, mobilize support, and put pressure on decision-makers to take action. Advocacy can influence public opinion, shape the political agenda, and ultimately lead to changes in laws and regulations that address important issues and promote positive social change.

Passion plays a crucial role in advocacy. It is the driving force that motivates individuals to take action, speak out, and work towards creating change. When people are passionate about an issue, they are more likely to dedicate their time, energy, and resources to advocating for it.

Collaboration is also important in advocacy. By working together, advocates can amplify their efforts, reach a wider audience, and have a greater impact. Collaboration allows advocates to pool their resources, expertise, and networks to achieve a common goal.

Advocacy is not without its challenges, but there are strategies that advocates can use to overcome resistance and pushback. By building coalitions, engaging with decision-makers, using storytelling techniques, and leveraging media and public relations strategies, advocates can continue their efforts and create lasting change.

Ultimately, advocacy has the power to create a better future for generations to come. By addressing important issues, challenging existing systems and structures, and promoting positive social change, advocates can create a more just, equitable, and sustainable world. Advocacy is a powerful tool for creating lasting change and making a difference in society.

Chapter 28: Breaking Down the Stigma: Why Therapy is for Everyone

Mental health is a crucial aspect of overall well-being, yet it is often overlooked or stigmatized in society. Therapy plays a vital role in maintaining and improving mental health, providing individuals with the tools and support they need to navigate life's challenges. In this article, we will explore the importance of mental health, debunk common myths surrounding therapy, discuss the benefits of therapy, and delve into how therapy can help individuals in various aspects of their lives.

The Importance of Mental Health

Mental health is just as important as physical health. It encompasses our emotional, psychological, and social well-being, affecting how we think, feel, and act. Good mental health allows us to cope with stress, form and maintain healthy relationships, make sound decisions, and live fulfilling lives.

When our mental health is compromised, it can have a significant impact on our overall well-being. Mental health disorders such as anxiety and depression can lead to decreased productivity, impaired relationships, and even physical health problems. It is essential to prioritize mental health and seek help when needed to prevent these negative consequences.

The Myths Surrounding Therapy

There are several common misconceptions about therapy that can prevent individuals from seeking the help they need. One myth is that therapy is only for people with severe mental health issues. In reality, therapy can benefit anyone who wants to improve their mental well-being or work through personal challenges.

Another myth is that therapy is a sign of weakness or failure. This stigma often prevents individuals from seeking help because they fear judgment or believe they should be able to handle their problems on their own. However, seeking therapy is a sign of strength and self-awareness, as it shows a willingness to address and work through personal issues.

A third myth is that therapy is a quick fix or that therapists will simply tell you what to do. Therapy is a collaborative process that requires active participation from the individual seeking help. Therapists provide guidance, support, and tools, but the individual must be willing to put in the effort to make lasting changes.

The Benefits of Therapy

Therapy offers a wide range of benefits that can improve mental health and overall well-being. One of the primary benefits is improved mental health. Therapy provides individuals with a safe space to explore their thoughts and emotions, helping them gain insight into their behaviors and patterns. Through therapy, individuals can develop healthier coping mechanisms, manage stress more effectively, and reduce symptoms of mental health disorders.

Therapy also has a positive impact on relationships. By improving self-awareness and communication skills, individuals can develop healthier and more fulfilling relationships with romantic partners, family members, and friends. Therapy can help individuals address underlying issues that may be affecting their relationships and provide them with tools to navigate conflicts and improve emotional intimacy.

Another benefit of therapy is increased self-awareness. Through therapy, individuals can gain a deeper understanding of themselves, their values, and their goals. This self-awareness allows individuals to make more informed decisions, set realistic goals, and live more authentic lives.

How Therapy Can Help You

Therapy can help individuals in various ways depending on their specific needs and goals. For example, therapy can be beneficial for managing anxiety or depression. Therapists can teach individuals coping strategies to manage symptoms, challenge negative thought patterns, and develop healthier habits.

Therapy is also effective in improving communication skills. Many individuals struggle with expressing their needs or emotions effectively, leading to misunderstandings and conflicts in relationships. Therapists can provide guidance on assertive communication techniques, active listening skills, and conflict resolution strategies.

Additionally, therapy can help individuals develop coping strategies for dealing with stress. Stress is a common part of life, but when it becomes overwhelming or chronic, it can have a detrimental impact on mental health. Therapists can help individuals identify stress triggers, develop healthy coping mechanisms, and create self-care routines to manage stress effectively.

The Different Types of Therapy Available

There are various types of therapy available, each with its own approach and techniques. One common type is cognitive-behavioral therapy (CBT), which focuses on identifying and changing negative thought patterns and behaviors. CBT is often used to treat anxiety, depression, and other mental health disorders.

Psychoanalytic therapy, on the other hand, delves into the unconscious mind to explore unresolved conflicts and childhood experiences that may be influencing current behaviors and emotions. This type of therapy aims to bring these unconscious processes to conscious awareness, allowing individuals to gain insight and make changes.

Group therapy is another type of therapy that involves a small group of individuals who meet regularly to discuss their experiences, challenges, and goals. Group therapy provides a supportive environment where individuals can learn from others, gain different perspectives, and develop a sense of belonging.

Overcoming the Fear of Seeking Help

Many individuals have fears or reservations about seeking therapy. Common fears include the fear of being judged, the fear of opening up about personal issues, or the fear that therapy won't work. It is important to remember that therapists are trained professionals who provide a safe and non-judgmental space for individuals to explore their thoughts and emotions.

To overcome the fear of seeking help, it can be helpful to educate oneself about therapy and its benefits. Reading books or articles about therapy, talking to friends or family members who have had positive experiences with therapy, or even reaching out to therapists for a consultation can help alleviate fears and provide a better understanding of what to expect.

How Therapy Can Improve Your Relationships

Therapy can have a significant impact on improving relationships with others. By gaining self-awareness and developing healthier communication skills, individuals can navigate conflicts more effectively and build stronger emotional connections with their loved ones.

In therapy, individuals can explore their own patterns and behaviors that may be contributing to relationship difficulties. Therapists can provide guidance on setting boundaries, expressing needs and emotions, and developing empathy and understanding for others. Through therapy, individuals can learn to communicate more effectively, resolve conflicts in a healthy manner, and build trust and intimacy in their relationships.

The Role of Therapy in Managing Stress

Stress is a common part of life, but when it becomes overwhelming or chronic, it can have a detrimental impact on mental health. Therapy can play a crucial role in managing stress by helping individuals identify stress triggers, develop healthy coping mechanisms, and create self-care routines.

Therapists can teach individuals relaxation techniques such as deep breathing exercises, mindfulness meditation, or progressive muscle relaxation. These techniques can help individuals reduce stress levels and promote a sense of calm and well-being.

Additionally, therapists can help individuals identify unhealthy coping mechanisms such as substance abuse or avoidance behaviors and provide alternative strategies for managing stress. By developing healthier coping mechanisms, individuals can reduce the negative impact of stress on their mental health and overall well-being.

The Connection Between Therapy and Self-Care

Therapy is not only a form of self-care but also an essential component of it. Self-care involves taking deliberate actions to prioritize one's physical, emotional, and mental well-being. Therapy provides individuals with the tools and support they need to address personal challenges, improve mental health, and develop healthier habits.

By seeking therapy, individuals are actively investing in their own well-being and demonstrating self-compassion. Therapy allows individuals to explore their thoughts and emotions in a safe space, gain insight into their behaviors and patterns, and develop strategies for self-improvement.

In addition to therapy sessions, therapists may also provide homework assignments or recommend self-help resources such as books or online courses. These additional tools can further support an individual's self-care journey and provide ongoing guidance and support outside of therapy sessions.

How Therapy Can Help You Achieve Your Goals

Therapy can be a valuable tool for setting and achieving personal and professional goals. By gaining self-awareness, individuals can identify their values, strengths, and areas for growth. Therapists can help individuals set realistic and achievable goals, develop action plans, and provide accountability and support throughout the process.

Therapy can also help individuals overcome obstacles or limiting beliefs that may be hindering their progress. By exploring underlying fears or self-doubt, individuals can develop strategies to overcome these barriers and move closer to their goals.

Additionally, therapy can provide individuals with a sense of purpose and direction. Through therapy, individuals can gain clarity on their passions, interests, and values, allowing them to make more informed decisions about their personal and professional lives.

The Future of Mental Health Treatment

The field of mental health treatment is constantly evolving, with new approaches and technologies emerging to improve accessibility and effectiveness. One emerging trend is teletherapy, which allows individuals to receive therapy remotely through video calls or phone sessions. Teletherapy eliminates geographical barriers and provides greater flexibility for individuals who may have difficulty accessing traditional in-person therapy.

Virtual reality therapy is another innovative approach that is gaining traction in the field of mental health treatment. This form of therapy uses virtual reality technology to create simulated environments where individuals can confront and overcome their fears or traumas in a controlled and safe manner.

Art therapy, animal-assisted therapy, and mindfulness-based therapies are also becoming more widely recognized as effective approaches to mental health treatment. These alternative therapies provide individuals with unique ways to express themselves, connect with others, and develop coping strategies.

Mental health is a crucial aspect of overall well-being, and therapy plays a vital role in maintaining and improving it. By debunking common myths surrounding therapy and highlighting its benefits, we hope to encourage individuals to seek help if needed. Therapy can help individuals manage anxiety or depression, improve communication skills, develop coping strategies, and achieve personal and professional goals. As the field of mental health treatment continues to evolve, individuals can expect greater accessibility and innovative approaches to therapy. It is essential to prioritize mental health and seek therapy when needed to live a fulfilling and balanced life.

Chapter 29: Unlock Your Potential: How Specialized Programs Can Help You Achieve Your Goals

Unlocking your potential is the process of discovering and utilizing your unique talents, abilities, and strengths to achieve personal and professional growth. It involves tapping into your inner resources and pushing yourself beyond your comfort zone to reach new heights of success. By unlocking your potential, you can unleash your true capabilities and achieve things you never thought possible.

Unlocking your potential is crucial for personal and professional growth because it allows you to maximize your abilities and achieve your goals. When you tap into your full potential, you can accomplish more, overcome challenges, and make a greater impact in your personal and professional life. It also helps you build confidence, develop new skills, and expand your horizons. By unlocking your potential, you can create a fulfilling and successful life.

The Benefits of Specialized Programs for Achieving Your Goals

Specialized programs are designed to help individuals achieve specific goals or develop specific skills. These programs provide focused training, guidance, and support to help individuals unlock their potential in a particular area. Whether it's a program for career advancement, entrepreneurship, personal development, or any other field, specialized programs offer numerous benefits for achieving your goals.

One of the key benefits of specialized programs is that they provide structured guidance and support. These programs are designed by experts in the field who have a deep understanding of the challenges and requirements for success. They provide step-by-step guidance, resources, and tools to help you navigate the path towards achieving your goals. This structured approach can save you time and effort by providing a clear roadmap for success.

Specialized programs also offer a supportive community of like-minded individuals who are on a similar journey. This community provides a valuable network of support, encouragement, and accountability. Being surrounded by others who share similar goals and aspirations can inspire you to push yourself further and stay motivated throughout the process.

Examples of specialized programs include career coaching programs, entrepreneurship programs, leadership development programs, and personal development programs. These programs are designed to provide individuals with the knowledge, skills, and support they need to unlock their potential in a specific area and achieve their goals.

Identifying Your Goals and Creating a Plan for Success

Setting goals is an essential step in unlocking your potential. Goals provide direction and purpose, and they help you stay focused and motivated. When setting goals, it's important to be specific, measurable, achievable, relevant, and time-bound (SMART). This means that your goals should be clear, quantifiable, realistic, relevant to your overall vision, and have a deadline.

To identify your goals, start by reflecting on your passions, interests, and values. What are the things that truly matter to you?

What do you want to achieve in your personal and professional life? Once you have a clear understanding of your values and aspirations, you can start setting specific goals that align with them.

Once you have identified your goals, it's important to create a plan for success. This plan should outline the steps you need to take to achieve your goals and the resources you will need along the way. Break down your goals into smaller, manageable tasks and create a timeline for completing each task. This will help you stay organized and focused on your journey towards unlocking your potential.

Overcoming Obstacles and Challenges Along the Way

As you work towards unlocking your potential, you are likely to encounter obstacles and challenges along the way. These obstacles can come in various forms, such as self-doubt, fear of failure, lack of resources or support, or external circumstances beyond your control. However, it's important to remember that obstacles are a natural part of the journey towards success.

One common obstacle is self-doubt. Many people struggle with feelings of inadequacy or imposter syndrome when trying to unlock their potential. It's important to recognize that these feelings are normal and that everyone experiences them at some point. The key is to challenge these negative thoughts and beliefs and replace them with positive affirmations and self-belief.

Another common obstacle is fear of failure. Many people are afraid to take risks or step outside their comfort zone because they fear failure. However, it's important to remember that failure is not the end of the road, but rather a stepping stone towards success. Embrace failure as an opportunity to learn and grow, and don't let it hold you back from unlocking your potential.

Lack of resources or support can also be a significant obstacle. It's important to seek out the resources and support you need to overcome these challenges. This could involve reaching out to mentors or coaches, joining a supportive community, or investing in specialized programs that can provide the guidance and support you need.

The Role of Accountability and Support in Achieving Your Goals

Accountability and support play a crucial role in achieving your goals and unlocking your potential. When you have someone holding you accountable, it becomes easier to stay motivated, focused, and on track towards your goals. Additionally, having a support system can provide encouragement, guidance, and feedback along the way.

There are different types of accountability and support that you can utilize. One option is to find an accountability partner or join a mastermind group. An accountability partner is someone who shares similar goals and aspirations and can hold you accountable for taking action towards your goals. A mastermind group is a community of like-minded individuals who meet regularly to support each other's growth and success.

Another option is to work with a coach or mentor. A coach or mentor can provide personalized guidance, support, and feedback based on their expertise and experience. They can help you identify your strengths and weaknesses, set realistic goals, develop strategies for success, and overcome obstacles along the way.

To find accountability and support, start by reaching out to your existing network. Look for individuals who share similar goals or interests and who can provide the support and accountability you need. You can also join online communities or forums related to your field of interest to connect with like-minded individuals.

Finding the Right Specialized Program for Your Needs and Interests

When it comes to choosing a specialized program, it's important to consider your needs, interests, and goals. Not all programs are created equal, and what works for one person may not work for another. Here are some factors to consider when choosing a specialized program:

1. Relevance: Does the program align with your goals and aspirations? Does it provide the knowledge, skills, and support you need to unlock your potential in a specific area?

2. Expertise: Who is behind the program? Are they experts in their field with a proven track record of success? Do they have the knowledge and experience to guide you towards achieving your goals?

3. Structure: What is the structure of the program? Does it provide a clear roadmap for success? Does it offer step-by-step guidance, resources, and tools to help you navigate the path towards achieving your goals?

4. Support: What kind of support does the program offer? Does it provide a supportive community of like-minded individuals who can offer encouragement, feedback, and accountability? Does it offer personalized coaching or mentorship?

5. Cost: What is the cost of the program? Is it within your budget? Does it offer any payment plans or scholarships?

To research and evaluate specialized programs, start by reading reviews and testimonials from past participants. Look for programs that have a track record of success and positive feedback from participants. You can also reach out to individuals who have completed the program to get their insights and recommendations.

Before enrolling in a specialized program, ask questions to ensure that it's the right fit for you. Some questions to consider include:

- What are the program's goals and objectives?
- What is the curriculum or content of the program?
- What kind of support and resources are provided?
- What is the time commitment required?
- What is the cost of the program?
- Are there any prerequisites or requirements for enrollment?

The Impact of Personalized Coaching and Mentorship on Your Success

Personalized coaching and mentorship can have a significant impact on your success in unlocking your potential. A coach or mentor can provide personalized guidance, support, and feedback based on their expertise and experience. They can help you identify your strengths and weaknesses, set realistic goals, develop strategies for success, and overcome obstacles along the way.

One of the key benefits of personalized coaching and mentorship is that it provides accountability. When you have someone holding you accountable, it becomes easier to stay motivated, focused, and on track towards your goals. A coach or mentor can help you set clear goals, develop action plans, and hold you accountable for taking consistent action towards your goals.

Another benefit is that a coach or mentor can provide valuable insights and feedback. They can help you identify blind spots, challenge limiting beliefs, and provide guidance on how to overcome obstacles. They can also offer advice based on their own experiences and help you navigate challenges more effectively.

To find a coach or mentor, start by reaching out to your existing network. Look for individuals who have achieved success in your field of interest and who can provide guidance and support. You can also join professional organizations or attend networking events to connect with potential coaches or mentors.

When working with a coach or mentor, it's important to establish clear expectations and goals from the beginning. Be open to feedback and willing to take action on their recommendations. Remember that their role is to guide and support you, but ultimately, it's up to you to take responsibility for your own growth and success.

Chapter 30: Breaking Down Barriers: Strategies for Overcoming Peer Relationship Challenges

Positive peer relationships are crucial for the social and emotional development of individuals, especially during adolescence. These relationships provide a sense of belonging, support, and validation, which are essential for overall well-being. Positive peer relationships can have a significant impact on various aspects of life, including academic success, mental health, and personal growth. In this article, we will explore the importance of positive peer relationships, common barriers to healthy relationships, the impact of social media on peer relationships, and strategies for developing effective communication skills, empathy, and understanding.

Understanding the Importance of Positive Peer Relationships

Positive peer relationships refer to connections between individuals that are characterized by mutual respect, trust, and support. These relationships play a vital role in shaping one's identity and self-esteem. When individuals have positive peer relationships, they feel accepted and valued for who they are, which boosts their confidence and self-worth.

There are numerous benefits to cultivating positive peer relationships. Firstly, these relationships provide emotional support during challenging times. Having friends who understand and empathize with one's struggles can help alleviate stress and promote mental well-being. Secondly, positive peer relationships foster a sense of belonging and connectedness. When individuals feel like they belong to a group or community, they are more likely to engage in prosocial behaviors and develop a sense of purpose. Lastly, positive peer relationships can enhance personal growth by exposing individuals to different perspectives and experiences. Through interactions with peers, individuals can learn new skills, broaden their horizons, and develop a greater understanding of themselves and others.

Examples of positive peer relationships include friendships built on trust and respect, mentorship programs where older students guide younger ones, and support groups where individuals facing similar challenges come together to share their experiences and provide encouragement.

Identifying Common Barriers to Healthy Peer Relationships

While positive peer relationships are essential for personal growth and well-being, there are several barriers that can hinder their development. These barriers include a lack of communication skills, fear of rejection, bullying and harassment, and cultural and diversity differences.

1. Lack of communication skills: Effective communication is the foundation of any healthy relationship. However, many individuals struggle with expressing their thoughts and emotions clearly. This can lead to misunderstandings, conflicts, and a breakdown in relationships. Developing strong communication skills is crucial for building positive peer relationships.

2. Fear of rejection: Fear of rejection is a common barrier to forming meaningful connections with peers. This fear can stem from past experiences of rejection or a lack of self-confidence. Individuals who fear rejection may avoid social interactions or hesitate to express

their true selves, which can hinder the development of positive peer relationships.

3. Bullying and harassment: Bullying and harassment can have a detrimental impact on peer relationships. Individuals who experience bullying may feel isolated, anxious, and unworthy of forming connections with others. Additionally, witnessing bullying can create a culture of fear and mistrust among peers, making it challenging to establish positive relationships.

4. Cultural and diversity differences: Cultural and diversity differences can create barriers to understanding and acceptance among peers. When individuals come from different backgrounds or have different beliefs and values, it can be challenging to find common ground and build connections. Lack of understanding and respect for cultural and diversity differences can lead to stereotypes, prejudice, and discrimination.

The Impact of Social Media on Peer Relationships

In today's digital age, social media plays a significant role in shaping peer relationships. While social media platforms offer opportunities for connection and self-expression, they also present challenges that can impact the quality of peer relationships.

Positive effects of social media on peer relationships include the ability to connect with individuals from different geographical locations, share experiences and interests, and find support communities for specific issues or challenges. Social media can also provide a platform for individuals to showcase their talents, creativity, and achievements, which can boost self-esteem and foster positive peer interactions.

However, there are also negative effects of social media on peer relationships. The constant exposure to carefully curated and filtered versions of others' lives can lead to feelings of inadequacy and comparison. This can create a toxic environment where individuals feel pressured to conform to unrealistic standards and may struggle with self-acceptance. Additionally, cyberbullying and online harassment are prevalent issues on social media platforms, which can have severe consequences on individuals' mental health and well-being.

To use social media to enhance peer relationships, it is essential to be mindful of one's online presence and interactions. This includes being authentic, respectful, and supportive in online interactions, as well as setting boundaries and taking breaks when needed. It is also crucial to remember that social media is just one aspect of peer relationships and should not replace face-to-face interactions and genuine connections.

Developing Effective Communication Skills

Effective communication skills are vital for building positive peer relationships. Good communication allows individuals to express their thoughts and emotions clearly, listen actively, and resolve conflicts constructively. Here are some tips for improving communication skills:

1. Active listening: Practice active listening by giving your full attention to the speaker, maintaining eye contact, and avoiding interruptions. Show empathy by acknowledging the speaker's feelings and summarizing their main points.

· 2. Assertiveness: Be assertive in expressing your thoughts, feelings, and needs while respecting the rights and boundaries of others. Use "I" statements to communicate your perspective without blaming or attacking others.

3. Nonverbal communication: Pay attention to your body language, facial expressions, and tone of voice when communicating with others. Nonverbal cues can convey messages that complement or contradict your words.

4. Conflict resolution: Learn strategies for resolving conflicts in a constructive manner, such as active listening, finding common ground, and seeking win-win solutions. Avoid personal attacks or defensiveness during conflicts.

Building Empathy and Understanding

Empathy is the ability to understand and share the feelings of others. It is a crucial skill for building positive peer relationships as it allows individuals to connect on a deeper level and show compassion towards others. Here are some tips for building empathy and understanding:

1. Practice active listening: When someone shares their experiences or emotions, listen attentively and try to understand their perspective without judgment. Reflect back on what they have said to show that you are actively engaged in the conversation.

2. Put yourself in their shoes: Imagine how you would feel if you were in the other person's situation. This exercise can help you develop a greater understanding of their emotions and experiences.

3. Seek diverse perspectives: Engage with individuals from different backgrounds, cultures, and experiences. This exposure can broaden your understanding of the world and help you develop empathy towards others.

4. Practice kindness and compassion: Show kindness and compassion towards others in your daily interactions. Small acts of kindness can go a long way in building positive peer relationships.

Cultivating a Positive Mindset

A positive mindset is essential for fostering positive peer relationships. When individuals have a positive outlook, they are more likely to approach interactions with optimism, resilience, and openness. Here are some tips for cultivating a positive mindset:

1. Practice gratitude: Take time each day to reflect on the things you are grateful for. This practice can shift your focus towards the positive aspects of life and enhance your overall well-being.

2. Challenge negative thoughts: Notice when negative thoughts arise and challenge them with more positive and realistic perspectives. Replace self-critical thoughts with self-compassion and encouragement.

3. Surround yourself with positivity: Surround yourself with people who uplift and inspire you. Avoid toxic relationships or environments that bring you down.

4. Take care of your physical and mental health: Engage in activities that promote your physical and mental well-being, such as exercise, mindfulness, and self-care. Taking care of yourself can contribute to a positive mindset.

Overcoming Fear of Rejection

Fear of rejection can hinder the development of positive peer relationships. Overcoming this fear is crucial for building connections and forming meaningful bonds with others. Here are some tips for overcoming fear of rejection:

1. Challenge negative beliefs: Identify and challenge any negative beliefs you may have about yourself or your worthiness of forming connections. Remind yourself that everyone experiences rejection at some point, and it does not define your value as a person.

2. Take small steps: Start by engaging in low-risk social interactions and gradually increase your comfort level. This could involve joining a club or group with shared interests or initiating conversations with classmates or colleagues.

3. Focus on self-acceptance: Cultivate self-acceptance and self-compassion by recognizing your strengths, embracing your uniqueness, and practicing self-care. When you accept and love yourself, the fear of rejection becomes less powerful.

4. Seek support: Reach out to trusted friends, family members, or professionals who can provide support and guidance as you navigate your fear of rejection. Sometimes, talking about your fears can help alleviate their intensity.

Addressing Bullying and Harassment

Bullying and harassment can have a detrimental impact on peer relationships. It is essential to address these issues to create a safe and inclusive environment for all individuals. Here are some tips for addressing bullying and harassment:

1. Speak up: If you witness bullying or harassment, speak up against it in a calm and assertive manner. Let the individuals involved

know that their behavior is not acceptable and that it has consequences.

2. Report incidents: If you are a victim of bullying or harassment, report the incidents to a trusted adult, such as a teacher, counselor, or parent. They can provide support and take appropriate actions to address the situation.

3. Promote empathy and kindness: Encourage empathy and kindness among peers by modeling these behaviors yourself and promoting a culture of respect and inclusivity.

4. Educate others: Raise awareness about the impact of bullying and harassment by organizing workshops, presentations, or campaigns that educate individuals about the consequences of such behaviors. Education is key to prevention.

Navigating Cultural and Diversity Differences

Cultural and diversity differences can enrich peer relationships by providing opportunities for learning, growth, and understanding. However, it is essential to navigate these differences with respect and sensitivity. Here are some tips for navigating cultural and diversity differences:

1. Educate yourself: Take the initiative to learn about different cultures, traditions, and perspectives. This can help you develop a greater understanding and appreciation for diversity.

2. Ask questions: If you are unsure about something related to another person's culture or background, ask respectful questions to gain clarity. Be open-minded and receptive to their responses.

3. Respect boundaries: Recognize that individuals may have different boundaries based on their cultural or personal beliefs.

Respect these boundaries and avoid making assumptions or judgments.

4. Foster inclusivity: Create an inclusive environment where individuals from different backgrounds feel welcome and valued. Encourage open dialogue, celebrate diversity, and challenge stereotypes or biases.

Seeking Support from Trusted Adults

Seeking support from trusted adults is crucial for navigating peer relationships, especially during challenging times. Trusted adults can provide guidance, advice, and a safe space to express concerns or seek validation. Here are some tips for identifying trusted adults:

1. Family members: Family members can be a source of support and guidance during difficult times. They know you well and can provide valuable insights and advice.

2. Teachers or counselors: Teachers or school counselors are trained professionals who can offer support and guidance in navigating peer relationships. They can provide resources, mediation, or referrals to other professionals if needed.

3. Mentors or coaches: Mentors or coaches can provide guidance and support in specific areas of interest or personal growth. They can offer valuable insights and advice based on their own experiences.

4. Community leaders or religious figures: Community leaders or religious figures can provide a sense of belonging and support. They can offer guidance based on their knowledge and experience.

Celebrating Successes and Encouraging Growth

Celebrating successes and encouraging growth in peer relationships is essential for fostering a positive and supportive environment. Recognizing achievements and milestones can boost self-esteem and strengthen bonds among peers. Here are some tips for celebrating successes and encouraging growth:

1. Acknowledge achievements: Take the time to acknowledge and celebrate the achievements of your peers. This can be done through verbal praise, written notes, or small gestures of appreciation.

2. Offer support: Offer support and encouragement to your peers when they face challenges or setbacks. Let them know that you believe in their abilities and are there to support them.

3. Collaborate and learn from each other: Engage in collaborative projects or activities where you can learn from each other's strengths and skills. This can foster a sense of teamwork and mutual growth.

4. Provide constructive feedback: When providing feedback, focus on constructive criticism that helps individuals improve rather than tearing them down. Offer suggestions for growth and improvement in a supportive manner.

Positive peer relationships are essential for personal growth, well-being, and social development. They provide a sense of belonging, support, and validation that contribute to overall happiness and success. By understanding the importance of positive peer relationships, identifying common barriers, developing effective communication skills, building empathy, cultivating a positive mindset, overcoming fear of rejection, addressing bullying and harassment, navigating cultural and diversity differences, seeking support from trusted adults, and celebrating successes, individuals can cultivate meaningful connections with their peers. It is through these connections that individuals can thrive and reach their full potential.

Chapter 31: Developing Essential Skills and Knowledge to Reach Your Full Potential

Developing essential skills and knowledge is crucial for reaching your full potential. These skills and knowledge can help you overcome challenges, adapt to change, and achieve your goals. Here are some essential skills and knowledge areas to focus on:

1. Communication: Effective communication is essential for building relationships, resolving conflicts, and conveying your ideas and thoughts. Focus on developing both verbal and written communication skills.

2. Leadership: Leadership skills are important for taking initiative, inspiring others, and driving change. Develop skills such as decision-making, problem-solving, and emotional intelligence.

3. Time management: Time management skills are crucial for staying organized, prioritizing tasks, and maximizing productivity. Learn how to set goals, plan your time effectively, and manage distractions.

4. Emotional intelligence: Emotional intelligence is the ability to recognize and manage your own emotions and the emotions of others. It involves skills such as self-awareness, empathy, and relationship management.

5. Financial literacy: Financial literacy is the knowledge and understanding of financial concepts such as budgeting, saving, investing, and managing debt. Develop basic financial literacy skills to make informed decisions about your personal and professional finances.

6. Networking: Networking skills are important for building relationships, expanding your professional network, and creating opportunities. Learn how to effectively network both online and offline.

To develop these essential skills and knowledge areas, consider taking courses or workshops, reading books or articles, attending seminars or conferences, or seeking out mentors or coaches who can provide guidance in these areas. Continuous learning and development are key to unlocking your potential and staying ahead in today's rapidly changing world.

Building a Strong Mindset and Resilience for Long-Term Success

Building a strong mindset and resilience is crucial for long-term success in unlocking your potential. Your mindset determines how you perceive challenges, setbacks, and failures, and it plays a significant role in your ability to bounce back and keep moving forward. Here are some strategies for building a strong mindset and resilience:

1. Cultivate a growth mindset: A growth mindset is the belief that your abilities and intelligence can be developed through hard work, dedication, and perseverance. Embrace challenges, view failures as opportunities for growth, and believe in your ability to learn and improve.

2. Practice self-care: Taking care of your physical, mental, and emotional well-being is crucial for building resilience. Make time for activities that recharge and rejuvenate you, such as exercise, meditation, hobbies, or spending time with loved ones.

3. Surround yourself with positive influences: Surround yourself with positive, supportive people who believe in your potential and

encourage you to keep going. Avoid negative influences or toxic relationships that can drain your energy and hinder your progress.

4. Practice gratitude: Cultivating an attitude of gratitude can help shift your focus from what's not working to what is working in your life. Take time each day to reflect on the things you are grateful for and appreciate the progress you have made.

5. Set realistic expectations: Setting realistic expectations for yourself can help prevent feelings of overwhelm or burnout. Break down your goals into smaller, manageable tasks and celebrate each milestone along the way.

6. Learn from setbacks: Instead of dwelling on setbacks or failures, use them as opportunities for learning and growth. Reflect on what went wrong, identify lessons learned, and adjust your approach moving forward.

Building a strong mindset and resilience takes time and practice. Be patient with yourself and remember that it's a journey. By cultivating a strong mindset and resilience, you can overcome obstacles, bounce back from setbacks, and continue moving towards unlocking your full potential.

The Power of Networking and Community in Achieving Your Goals

Networking and community play a powerful role in achieving your goals and unlocking your potential. Networking involves building relationships with individuals who can provide support, guidance, and opportunities. Community refers to a group of like-minded individuals who share similar goals and aspirations.

Networking is important because it allows you to tap into the knowledge, resources, and connections of others. By building a strong network, you can gain access to new opportunities, learn from others' experiences, and receive support and guidance along your journey. Networking can also help you build your personal brand and reputation, which can open doors for future collaborations or career advancements.

Community is important because it provides a sense of belonging and support. Being part of a community of like-minded individuals who share similar goals and aspirations can provide encouragement, motivation, and accountability. It can also provide a safe space to share ideas, ask for feedback, and learn from others' experiences.

To build a strong network and community, start by reaching out to your existing network. Attend networking events, join professional organizations or industry groups, or participate in online communities or forums related to your field of interest. Be proactive in building relationships and offering support to others. Remember that networking is a two-way street, and it's important to give as much as you receive.

Taking Action to Unlock Your Potential with Specialized Programs

Unlocking your potential is a lifelong journey that requires continuous learning, growth, and self-reflection. By taking advantage of specialized programs, setting clear goals, overcoming obstacles, seeking accountability and support, developing essential skills and knowledge, building a strong mindset and resilience, and leveraging the power of networking and community, you can unlock your full potential and achieve personal and professional success. Specialized programs provide the necessary tools, resources, and guidance to help you navigate your unique path and reach your goals. Whether it's a leadership development program, a career coaching program, or a skills training program, these specialized programs offer targeted support and expertise to help you unlock your potential in specific areas. By actively participating in these programs, you can gain valuable insights, acquire new skills, and develop a deeper understanding of yourself and your capabilities. Additionally, setting clear goals and regularly assessing your progress can help you stay focused and motivated on your journey towards unlocking your potential. Overcoming obstacles is an inevitable part of the process, but by embracing challenges and learning from setbacks, you can grow stronger and more resilient. Seeking accountability and support from mentors, coaches, or peers can provide valuable guidance and encouragement along the way. Developing essential skills and knowledge is crucial for unlocking your potential. Whether it's honing your communication skills, improving your problem-solving abilities, or expanding your knowledge in a specific field, continuous learning is key to personal and professional growth. Building a strong mindset and resilience is also essential for unlocking your potential. Cultivating a positive attitude, embracing failure as a learning opportunity, and staying persistent in the face of challenges can help you overcome obstacles and achieve success. Finally, leveraging the power of networking and community can open doors to new opportunities and connections that can propel you forward on your journey. By surrounding yourself with like-minded individuals who share similar goals and aspirations, you can gain valuable insights, support, and inspiration. In conclusion, unlocking your potential requires taking action and actively engaging in specialized programs that provide the necessary tools, resources, and support to help you reach your goals. By continuously learning, setting clear goals, overcoming obstacles, seeking accountability and support, developing essential skills and knowledge, building a strong mindset and resilience, and leveraging the power of networking and community, you can unlock your full potential and achieve personal and professional success.

Chapter 32: The Art of Listening: Tips for Effective Communication in the Workplace

Listening is a fundamental skill that plays a crucial role in the workplace. Effective listening is essential for clear communication, building relationships, and fostering collaboration among coworkers. In today's fast-paced and technology-driven world, it can be easy to overlook the importance of listening. However, by actively practicing and improving our listening skills, we can create a more productive and harmonious work environment.

The Importance of Listening in the Workplace

Listening is crucial in the workplace for several reasons. First and foremost, it is essential for effective communication. When we listen attentively to our colleagues, we can better understand their needs, concerns, and ideas. This understanding allows us to respond appropriately and provide valuable input. On the other hand, poor listening can lead to misunderstandings, miscommunication, and even conflicts.

Furthermore, listening is vital for building trust and rapport among coworkers. When we actively listen to others, we show them that we value their opinions and perspectives. This fosters a sense of respect and appreciation, which in turn strengthens relationships in the workplace. Conversely, when we fail to listen or dismiss others' ideas without consideration, it can create a negative and hostile work environment.

How Listening Can Improve Workplace Relationships

Active listening is a powerful tool for improving communication and relationships among coworkers. When we actively listen to others, we demonstrate empathy and understanding. This creates a safe space for open and honest dialogue, where individuals feel comfortable expressing their thoughts and concerns.

Active listening also promotes collaboration and teamwork. By truly hearing what others have to say, we can identify common goals and find solutions that benefit everyone involved. This collaborative approach leads to better decision-making and problem-solving, as diverse perspectives are taken into account.

For example, imagine a team working on a project where each member actively listens to one another's ideas and concerns. By valuing each other's input and working together to find common ground, the team can develop a more comprehensive and innovative solution. This not only improves the quality of the work but also strengthens the bond between team members.

The Benefits of Active Listening in the Workplace

Active listening offers numerous benefits in the workplace. Firstly, it enhances understanding. When we actively listen to others, we gain a deeper comprehension of their thoughts, feelings, and perspectives. This understanding allows us to respond more effectively and make informed decisions.

Active listening also promotes problem-solving. By truly hearing what others have to say, we can identify the root causes of issues and work together to find solutions. This collaborative approach leads to more effective problem-solving and prevents recurring problems.

Additionally, active listening is crucial for conflict resolution. When conflicts arise in the workplace, active listening allows us to understand the underlying issues and address them in a constructive manner. By actively listening to all parties involved, we can find common ground and reach a resolution that satisfies everyone.

For instance, imagine a situation where two coworkers have a disagreement about a project's direction. By actively listening to each other's concerns and perspectives, they can identify the underlying issues and find a compromise that meets both of their needs. This not only resolves the conflict but also strengthens their working relationship.

Common Listening Barriers and How to Overcome Them

While listening is essential, there are several common barriers that can hinder effective listening in the workplace. One common barrier is distractions. In today's digital age, it is easy to get distracted by emails, notifications, or other tasks while someone is speaking. To overcome this barrier, it is important to practice mindfulness and be fully present in the conversation. This means putting away distractions and giving our full attention to the speaker.

Another common barrier is biases or preconceived notions. We all have our own biases based on our experiences and beliefs, which can influence how we interpret information. To overcome this barrier, it is important to practice self-awareness and actively challenge our biases. By being open-minded and willing to consider different perspectives, we can overcome biases and truly listen to others.

Additionally, language barriers can also hinder effective listening in the workplace. In multicultural or multinational workplaces, it is important to be aware of language differences and make an effort to bridge the gap. This can be done by using simple and clear language, asking for clarification when needed, and being patient with non-native speakers.

The Role of Nonverbal Communication in Listening

Nonverbal communication plays a significant role in listening. In fact, research suggests that nonverbal cues account for a large portion of our communication. Body language, facial expressions, and tone of voice can all convey important information that complements or contradicts verbal messages.

For example, imagine a coworker who is speaking confidently about a project but is fidgeting nervously and avoiding eye contact. These nonverbal cues may indicate that they are not as confident as they appear, and there may be underlying concerns or uncertainties. By paying attention to these nonverbal cues, we can gain a deeper understanding of the speaker's true thoughts and feelings.

Similarly, tone of voice can greatly impact how a message is received. A harsh or condescending tone can make the listener defensive or disengaged, while a warm and empathetic tone can create a sense of trust and openness. By being mindful of our own tone of voice and paying attention to others', we can enhance our listening skills and improve communication in the workplace.

Techniques for Improving Your Listening Skills

Improving listening skills requires practice and intentionality. Here are some practical tips for enhancing your listening skills in the workplace:

1. Practice active listening: Active listening involves fully engaging with the speaker and demonstrating your attentiveness through verbal and nonverbal cues. This includes maintaining eye contact, nodding or using other affirmative gestures, and providing verbal feedback such as paraphrasing or summarizing.

2. Avoid interrupting: Interrupting can disrupt the flow of conversation and make the speaker feel unheard or disrespected. Instead, allow the speaker to finish their thoughts before responding or asking questions.

3. Paraphrase and summarize: Paraphrasing and summarizing what the speaker has said not only demonstrates your understanding but also allows for clarification and confirmation. This shows the speaker that you are actively listening and engaged in the conversation.

4. Minimize distractions: As mentioned earlier, distractions can hinder effective listening. Minimize distractions by putting away electronic devices, finding a quiet space for conversations, and focusing your attention solely on the speaker.

5. Be patient: Sometimes, it takes time for individuals to articulate their thoughts or express themselves fully. Be patient and give them the space they need to communicate effectively.

By incorporating these techniques into your daily interactions, you can significantly improve your listening skills and create a more positive and productive work environment.

How to Listen with Empathy and Understanding

Empathy is a crucial component of effective listening. When we listen with empathy, we not only hear the words being spoken but also try to understand the speaker's emotions, perspectives, and experiences. This deep level of understanding allows us to respond in a compassionate and supportive manner.

To listen with empathy, it is important to reflect the speaker's feelings and perspectives. This can be done by using phrases such as "It sounds like you're feeling..." or "I can understand why you might think that..." By acknowledging and validating the speaker's emotions and perspectives, we create a safe space for them to express themselves fully.

It is also important to suspend judgment when listening with empathy. Instead of immediately forming opinions or jumping to conclusions, try to approach the conversation with an open mind. This allows for a more objective understanding of the speaker's thoughts and feelings.

For example, imagine a coworker who is expressing frustration about a recent project. Instead of dismissing their concerns or offering immediate solutions, listen with empathy by acknowledging their frustration and asking open-ended questions to better understand their perspective. This not only shows that you care about their feelings but also allows for a more meaningful and productive conversation.

The Art of Asking Effective Questions to Enhance Listening

Asking effective questions is an important skill that enhances listening and understanding. By asking thoughtful and relevant questions, we can encourage the speaker to elaborate on their thoughts and provide more information. This not only deepens our understanding but also shows the speaker that we are actively engaged in the conversation.

Open-ended questions are particularly effective in encouraging the speaker to share more information. These questions cannot be answered with a simple "yes" or "no" and require the speaker to provide more details or explanations. Examples of open-ended questions include "Can you tell me more about that?" or "How did you come to that conclusion?"

Clarifying questions are also useful in enhancing listening and understanding. These questions seek to clarify any ambiguities or uncertainties in the speaker's message. Examples of clarifying questions include "Could you please explain what you mean by that?" or "Can you give me an example?"

By incorporating these questioning techniques into your conversations, you can enhance your listening skills and gain a deeper understanding of others' thoughts and perspectives.

The Connection Between Listening and Productivity in the Workplace

Listening has a direct impact on productivity in the workplace. When individuals feel heard and understood, they are more likely to be engaged and motivated in their work. This leads to increased productivity and efficiency.

Effective listening also prevents misunderstandings and errors. By actively listening to instructions or feedback, individuals can ensure that they have a clear understanding of what is expected of them. This reduces the likelihood of mistakes or miscommunication, saving time and resources.

Furthermore, listening promotes collaboration and teamwork. When individuals actively listen to each other's ideas and perspectives, they can work together more effectively towards a common goal. This collaborative approach leads to better outcomes and increased efficiency.

For example, imagine a team working on a tight deadline. By actively listening to each other's suggestions and concerns, they can identify potential roadblocks or inefficiencies and find solutions together. This not only improves the quality of the work but also allows the team to meet the deadline more efficiently.

How to Foster a Culture of Listening in Your Workplace

Creating a workplace culture that values listening and communication requires effort from both leaders and employees. Here are some tips for fostering a culture of listening in your workplace:

1. Lead by example: Leaders play a crucial role in setting the tone for the workplace culture. By actively listening to their employees, leaders demonstrate the importance of listening and create an environment where everyone feels heard and valued.

2. Encourage open communication: Create opportunities for open and honest communication, such as team meetings or feedback sessions. Encourage employees to share their thoughts, concerns, and ideas without fear of judgment or reprisal.

3. Provide training and resources: Offer training programs or workshops on effective communication and listening skills. Provide

resources such as books or articles that employees can refer to for further development.

4. Foster a supportive environment: Create a safe space where individuals feel comfortable expressing themselves without fear of criticism or ridicule. Encourage empathy, respect, and understanding among coworkers.

5. Recognize and reward active listening: Acknowledge and appreciate individuals who demonstrate active listening skills. This can be done through verbal recognition, rewards, or other forms of appreciation.

By implementing these strategies, you can foster a workplace culture that values listening and communication, leading to improved collaboration, productivity, and job satisfaction.

The Role of Technology in Enhancing Workplace Communication and Listening

Technology plays a significant role in enhancing workplace communication and listening. With the advent of various tools and platforms, individuals can now communicate and collaborate more effectively, regardless of geographical barriers.

For instance, video conferencing tools allow for face-to-face communication, even when individuals are located in different parts of the world. This enhances listening by allowing participants to observe nonverbal cues and engage in real-time conversations.

Collaboration platforms such as project management software or shared document platforms enable teams to work together seamlessly. These tools facilitate effective listening by providing a centralized space for sharing ideas, providing feedback, and tracking progress.

Additionally, instant messaging platforms or email allow for quick and efficient communication. While these tools may not provide the same level of nuance as face-to-face communication, they still play a valuable role in enhancing listening by providing a platform for ongoing dialogue and information sharing.

It is important to note that while technology can enhance workplace communication and listening, it should not replace face-to-face interactions entirely. In-person conversations still offer the richest form of communication, allowing for the full range of nonverbal cues and nuances.

Listening is a critical skill that plays a vital role in the workplace. Effective listening enhances communication, builds relationships, and fosters collaboration among coworkers. By actively practicing and improving our listening skills, we can create a more productive and harmonious work environment.

To prioritize listening in your own workplace, start by recognizing the importance of active listening and its impact on productivity and relationships. Incorporate techniques such as active listening, paraphrasing, and asking effective questions into your daily interactions. Foster a culture of listening by leading by example, encouraging open communication, and providing training and resources.

By prioritizing listening in the workplace, you can create a positive and supportive environment where individuals feel heard, valued, and motivated to contribute their best work.

Chapter 33: 10 Steps to Achieving True Independence in Your Life

Independence is defined as the ability to think and act freely, without being influenced or controlled by others. It is the state of being self-reliant and self-sufficient, where one can make decisions and take actions based on their own beliefs and values. Independence is important because it allows individuals to have control over their own lives, make choices that align with their goals and priorities, and ultimately lead a fulfilling and meaningful life.

Having independence can greatly improve your life in various ways. It gives you the freedom to pursue your passions and interests, without being limited by the expectations or opinions of others. It allows you to take risks and explore new opportunities, which can lead to personal growth and development. Independence also fosters a sense of empowerment and self-confidence, as you become more capable of handling challenges and making decisions on your own.

Step 1: Identify Your Goals and Priorities

The first step towards achieving independence is to identify your goals and priorities. This involves taking the time to reflect on what truly matters to you and what you want to achieve in different areas of your life. By having clear goals and priorities, you can create a roadmap for yourself and make decisions that align with your values.

To identify your goals and priorities, start by asking yourself some important questions. What do you want to accomplish in your career? What kind of relationships do you want to have? How do you want to spend your free time? Consider both short-term and long-term goals, as well as different aspects of your life such as personal, professional, and social.

Once you have identified your goals and priorities, write them down and create a plan for how you will achieve them. This will help you stay focused and motivated, as well as provide a sense of direction in your journey towards independence.

Step 2: Develop a Plan of Action

After identifying your goals and priorities, the next step is to develop a plan of action. A plan of action is a detailed outline of the steps you need to take in order to achieve your goals. It helps you stay organized, track your progress, and make adjustments along the way.

To develop a plan of action, break down your goals into smaller, manageable tasks. Determine what specific actions you need to take in order to move closer to your goals. Set deadlines for each task and create a timeline for when you want to achieve certain milestones.

Having a plan of action is important because it provides structure and accountability. It helps you stay focused and motivated, as well as measure your progress towards your goals. By breaking down your goals into smaller tasks, you can also avoid feeling overwhelmed and increase your chances of success.

Step 3: Take Responsibility for Your Decisions

Taking responsibility for your decisions is a crucial step towards achieving independence. It means acknowledging that you have the power to make choices and accepting the consequences that come with them. By taking responsibility for your decisions, you are taking ownership of your life and actively shaping your own future.

To take responsibility for your decisions, start by being aware of the choices you make on a daily basis. Reflect on the reasons behind your decisions and consider how they align with your goals and priorities. If you make a mistake or face a setback, instead of blaming others or external circumstances, take ownership of the situation and learn from it.

Taking responsibility is important because it empowers you to take control of your life. It allows you to learn from your mistakes, grow from challenges, and make better decisions in the future. By taking responsibility for your decisions, you become more self-reliant and less dependent on others for validation or guidance.

Step 4: Build a Support System

Building a support system is essential for achieving independence. A support system consists of people who provide encouragement, guidance, and assistance as you work towards your goals. They can be friends, family members, mentors, or even professional networks.

To build a support system, start by identifying the people in your life who are supportive and share similar values or goals. Reach out to them and express your desire for independence and personal growth. Seek their advice and guidance, and be open to their feedback and suggestions.

Having a support system is important because it provides a sense of community and belonging. It gives you access to different perspectives and resources that can help you overcome challenges and achieve your goals. A support system also provides emotional support and motivation, especially during difficult times.

Step 5: Learn to Manage Your Finances

Learning to manage your finances is a crucial aspect of achieving independence. It involves understanding your income, expenses, and financial goals, as well as making informed decisions about saving, investing, and budgeting.

To manage your finances effectively, start by creating a budget that outlines your income and expenses. Track your spending habits and identify areas where you can cut back or save money. Set financial goals for yourself, such as saving for a down payment on a house or paying off debt, and create a plan for how you will achieve them.

Managing your finances is important because it provides financial security and freedom. It allows you to make choices based on what is best for your long-term financial well-being, rather than being limited by financial constraints. By being in control of your finances, you can also reduce stress and anxiety related to money.

Step 6: Embrace Change and Adaptability

Embracing change and adaptability is crucial for achieving independence. Life is constantly changing, and being able to adapt to new circumstances and challenges is essential for personal growth and success.

To embrace change and adaptability, start by developing a growth mindset. This means being open to new ideas, perspectives, and experiences. Embrace challenges as opportunities for learning and growth, and be willing to step outside of your comfort zone.

Embracing change and adaptability is important because it allows you to navigate through life's ups and downs with resilience and flexibility. It enables you to overcome obstacles, seize new opportunities, and make the most out of every situation. By embracing change, you can also discover new passions and interests that can contribute to your overall sense of independence.

Step 7: Cultivate Self-Confidence and Self-Esteem

Cultivating self-confidence and self-esteem is essential for achieving independence. It involves believing in yourself, recognizing your worth, and having a positive self-image.

To cultivate self-confidence and self-esteem, start by practicing self-compassion and self-acceptance. Be kind to yourself and acknowledge your strengths and accomplishments. Surround yourself with positive influences and engage in activities that make you feel good about yourself.

Cultivating self-confidence and self-esteem is important because it allows you to trust in your abilities and make decisions with conviction. It helps you overcome self-doubt and fear of failure, which can often hold you back from pursuing your goals. By cultivating self-confidence and self-esteem, you can also inspire others and become a role model for independence.

Step 8: Practice Self-Care and Wellness

Practicing self-care and wellness is crucial for achieving independence. It involves taking care of your physical, mental, and emotional well-being, as well as prioritizing your needs and boundaries.

To practice self-care and wellness, start by identifying activities that bring you joy and relaxation. Make time for hobbies, exercise regularly, get enough sleep, eat nutritious meals, and engage in activities that promote mental well-being such as meditation or journaling.

Practicing self-care and wellness is important because it allows you to recharge and rejuvenate, which is essential for maintaining a healthy and balanced lifestyle. It also helps you manage stress and prevent burnout, which can hinder your progress towards independence. By prioritizing self-care and wellness, you can show up as your best self and have the energy and resilience to pursue your goals.

Step 9: Continuously Learn and Grow

Continuously learning and growing is essential for achieving independence. It involves seeking new knowledge, skills, and experiences that contribute to your personal and professional development.

To continuously learn and grow, start by setting aside time for learning and self-improvement. Read books, take courses, attend workshops or conferences, or engage in activities that challenge you and expand your horizons. Seek feedback from others and be open to constructive criticism.

Continuously learning and growing is important because it keeps you curious, adaptable, and relevant in a rapidly changing world. It allows you to stay ahead of the curve, acquire new skills that can contribute to your independence, and discover new passions or interests along the way. By continuously learning and growing, you can also inspire others and contribute to the betterment of society.

Step 10: Celebrate Your Achievements and Maintain Your Independence

The final step towards achieving independence is to celebrate your achievements and maintain your independence. Celebrating your achievements allows you to acknowledge your hard work and progress, while maintaining your independence ensures that you continue to make choices that align with your goals and priorities.

To celebrate your achievements, take the time to reflect on how far you have come and the obstacles you have overcome. Reward yourself for reaching milestones or accomplishing goals, whether it's treating yourself to something special or simply taking a moment to appreciate your efforts.

To maintain your independence, continue to prioritize your goals and priorities. Regularly assess your progress and make adjustments as needed. Stay connected with your support system and seek their guidance or feedback when necessary. Remember that achieving independence is an ongoing journey, and it requires consistent effort and commitment.

Conclusion:

In conclusion, independence is a fundamental aspect of leading a fulfilling and meaningful life. By following the 10 steps outlined in this article, you can take control of your life, make choices that align with your goals and priorities, and ultimately achieve independence. Remember that achieving independence is a journey, and it requires consistent effort and commitment. So take action today and start working towards your goals and dreams. You have the power to create the life you desire.

Chapter 34: Mastering Executive Functioning: The Key to Success in Life

Executive functioning refers to a set of cognitive skills that are essential for managing and regulating one's thoughts, emotions, and behaviors. These skills play a crucial role in our daily lives, helping us to plan, organize, problem-solve, make decisions, and achieve our goals. Without strong executive functioning skills, individuals may struggle with tasks such as time management, attention and focus, emotional regulation, and decision making. In this article, we will explore the importance of executive functioning skills and provide strategies for developing and improving these skills.

Understanding Executive Functioning: What is it and Why is it Important?

Executive functioning can be defined as the set of mental processes that enable individuals to plan, organize, problem-solve, and regulate their behavior in order to achieve their goals. These skills are controlled by the prefrontal cortex of the brain and develop throughout childhood and adolescence. They continue to develop into adulthood but can also be improved through practice and training.

Executive functioning is important because it allows individuals to effectively manage their time, attention, and emotions. It helps us to set goals, create plans to achieve those goals, stay focused on tasks, regulate our emotions in order to make rational decisions, and adapt to changing circumstances. Without strong executive functioning skills, individuals may struggle with tasks such as completing assignments on time, staying organized, managing their emotions in stressful situations, and making sound decisions.

The Role of Executive Functioning in Achieving Success in Life

Executive functioning skills are crucial for achieving success in various aspects of life. Individuals with strong executive functioning skills are better able to set goals and create plans to achieve those goals. They are able to stay focused on tasks and manage their time effectively. They are also better able to regulate their emotions and make rational decisions.

Many successful individuals have strong executive functioning skills. For example, successful entrepreneurs often possess excellent planning and organization skills, allowing them to create and execute business plans effectively. Successful athletes often have strong attention and focus skills, enabling them to stay focused on their training and perform at their best. Successful leaders often have strong decision-making skills, allowing them to make sound decisions in high-pressure situations.

Common Challenges Faced by Individuals with Poor Executive Functioning

Individuals with poor executive functioning skills may face a number of challenges in their daily lives. They may struggle with tasks such as time management, organization, attention and focus, emotional regulation, and decision making.

Common symptoms of poor executive functioning include difficulty with planning and organizing tasks, trouble staying focused on tasks, impulsivity, difficulty managing time effectively, difficulty regulating emotions, and difficulty making decisions.

These challenges can have a significant impact on daily life. For example, individuals with poor executive functioning skills may struggle to complete assignments on time or stay organized. They may have difficulty paying attention in class or at work. They may struggle to regulate their emotions in stressful situations or make impulsive decisions without considering the consequences.

Developing Executive Functioning Skills: Tips and Strategies

Fortunately, executive functioning skills can be developed and improved with practice and training. Here are some strategies for improving executive functioning skills:

1. Break tasks into smaller steps: Breaking tasks into smaller steps can make them more manageable and easier to complete. This can help individuals with poor executive functioning skills to stay organized and focused on the task at hand.

2. Use visual aids: Visual aids such as calendars, to-do lists, and charts can help individuals with poor executive functioning skills to stay organized and manage their time effectively. These visual aids can serve as reminders of tasks that need to be completed and help individuals prioritize their activities.

3. Practice mindfulness: Mindfulness exercises can help individuals improve their attention and focus skills. Mindfulness involves paying attention to the present moment without judgment. By practicing mindfulness regularly, individuals can train their brains to stay focused on tasks and reduce distractions.

4. Engage in physical exercise: Physical exercise has been shown to improve executive functioning skills. Regular exercise can help individuals improve their attention, focus, and decision-making skills.

5. Seek support: Individuals with poor executive functioning skills may benefit from seeking support from a therapist or coach who specializes in executive functioning. These professionals can provide strategies and techniques to help individuals improve their executive functioning skills.

The Importance of Time Management in Mastering Executive Functioning

Time management is a crucial skill for mastering executive functioning. Effective time management allows individuals to prioritize tasks, allocate time for each task, and stay on track with their goals.

Tips for improving time management skills include:

1. Set goals: Setting clear and specific goals can help individuals prioritize their tasks and allocate time for each task. By setting goals, individuals can stay focused and motivated to complete their tasks.

2. Create a schedule: Creating a schedule can help individuals allocate time for each task and stay organized. It can also help individuals identify any gaps in their schedule and make adjustments as needed.

3. Use timers and alarms: Timers and alarms can help individuals stay on track with their tasks and manage their time effectively. Setting timers for specific tasks can help individuals stay focused and avoid getting distracted.

4. Avoid multitasking: Multitasking can actually decrease productivity and make it more difficult to manage time effectively. Instead of trying to do multiple tasks at once, it is better to focus on one task at a time and give it your full attention.

How to Improve Attention and Focus for Better Executive Functioning

Attention and focus are essential skills for executive functioning. Improving attention and focus can help individuals stay on task, avoid distractions, and complete tasks more efficiently.

Strategies for improving attention and focus include:

1. Minimize distractions: Minimizing distractions in your environment can help you stay focused on your tasks. This can include turning off notifications on your phone, finding a quiet place to work, and using noise-cancelling headphones if necessary.

2. Practice mindfulness: Mindfulness exercises, such as meditation or deep breathing, can help improve attention and focus. By practicing mindfulness regularly, individuals can train their brains to stay focused on tasks and reduce distractions.

3. Break tasks into smaller steps: Breaking tasks into smaller steps can make them more manageable and easier to focus on. By focusing on one step at a time, individuals can avoid feeling overwhelmed and stay focused on the task at hand.

4. Take regular breaks: Taking regular breaks can actually improve attention and focus. Short breaks can help individuals recharge their energy and maintain focus for longer periods of time.

The Role of Emotional Regulation in Executive Functioning

Emotional regulation is an important aspect of executive functioning. It involves the ability to recognize and manage one's emotions in order to make rational decisions and regulate behavior.

Tips for improving emotional regulation skills include:

1. Practice self-awareness: Developing self-awareness can help individuals recognize their emotions and understand how they are affecting their thoughts and behaviors. This can help individuals regulate their emotions more effectively.

2. Use relaxation techniques: Relaxation techniques such as deep breathing, progressive muscle relaxation, or guided imagery can help individuals calm their emotions and reduce stress.

3. Seek support: Individuals who struggle with emotional regulation may benefit from seeking support from a therapist or counselor who specializes in emotion regulation. These professionals can provide strategies and techniques to help individuals manage their emotions more effectively.

4. Engage in activities that promote emotional well-being: Engaging in activities that promote emotional well-being, such as exercise, spending time with loved ones, or engaging in hobbies, can help individuals regulate their emotions and improve their overall well-being.

The Benefits of Planning and Organization in Mastering Executive Functioning

Planning and organization skills are essential for mastering executive functioning. These skills allow individuals to set goals, create plans to achieve those goals, and stay organized throughout the process.

Tips for improving planning and organization skills include:

1. Set clear and specific goals: Setting clear and specific goals can help individuals prioritize their tasks and create plans to achieve those goals. By setting goals, individuals can stay focused and motivated to complete their tasks.

2. Break tasks into smaller steps: Breaking tasks into smaller steps can make them more manageable and easier to complete. This can help individuals stay organized and focused on the task at hand.

3. Use visual aids: Visual aids such as calendars, to-do lists, and charts can help individuals stay organized and manage their time effectively. These visual aids can serve as reminders of tasks that need to be completed and help individuals prioritize their activities.

4. Create a routine: Creating a routine can help individuals stay organized and manage their time effectively. By following a consistent routine, individuals can develop habits that support their planning and organization skills.

Executive Functioning and Decision Making: Tips for Making Better Choices

Executive functioning skills play a crucial role in decision making. These skills allow individuals to consider different options, weigh the pros and cons, and make rational decisions based on their goals and values.

Tips for making better decisions include:

1. Gather information: Before making a decision, it is important to gather as much information as possible about the options available. This can involve conducting research, seeking advice from experts, or consulting with trusted individuals.

2. Consider the pros and cons: Consider the potential benefits and drawbacks of each option before making a decision. This can help individuals make more informed choices that align with their goals and values.

3. Reflect on values and priorities: Reflecting on one's values and priorities can help individuals make decisions that are in line with their personal beliefs and long-term goals.

4. Take time to think: Taking time to think before making a decision can help individuals avoid impulsive choices and consider all the relevant factors. It is important to give yourself enough time to weigh the pros and cons and make a decision that feels right for you.

The Impact of Executive Functioning on Academic and Career Success

Executive functioning skills have a significant impact on academic and career success. These skills are crucial for managing time, staying organized, staying focused on tasks, regulating emotions, and making sound decisions.

In academic settings, strong executive functioning skills can help students stay organized, manage their time effectively, complete assignments on time, stay focused in class, regulate their emotions during exams or presentations, and make informed decisions about their education and career goals.

In the workplace, strong executive functioning skills can help individuals manage their time effectively, stay organized, meet deadlines, stay focused on tasks, regulate their emotions in high-pressure situations, and make sound decisions that contribute to their professional success.

Many successful individuals possess strong executive functioning skills. For example, successful entrepreneurs often have excellent planning and organization skills, allowing them to create and execute business plans effectively. Successful athletes often have strong attention and focus skills, enabling them to stay focused on their training and perform at their best. Successful leaders often have strong decision-making skills, allowing them to make sound decisions in high-pressure situations.

How to Support Children and Adolescents in Developing Strong Executive Functioning Skills

Supporting children and adolescents in developing strong executive functioning skills is crucial for their academic and personal success. Parents and educators can play a key role in helping children and adolescents develop these skills.

Strategies for supporting children and adolescents in developing executive functioning skills include:

1. Provide structure: Providing structure can help children and adolescents develop routines and habits that support their planning and organization skills. This can involve creating schedules, setting clear expectations, and providing reminders for tasks that need to be completed.

2. Teach problem-solving skills: Teaching children and adolescents problem-solving skills can help them develop their executive functioning skills. Encourage them to think critically, consider different options, and weigh the pros and cons before making decisions.

3. Encourage self-reflection: Encouraging children and adolescents to reflect on their thoughts, emotions, and behaviors

can help them develop self-awareness and improve their emotional regulation skills. This can involve asking open-ended questions, encouraging journaling or self-reflection exercises, and providing a safe space for them to express their thoughts and feelings.

4. Provide opportunities for practice: Providing children and adolescents with opportunities to practice their executive functioning skills can help them develop and improve these skills. This can involve assigning age-appropriate tasks that require planning, organization, attention, and decision making.

In conclusion, executive functioning skills are essential for managing and regulating one's thoughts, emotions, and behaviors. These skills play a crucial role in our daily lives, helping us to plan, organize, problem-solve, make decisions, and achieve our goals. Without strong executive functioning skills, individuals may struggle with tasks such as time management, attention and focus, emotional regulation, and decision making.

Fortunately, executive functioning skills can be developed and improved with practice and training. Strategies for improving executive functioning skills include breaking tasks into smaller steps, using visual aids, practicing mindfulness, engaging in physical exercise, and seeking support from professionals who specialize in executive functioning.

Developing strong executive functioning skills is crucial for achieving success in various aspects of life. These skills are particularly important for academic and career success. Many successful individuals possess strong executive functioning skills, which allow them to set goals, stay organized, stay focused on tasks, regulate their emotions, and make sound decisions.

Parents and educators can play a key role in supporting children and adolescents in developing strong executive functioning skills.

By providing structure, teaching problem-solving skills, encouraging self-reflection, and providing opportunities for practice, parents and educators can help children and adolescents develop and improve their executive functioning skills.

Chapter 35: Breaking the Monotony: How to Spice Up Your Daily Routine

In today's fast-paced world, it's easy to fall into a monotonous routine. Wake up, go to work, come home, repeat. This repetitive cycle can have negative effects on our mental health and overall well-being. Breaking the monotony is essential for leading a more fulfilling life. By introducing variety and new experiences into our daily routines, we can stimulate our minds, boost our creativity, and find joy in the unexpected.

Recognizing the Signs of a Monotonous Routine

It's important to recognize the signs of a monotonous routine in order to break free from it. Some common signs include feeling bored or unmotivated, lacking enthusiasm for daily activities, and experiencing a sense of stagnation in life. If you find yourself going through the motions without any excitement or passion, it may be time to shake things up.

Take a moment to reflect on your own routine and identify any signs of monotony. Are you doing the same things day in and day out? Are you feeling uninspired or stuck in a rut? Recognizing these signs is the first step towards breaking free from the monotony and embracing a more fulfilling life.

Getting Out of Your Comfort Zone: Why It's Important

Stepping out of your comfort zone is essential for personal growth and development. When we stay within our comfort zones, we limit ourselves and miss out on new opportunities for learning and self-discovery. By pushing ourselves to try new things and face our fears, we can expand our horizons and gain confidence in ourselves.

There are many ways to get out of your comfort zone. It could be as simple as trying a new type of cuisine or taking a different route to work. Or it could be something more challenging like traveling to a new country or learning a new skill. The key is to push yourself beyond what feels safe and familiar. Embracing discomfort and uncertainty can lead to personal growth and a more fulfilling life.

Planning Your Day: Tips for Adding Variety

Adding variety to your daily routine doesn't have to be complicated. It can be as simple as planning ahead and incorporating small changes into your day. One way to do this is by trying a new coffee shop or restaurant for your morning pick-me-up. Instead of taking the same route to work every day, take a different one and see what new sights you discover along the way.

Another tip is to schedule time for activities that bring you joy and excitement. Whether it's going for a hike, attending a yoga class, or meeting up with friends for dinner, make sure to prioritize these activities in your daily or weekly schedule. By planning ahead, you can ensure that variety is incorporated into your day and that you have something to look forward to.

Incorporating Exercise into Your Routine: Benefits and Ideas

Exercise is not only beneficial for our physical health but also for our mental well-being. It releases endorphins, reduces stress, and improves our mood. Incorporating exercise into your routine is a great way to break the monotony and add variety to your day.

There are many ways to incorporate exercise into your routine. You could try a new workout class or join a sports team. If you prefer outdoor activities, consider going for a hike, bike ride, or swim. The key is to find an activity that you enjoy and that challenges you physically. By incorporating exercise into your routine, you'll not only improve your physical health but also add excitement and variety to your day.

Trying New Hobbies: Exploring Your Interests

Exploring new hobbies is another great way to break the monotony and add variety to your life. Hobbies allow us to explore our interests, learn new skills, and engage in activities that bring us joy and fulfillment.

There are countless hobbies to try, depending on your interests and preferences. If you enjoy being creative, you could try painting, drawing, or photography. If you're more inclined towards physical activities, you could try rock climbing, dancing, or martial arts. The key is to find something that sparks your curiosity and brings you joy. By trying new hobbies, you'll not only break the monotony but also discover new passions and interests.

Socializing: The Power of Human Connection

Socializing is an essential aspect of our well-being. It provides us with a sense of belonging, support, and connection. When we're stuck in a monotonous routine, it's easy to isolate ourselves and miss out on the benefits of human connection.

There are many ways to socialize and break free from the monotony. You could join a club or organization that aligns with your interests, attend networking events or conferences in your field, or simply reach out to friends and family for a catch-up session. By prioritizing socializing in your routine, you'll not only break the monotony but also strengthen your relationships and improve your overall well-being.

Taking Time for Self-Care: How to Relax and Recharge

Self-care is crucial for our mental health and overall well-being. It allows us to relax, recharge, and take care of ourselves amidst the chaos of daily life. When we're stuck in a monotonous routine, it's easy to neglect self-care and prioritize other responsibilities.

Taking time for self-care doesn't have to be complicated or time-consuming. It can be as simple as taking a bubble bath, practicing meditation or mindfulness, or indulging in a hobby that brings you joy. The key is to prioritize self-care in your routine and make it a non-negotiable part of your day. By taking care of yourself, you'll not only break the monotony but also improve your mental health and overall well-being.

Changing Your Environment: Simple Ways to Mix Things Up

Changing your environment is a powerful way to break the monotony and stimulate your creativity. When we're stuck in the same physical space day in and day out, it's easy to feel uninspired and stagnant.

There are many simple ways to change your environment. You could rearrange your furniture to create a new layout, declutter and organize your space, or work in a different coffee shop or co-working space. By changing your environment, you'll not only break the monotony but also boost your creativity and productivity.

Embracing Spontaneity: The Joy of Unplanned Adventures

Embracing spontaneity is a wonderful way to break free from the monotony and add excitement to your life. When we're stuck in a rigid routine, it's easy to become predictable and miss out on the joy of unplanned adventures.

There are many ways to embrace spontaneity. You could take a last-minute road trip to a nearby town or city, try a new restaurant without researching it first, or say yes to an invitation or opportunity that comes your way. By embracing spontaneity, you'll not only break the monotony but also experience the thrill of the unknown and create lasting memories.

Breaking the Monotony for a More Fulfilling Life

Breaking the monotony is essential for leading a more fulfilling life. By recognizing the signs of a monotonous routine, getting out of your comfort zone, planning your day with variety in mind, incorporating exercise into your routine, trying new hobbies, socializing, taking time for self-care, changing your environment, and embracing spontaneity, you can break free from the repetitive cycle and find joy in the unexpected.

It's important to remember that breaking the monotony doesn't have to be complicated or time-consuming. It can be as simple as trying a new coffee shop, joining a club, or taking a bubble bath. The key is to prioritize variety and new experiences in your daily routine. By doing so, you'll not only improve your mental health and overall well-being but also lead a more fulfilling and meaningful life. So go ahead, break the monotony and embrace the joy of variety!

Chapter 36: The Dos and Don'ts of Networking: Building Professional Relationships

Networking is the process of building and nurturing relationships with individuals who can provide support, guidance, and opportunities in your professional life. It involves connecting with people in your industry or field of interest, attending events, and actively engaging with others to create a strong network of contacts. Networking is crucial for career growth as it allows you to expand your knowledge, gain new perspectives, and open doors to new opportunities.

One of the key benefits of networking is the ability to tap into the hidden job market. Many job opportunities are never advertised publicly, and instead, are filled through referrals and recommendations. By building a strong network, you increase your chances of hearing about these hidden opportunities and being referred by someone within your network. Additionally, networking allows you to stay up-to-date with industry trends and developments, which can help you stay competitive in your field.

Dos of Networking: Tips for Making a Positive Impression

1. Research and prepare before attending events: Before attending a networking event, take the time to research the attendees and the organizations that will be present. This will allow you to have meaningful conversations and show genuine interest in others. Additionally, prepare some talking points or questions that you can use to start conversations and keep them flowing.

2. Dress appropriately: First impressions matter, so it's important to dress professionally when attending networking events. Dressing appropriately shows that you take yourself and your career seriously. It's better to be slightly overdressed than underdressed, as it demonstrates respect for the event and the people attending.

3. Be confident and approachable: Confidence is key when networking. Approach others with a smile, make eye contact, and introduce yourself confidently. Remember that everyone is at the event for the same reason - to meet new people and make connections - so don't be afraid to initiate conversations.

4. Listen actively and ask questions: Networking is not just about talking about yourself; it's about building relationships and showing genuine interest in others. Practice active listening by focusing on the person you're speaking with, asking open-ended questions, and showing curiosity about their experiences and perspectives.

5. Exchange business cards and follow up: At networking events, it's important to exchange business cards with the people you meet. This allows you to stay in touch and follow up after the event. Make sure to write a note on the back of each card you receive to help you remember the conversation and any follow-up actions you discussed.

Don'ts of Networking: Common Mistakes to Avoid

1. Being too pushy or aggressive: Networking is about building relationships, not making sales pitches. Avoid being too pushy or aggressive when approaching others. Instead, focus on creating a genuine connection and finding common ground.

2. Talking too much about yourself: While it's important to share information about yourself and your career, avoid dominating

the conversation and talking only about yourself. Remember to listen actively and show interest in others.

3. Forgetting to follow up: Following up is a crucial step in networking. If you fail to follow up after meeting someone, you miss out on the opportunity to continue building the relationship. Send a personalized follow-up email or message within a few days of the event to express your appreciation for the conversation and suggest next steps.

4. Being unprofessional or inappropriate: Networking events are professional settings, so it's important to maintain a level of professionalism at all times. Avoid engaging in inappropriate or unprofessional behavior that could damage your reputation.

5. Failing to show genuine interest in others: Building strong relationships requires showing genuine interest in others. Avoid being self-centered or only focused on what others can do for you. Instead, take the time to learn about others' experiences, goals, and challenges, and find ways to provide value or assistance.

Identifying Your Networking Goals: What Do You Want to Achieve?

Before diving into networking, it's important to identify your goals and what you hope to achieve through networking. This will help you focus your efforts and make the most of your time and energy. Start by defining your career goals and where you want to be in the future. Then, identify the people and organizations that can help you achieve those goals.

For example, if your goal is to advance in your current industry, you may want to connect with professionals who are already in leadership positions or who have experience in the areas you're interested in. If you're looking to switch careers, you may want to network with individuals who have successfully made similar transitions or who work in the industry you're interested in.

Once you have identified your goals and the people you want to connect with, set specific networking goals. These could include attending a certain number of networking events per month, reaching out to a certain number of new contacts each week, or securing a certain number of informational interviews. Setting specific goals will help keep you motivated and focused on building meaningful relationships.

Choosing the Right Networking Events: Where to Find Opportunities

There are various types of networking events and opportunities available, so it's important to choose the ones that align with your goals and interests. Here are some common places to find networking opportunities:

1. Industry events and conferences: Industry-specific events and conferences are great places to meet professionals in your field and stay up-to-date with the latest trends and developments. These events often feature keynote speakers, panel discussions, and networking sessions.

2. Professional associations and organizations: Joining professional associations or organizations related to your field can provide access to a network of like-minded individuals who share similar interests and goals. These associations often host networking events, workshops, and seminars.

3. Networking groups and meetups: Networking groups and meetups are informal gatherings where professionals from various

industries come together to connect and share ideas. These events are often focused on specific topics or industries and provide a more relaxed environment for networking.

4. Social events and gatherings: Networking doesn't always have to happen at formal events. Social events, such as parties, fundraisers, or community gatherings, can also provide opportunities to meet new people and make connections. Keep an eye out for social events that attract professionals in your industry or field.

Preparing for Networking Events: How to Make the Most of Your Time

To make the most of your time at networking events, it's important to prepare in advance. Here are some tips to help you prepare:

1. Researching the event and attendees: Before attending an event, research the event itself and the attendees who will be present. Look for information about the event's agenda, speakers, and any specific networking opportunities. Additionally, research the attendees to identify individuals you would like to connect with and learn more about their backgrounds and interests.

2. Setting goals and objectives: Set clear goals and objectives for each networking event you attend. These goals could include meeting a certain number of new people, learning about a specific topic or industry, or securing a follow-up meeting with a key contact. Having clear goals will help you stay focused and make the most of your time.

3. Preparing your elevator pitch: An elevator pitch is a concise summary of who you are, what you do, and what value you can bring to others. Prepare a short elevator pitch that highlights your

skills, experiences, and goals. Practice delivering it in a confident and engaging manner.

4. Bringing business cards and other materials: Make sure to bring an ample supply of business cards to networking events. Business cards are a professional way to exchange contact information with others. Additionally, consider bringing other materials such as brochures or samples of your work that can help showcase your skills and expertise.

5. Dressing appropriately: Dressing appropriately for networking events is crucial. Dress in a way that reflects the level of professionalism of the event and the industry you're in. It's better to be slightly overdressed than underdressed, as it shows respect for the event and the people attending.

Approaching People: How to Start a Conversation and Make a Connection

Approaching people at networking events can be intimidating, but with the right approach, it can lead to meaningful connections. Here are some tips for starting a conversation and making a connection:

1. Introducing yourself and making small talk: Approach someone with a smile, make eye contact, and introduce yourself confidently. Start with a simple greeting and then move on to small talk to break the ice. Small talk can include topics such as the event itself, the venue, or any common interests you may have.

2. Asking open-ended questions: Asking open-ended questions is a great way to keep conversations flowing and show genuine interest in others. Open-ended questions require more than a simple yes or no answer and encourage the other person to share more about

themselves. For example, instead of asking "Do you like your job?", ask "What do you enjoy most about your job?"

3. Listening actively and showing interest: Active listening is an important skill in networking. Show genuine interest in what the other person is saying by maintaining eye contact, nodding, and asking follow-up questions. Avoid interrupting or thinking about what you're going to say next while the other person is speaking.

4. Finding common ground: Look for common interests or experiences that you can connect on. This could be anything from shared hobbies or interests to similar career paths or goals. Finding common ground helps build rapport and makes conversations more enjoyable and memorable.

5. Offering to help or provide value: Networking is not just about what others can do for you; it's also about what you can do for others. Look for opportunities to provide value or assistance to the people you meet. This could be sharing a relevant article or resource, introducing them to someone in your network, or offering your expertise or advice.

Following Up: Tips for Maintaining Relationships After the Event

Following up is a crucial step in networking as it allows you to maintain and strengthen the relationships you've built. Here are some tips for following up after a networking event:

1. Sending a follow-up email or message: Within a few days of the event, send a personalized follow-up email or message to the people you met. Express your appreciation for the conversation and mention something specific that you discussed to help jog their memory. Use this opportunity to suggest next steps, such as scheduling a follow-up meeting or call.

2. Connecting on social media: If appropriate, connect with the people you met on social media platforms such as LinkedIn. This allows you to stay connected and continue building the relationship online. When sending a connection request, personalize the message and remind them of where you met.

3. Scheduling a follow-up meeting or call: If you had a particularly meaningful conversation with someone at the event, consider scheduling a follow-up meeting or call to continue the conversation. This allows you to dive deeper into topics of interest and explore potential collaboration or mentorship opportunities.

4. Providing value or assistance: Look for ways to provide value or assistance to the people you met. This could be sharing relevant resources, introducing them to someone in your network, or offering your expertise or advice. Providing value helps strengthen the relationship and shows that you're invested in their success.

5. Staying in touch regularly: Networking is an ongoing process, so it's important to stay in touch with your contacts regularly. This can be as simple as sending occasional updates or articles of interest, inviting them to industry events or webinars, or scheduling regular catch-up calls or meetings. Regular communication helps maintain the relationship and keeps you top of mind.

Building Your Personal Brand: How to Present Yourself Professionally

Building a strong personal brand is essential for networking success. Your personal brand is how you present yourself to others and how you're perceived in your industry or field. Here are some tips for building your personal brand:

1. Defining your personal brand: Start by defining what you want to be known for in your industry or field. Identify your unique strengths, skills, and experiences that set you apart from others. This will help you create a clear and compelling personal brand message.

2. Creating a professional image: Your professional image includes how you dress, how you communicate, and how you carry yourself. Dress professionally at networking events and in your day-to-day work life. Communicate clearly and confidently, both in person and in written communication. Pay attention to your body language and make sure it conveys confidence and professionalism.

3. Developing your online presence: In today's digital age, having a strong online presence is crucial for building your personal brand. Create a professional LinkedIn profile that highlights your skills, experiences, and achievements. Consider creating a personal website or blog where you can showcase your work and share your expertise.

4. Building a reputation for expertise and value: Position yourself as an expert in your field by sharing valuable content and insights with others. Write articles or blog posts, speak at industry events, or participate in webinars or podcasts. By consistently providing value to others, you will build a reputation as someone who is knowledgeable and trustworthy.

5. Maintaining consistency across all channels: Consistency is key when it comes to building your personal brand. Make sure that your messaging, tone, and visual identity are consistent across all channels - from your LinkedIn profile to your personal website to your social media profiles. This helps create a cohesive and memorable brand image.

Networking Online: Tips for Building Relationships on Social Media

In addition to in-person networking, social media platforms provide a powerful tool for building and maintaining professional relationships. Here are some tips for networking online:

1. Choosing the right platforms: There are numerous social media platforms available, so it's important to choose the ones that align with your goals and target audience. LinkedIn is the most popular platform for professional networking, but depending on your industry or field, other platforms such as Twitter or Instagram may also be valuable.

2. Building a strong profile and presence: Your social media profiles should reflect your personal brand and showcase your expertise and achievements. Make sure your profiles are complete, up-to-date, and visually appealing. Use keywords relevant to your industry in your profile descriptions to make it easier for others to find you.

3. Engaging with others and sharing valuable content: Engage with others by commenting on their posts, sharing their content, and participating in discussions or groups. This helps you build relationships and establish yourself as an active and engaged member of the community. Additionally, share valuable content of your own that is relevant to your industry or field.

4. Participating in online groups and communities: Joining online groups or communities related to your industry or field can provide opportunities for networking and learning from others. Participate in discussions, ask questions, and share your insights and experiences. This helps you connect with like-minded individuals and expand your network.

5. Using social media to connect with people you meet in person can be a great way to maintain and strengthen your relationships. By connecting on platforms like Facebook, Instagram, or LinkedIn, you can easily stay updated on each other's lives, share photos and memories, and even plan future meetups or events. Social media also

provides a convenient way to reach out and stay in touch, especially when distance or busy schedules make it difficult to meet up in person. Additionally, it allows you to engage with their posts, comment on their achievements, and show support for their endeavors. Overall, using social media as a tool to connect with people you meet in person can enhance your relationships and foster a sense of community even when you're not physically together.

Chapter 37: Breaking Down Barriers: Advocating for Individuals with Sensory Issues

Sensory issues are a common occurrence for many individuals, yet they often go unnoticed or misunderstood. These issues can have a significant impact on daily life, affecting everything from social interactions to academic performance. It is important to understand what sensory issues are and how they can affect individuals in order to provide the necessary support and accommodations.

Understanding Sensory Issues: What Are They and How Do They Affect Daily Life?

Sensory issues, also known as sensory processing disorder, occur when the brain has difficulty receiving and responding to information that comes in through the senses. This can result in an overreaction or underreaction to sensory stimuli such as touch, sound, taste, smell, and visual input.

There are several common types of sensory issues that individuals may experience. One example is hypersensitivity, where individuals are overly sensitive to certain sensory stimuli. For instance, they may find certain sounds or textures unbearable and may become overwhelmed or anxious in situations where these stimuli are present. On the other hand, individuals may also experience hyposensitivity, where they have a decreased sensitivity to sensory input. This can result in seeking out intense sensory experiences or having difficulty recognizing pain or temperature changes.

These sensory issues can have a profound impact on daily life. For example, individuals with sensory issues may struggle with social interactions due to their sensitivity to touch or sound. They may avoid crowded places or become overwhelmed in noisy environments. Additionally, sensory issues can affect academic performance, as individuals may have difficulty focusing or become easily distracted by sensory stimuli in the classroom.

The Importance of Advocating for Individuals with Sensory Issues

Advocacy plays a crucial role in ensuring that individuals with sensory issues receive the support and accommodations they need to thrive. By advocating for these individuals, we can help raise awareness about sensory issues and promote understanding and acceptance.

Advocacy efforts can have a significant impact on individuals with sensory issues. For example, advocacy has led to the implementation of sensory-friendly practices in various settings, such as schools, workplaces, and public spaces. These practices include providing quiet spaces, using visual schedules, and offering sensory breaks. By advocating for these accommodations, individuals with sensory issues can feel more comfortable and supported in their daily lives.

There have been many successful advocacy efforts that have resulted in positive changes for individuals with sensory issues. For instance, the Autism Society launched the Autism Friendly Initiative, which aims to make businesses and organizations more inclusive and accessible for individuals with sensory issues. Through this initiative, businesses and organizations receive training and resources to create sensory-friendly environments and provide appropriate accommodations.

Common Misconceptions About Sensory Issues and How to Address Them

There are several common misconceptions about sensory issues that can hinder understanding and support for individuals who experience them. One common misconception is that sensory issues are just a result of being picky or sensitive. However, sensory issues are a neurological condition that affects how the brain processes sensory information.

To address these misconceptions, education and awareness are key. By providing accurate information about sensory issues and their impact on daily life, we can help dispel these misconceptions. This can be done through workshops, training sessions, or informational materials that are accessible to the general public.

It is also important to emphasize that sensory issues are not a choice or something that can be easily overcome. Individuals with sensory issues may require specific accommodations or strategies to navigate their daily lives successfully. By understanding this, we can create a more inclusive and supportive environment for individuals with sensory issues.

Recognizing the Signs of Sensory Overload and How to Help

Sensory overload occurs when an individual's senses become overwhelmed by too much sensory input. This can lead to feelings of anxiety, stress, or even physical discomfort. It is important to recognize the signs of sensory overload in order to provide appropriate support and help.

Signs of sensory overload can vary from person to person, but some common indicators include becoming easily overwhelmed or irritable in noisy or crowded environments, covering ears or eyes to block out sensory input, or exhibiting repetitive behaviors as a way to self-soothe. If you notice these signs in someone, it is important to provide a calm and quiet environment and offer support and understanding.

There are several strategies that can help individuals experiencing sensory overload. One effective strategy is to provide a sensory break, where the individual can take a break from the overwhelming environment and engage in calming activities such as deep breathing or using sensory tools like fidget toys. Creating a sensory-friendly environment by reducing unnecessary noise or providing visual supports can also be helpful.

Supporting Sensory-Friendly Environments: Tips for Businesses and Organizations

Creating a sensory-friendly environment is crucial for individuals with sensory issues to feel comfortable and included. Businesses and organizations can play a significant role in supporting individuals with sensory issues by implementing sensory-friendly practices.

One tip for creating a sensory-friendly environment is to provide quiet spaces where individuals can retreat to when they become overwhelmed. These spaces should be free from excessive noise or bright lights and should offer calming activities such as soft seating or sensory tools. Visual supports such as visual schedules or social stories can also be beneficial in helping individuals navigate their surroundings.

Several businesses and organizations have already implemented sensory-friendly practices. For example, AMC Theatres offers sensory-friendly movie showings where the lights are dimmed, the volume is lowered, and there are no previews or advertisements. This allows individuals with sensory issues to enjoy the movie experience without feeling overwhelmed by the usual sensory stimuli.

Strategies for Parents and Caregivers of Children with Sensory Issues

Parents and caregivers play a crucial role in supporting children with sensory issues. There are several strategies that can help parents and caregivers navigate the challenges that come with raising a child with sensory issues.

One tip for parents and caregivers is to create a sensory-friendly home environment. This can include providing a designated quiet space where the child can retreat to when they become overwhelmed, using visual schedules or timers to help with transitions, and offering sensory tools such as weighted blankets or fidget toys.

Early intervention is also important for children with sensory issues. Seeking professional help from occupational therapists or other specialists can provide parents and caregivers with strategies and techniques to support their child's sensory needs. Additionally, connecting with other parents or support groups can provide a valuable source of information and support.

The Role of Occupational Therapy in Addressing Sensory Issues

Occupational therapy plays a crucial role in addressing sensory issues and helping individuals develop the necessary skills to navigate their daily lives. Occupational therapists are trained to assess and treat sensory processing difficulties and can provide individualized interventions to address specific needs.

Occupational therapy interventions for sensory issues may include activities that provide sensory input, such as swinging or jumping on a trampoline, as well as activities that help individuals regulate their sensory responses, such as deep pressure massage or deep breathing exercises. These interventions are designed to help individuals develop the necessary skills to process sensory information effectively and engage in daily activities without becoming overwhelmed.

Advocating for Sensory Accommodations in Schools and Workplaces

Sensory accommodations are essential for individuals with sensory issues to succeed in school and work environments. Advocating for these accommodations is crucial to ensure that individuals with sensory issues have equal access to education and employment opportunities.

Examples of sensory accommodations in schools include providing a quiet space for students to take breaks, allowing the use of noise-canceling headphones or fidget tools, and offering visual supports such as visual schedules or social stories. In the workplace, accommodations may include providing a quiet workspace, allowing flexible work hours to accommodate sensory needs, or providing access to sensory tools or equipment.

Advocating for these accommodations can be done by working with school administrators, teachers, or employers to raise awareness about sensory issues and the need for accommodations. Providing resources and information about sensory accommodations can also be helpful in advocating for these changes.

Empowering Individuals with Sensory Issues: Self-Advocacy and Assertiveness

Empowering individuals with sensory issues to advocate for themselves is crucial for their overall well-being and success. Self-advocacy and assertiveness skills can help individuals communicate their needs effectively and ensure that they receive the necessary support and accommodations.

One strategy for self-advocacy is to educate oneself about sensory issues and their impact on daily life. By understanding one's own sensory needs and how they affect daily functioning, individuals can better communicate their needs to others.

Assertiveness skills are also important in self-advocacy. This includes being able to express one's needs and preferences clearly and assertively, while also being respectful of others. Practicing assertiveness skills through role-playing or seeking support from a therapist or support group can help individuals develop these skills.

The Benefits of Sensory Integration Therapy and Other Treatments

Sensory integration therapy is a treatment approach that aims to help individuals with sensory issues develop the necessary skills to process sensory information effectively. This therapy involves engaging in activities that provide sensory input in a structured and controlled manner.

The benefits of sensory integration therapy can be significant. Research has shown that this therapy can improve sensory processing abilities, reduce sensory sensitivities, and enhance overall functioning in daily life. It can also help individuals develop self-regulation skills, improve attention and focus, and enhance social interactions.

In addition to sensory integration therapy, there are other treatments that can be beneficial for individuals with sensory issues. These may include cognitive-behavioral therapy, which focuses on changing negative thoughts and behaviors related to sensory issues, or medication management for individuals with co-occurring conditions such as anxiety or attention deficit hyperactivity disorder (ADHD).

Moving Forward: Continuing the Conversation and Breaking Down Barriers for Individuals with Sensory Issues

Continuing the conversation about sensory issues is crucial for raising awareness, promoting understanding, and breaking down barriers for individuals with sensory issues. By continuing to educate ourselves and others, we can create a more inclusive and supportive society.

Breaking down barriers for individuals with sensory issues can be done through various means. This includes advocating for policy changes that promote sensory-friendly practices in schools, workplaces, and public spaces. It also involves promoting acceptance and understanding through education and awareness campaigns.

There are several resources available for further education and advocacy about sensory issues. Organizations such as the Autism Society, the Sensory Processing Disorder Foundation, and the STAR Institute for Sensory Processing Disorder provide valuable information, resources, and support for individuals with sensory issues and their families.

Sensory issues have a significant impact on daily life, affecting everything from social interactions to academic performance. By understanding what sensory issues are and how they can affect individuals, we can provide the necessary support and accommodations to help them thrive.

Advocacy plays a crucial role in ensuring that individuals with sensory issues receive the support they need. By raising awareness, promoting understanding, and advocating for sensory accommodations, we can create a more inclusive and supportive environment for individuals with sensory issues.

It is important to recognize the signs of sensory overload and provide appropriate support when needed. Creating sensory-friendly environments in businesses and organizations is also crucial for individuals with sensory issues to feel comfortable and included.

Parents and caregivers play a crucial role in supporting children with sensory issues. Early intervention, creating a sensory-friendly home environment, and seeking professional help are important strategies for parents and caregivers.

Occupational therapy is an effective treatment approach for addressing sensory issues. Through individualized interventions, occupational therapists can help individuals develop the necessary skills to navigate their daily lives successfully.

Advocating for sensory accommodations in schools and workplaces is crucial to ensure that individuals with sensory issues have equal access to education and employment opportunities. Empowering individuals with sensory issues to advocate for themselves through self-advocacy and assertiveness skills is also important.

Sensory integration therapy and other treatments can provide significant benefits for individuals with sensory issues, improving sensory processing abilities, self-regulation skills, and overall functioning in daily life.

Continuing the conversation about sensory issues and breaking down barriers is crucial for creating a more inclusive and supportive society. By educating ourselves and others, advocating for policy changes, and promoting acceptance and understanding, we can create a world that is more inclusive for individuals with sensory issues.

Chapter 37: The Ultimate Guide to Finding the Perfect Accommodation for Your Next Trip

When planning a trip, one of the most important decisions you will make is choosing the right accommodation. The place where you stay can have a significant impact on your overall travel experience. It can either enhance your trip and make it more enjoyable, or it can detract from your experience and leave you feeling unsatisfied.

Finding the perfect accommodation is crucial because it sets the tone for your entire trip. It is your home away from home, and it should provide comfort, convenience, and a sense of security. Whether you are traveling for business or pleasure, having a comfortable and well-suited place to stay can make all the difference.

Determine Your Budget: Tips for Setting a Realistic Accommodation Budget

Before you start searching for accommodation options, it is important to determine your budget. Setting a realistic budget will help you narrow down your choices and ensure that you are not overspending on accommodation.

When setting a budget, consider factors such as the duration of your stay, the location you are visiting, and the type of accommodation you prefer. Keep in mind that prices can vary depending on the time of year and demand, so it is important to do some research and compare prices.

To find affordable accommodation options, consider staying in budget hotels or hostels, or look for deals and discounts online.

Another option is to consider alternative accommodations such as vacation rentals or homestays, which can often be more cost-effective than traditional hotels.

Location, Location, Location: How to Choose the Best Neighborhood for Your Stay

Choosing the right neighborhood for your stay is essential to ensure that you have easy access to the attractions and amenities you desire. When choosing a neighborhood, consider factors such as proximity to public transportation, safety, and the type of atmosphere you prefer.

Researching neighborhoods before booking your accommodation can help you make an informed decision. Look for information on the neighborhood's safety record, the availability of public transportation, and the proximity to attractions and amenities. You can also read reviews and ask for recommendations from friends or fellow travelers who have visited the area before.

Hotel or Airbnb: Pros and Cons of Each Accommodation Option

When it comes to choosing accommodation, two popular options are hotels and Airbnb. Each option has its own benefits and drawbacks, and it is important to consider your preferences and needs before making a decision.

Hotels offer convenience and a range of amenities such as room service, housekeeping, and on-site restaurants. They also provide a level of security and peace of mind. However, hotels can be more expensive than other accommodation options, especially in popular tourist destinations.

On the other hand, Airbnb offers a more personalized and local experience. It allows you to stay in someone's home or apartment, giving you a taste of what it's like to live in the area. Airbnb can also be more cost-effective, especially for longer stays or for larger groups. However, it may not offer the same level of service and amenities as hotels, and there may be less consistency in terms of quality.

Amenities: What to Look for in Accommodation Amenities

When choosing accommodation, it is important to consider the amenities that are important to you. Different travelers have different needs and preferences, so it is important to prioritize amenities based on what is most important to you.

Common amenities to look for include free Wi-Fi, breakfast included, a fitness center or pool, on-site parking, and a 24-hour front desk. Other amenities that may be important to some travelers include a kitchenette or full kitchen, laundry facilities, and pet-friendly options.

Consider what amenities are essential for your comfort and convenience during your stay. Make a list of must-have amenities and use it as a guide when searching for accommodation options.

Reviews and Ratings: How to Use Online Reviews to Find the Perfect Accommodation

One of the most valuable resources when searching for accommodation is online reviews and ratings. Reading reviews from previous guests can give you insight into the quality and experience of staying at a particular property.

When evaluating reviews and ratings, it is important to consider the overall consensus rather than focusing on one or two negative reviews. Look for patterns in the reviews and pay attention to comments about cleanliness, customer service, and the accuracy of the property description.

It is also helpful to read reviews from travelers who have similar preferences and needs as you. If you are traveling with children, for example, look for reviews from families who have stayed at the property. Their experiences and insights can help you make a more informed decision.

Safety and Security: Tips for Ensuring Your Accommodation is Safe and Secure

Safety and security should be a top priority when choosing accommodation. Before booking a property, consider factors such as the neighborhood's safety record, the security measures in place at the property, and the availability of emergency services.

When evaluating safety and security, look for properties that have secure entrances, well-lit common areas, and 24-hour front desk service. It is also important to consider factors such as fire safety measures, the availability of smoke detectors and fire extinguishers, and the presence of security cameras.

Reading reviews can also provide insight into the safety and security of a property. Look for comments about any safety concerns or incidents that previous guests may have experienced.

Accessibility: How to Choose Accommodation that Meets Your Accessibility Needs

If you have accessibility needs, it is important to choose accommodation that can accommodate your requirements. When evaluating accessibility, consider factors such as wheelchair accessibility, accessible bathrooms, and the availability of elevators or ramps.

Before booking accommodation, contact the property directly to inquire about their accessibility features. Ask specific questions about any accommodations they have for guests with disabilities and request photos or additional information if needed.

It is also helpful to read reviews from travelers with accessibility needs. Their experiences can provide valuable insights into the accessibility of a property and help you make an informed decision.

Group Travel: Tips for Finding Accommodation for Large Groups

Traveling with a large group can present unique challenges when it comes to finding accommodation. When traveling with a group, consider factors such as the number of rooms needed, the availability of common areas, and the proximity to attractions and amenities.

To find accommodation for large groups, consider options such as vacation rentals or apartments that can accommodate multiple guests. Look for properties that have multiple bedrooms or suites, as well as common areas where the group can gather.

It is also important to book accommodation well in advance when traveling with a large group. Popular properties can fill up quickly, so it is best to secure your accommodations as early as possible.

Pet-Friendly Accommodation: How to Find the Perfect Accommodation for You and Your Furry Friend

If you are traveling with pets, it is important to find accommodation that is pet-friendly. Not all properties allow pets, so it is important to do some research and find accommodations that welcome furry friends.

When searching for pet-friendly accommodation, consider factors such as the size and breed restrictions, any additional fees or deposits required, and the availability of pet-friendly amenities such as dog parks or walking trails.

It is also helpful to read reviews from travelers who have stayed at the property with their pets. Their experiences can provide insight into how accommodating the property is for pets and whether they had a positive experience.

Final Tips for Finding the Perfect Accommodation for Your Next Trip

Finding the perfect accommodation for your next trip requires careful consideration of your budget, preferences, and needs. By setting a realistic budget, researching neighborhoods, and considering factors such as amenities, reviews, safety, accessibility, and group travel, you can find the perfect accommodation that meets your requirements.

Remember to prioritize your needs and preferences when choosing accommodation. What is important to one traveler may not be as important to another, so it is important to consider what matters most to you.

By taking the time to find the perfect accommodation, you can enhance your travel experience and ensure that you have a comfortable and enjoyable stay. Happy travels!

Chapter 38: Why Support Services are Essential for Your Mental Health and Well-being

Mental health is just as important as physical health. It affects every aspect of our lives, from our relationships to our ability to work and function in society. However, there is still a stigma surrounding mental health that can make it difficult for individuals to seek help. This is where support services come in. Support services can provide individuals with the tools and resources they need to manage their mental health concerns and improve their overall well-being.

The Role of Support Services in Promoting Mental Wellness

Support services play a crucial role in promoting mental wellness. They can help individuals develop coping skills and resilience, which are essential for managing stress and navigating life's challenges. By providing a safe space for individuals to express their emotions, support services can also help individuals feel less isolated and alone.

One of the key benefits of support services is that they provide individuals with a sense of community and belonging. Many people who struggle with mental health issues often feel isolated and misunderstood. Support groups, therapy sessions, and online forums can provide a space where individuals can connect with others who are going through similar experiences. This sense of connection can be incredibly powerful and can help individuals feel less alone in their journey towards mental wellness.

The Different Types of Support Services Available for Mental Health

There are various types of support services available for mental health. Therapy and counseling are perhaps the most well-known forms of support services. These sessions provide individuals with a safe and confidential space to discuss their concerns and work through their emotions with a trained professional.

Support groups are another valuable resource for individuals struggling with mental health issues. These groups bring together individuals who are facing similar challenges, allowing them to share their experiences, offer support, and learn from one another.

Hotlines and crisis services are available for individuals who are in immediate need of assistance or are experiencing a mental health crisis. These services provide a lifeline for individuals who may be feeling overwhelmed or in danger.

In addition to these traditional support services, there are also online resources and forums that individuals can access from the comfort of their own homes. These resources provide information, support, and a sense of community for individuals who may not have access to in-person support services.

How Support Services Can Help You Manage Stress and Anxiety

Stress and anxiety are common mental health concerns that many individuals face on a daily basis. Support services can play a crucial role in helping individuals manage these issues.

Support services can provide individuals with tools and techniques for managing stress and anxiety. This may include relaxation exercises, breathing techniques, and mindfulness practices. By learning these skills, individuals can develop a greater sense of control over their emotions and reduce the impact of stress and anxiety on their daily lives.

Support services can also help individuals identify triggers and develop coping strategies. By understanding what causes their stress or anxiety, individuals can work with support professionals to develop personalized strategies for managing these triggers. This may involve setting boundaries, practicing self-care, or seeking additional support when needed.

During times of stress, support services can provide a sense of calm and comfort. Whether it's through therapy sessions, support group meetings, or crisis hotlines, knowing that there is someone there to listen and offer guidance can be incredibly reassuring.

The Benefits of Seeking Professional Support for Mental Health Concerns

While support from friends and family is important, seeking professional support for mental health concerns can provide a higher level of care and expertise. Mental health professionals have the training and experience to diagnose mental health conditions accurately and develop an appropriate treatment plan.

Professional support can also help individuals manage more severe mental health concerns. Conditions such as depression, bipolar disorder, and schizophrenia often require specialized treatment and medication management. Mental health professionals can provide the necessary guidance and support to help individuals manage these conditions effectively.

In addition to diagnosis and treatment, professional support can also provide individuals with a safe and non-judgmental space to explore their thoughts and emotions. This can be particularly valuable for individuals who may not feel comfortable discussing their concerns with friends or family members.

How Support Services Can Help You Build Resilience and Coping Skills

Resilience and coping skills are essential for managing mental health concerns and navigating life's challenges. Support services can play a crucial role in helping individuals develop these skills.

Support services can help individuals develop healthy coping mechanisms. This may involve learning new ways to manage stress, practicing self-care, or seeking support from others. By developing these skills, individuals can become better equipped to handle difficult situations and bounce back from setbacks.

Support services also provide a safe space for individuals to practice resilience. Through therapy sessions, support groups, and online forums, individuals can share their experiences, learn from others, and gain confidence in their ability to overcome challenges.

By building resilience and coping skills, individuals can develop a greater sense of control over their mental health. They can become more proactive in managing their concerns and feel empowered to take steps towards their own well-being.

The Importance of Peer Support in Mental Health Recovery

Peer support is an invaluable resource for individuals on their mental health recovery journey. Connecting with others who have experienced similar challenges can provide a sense of community and belonging.

Peer support offers a unique perspective and understanding of mental health concerns. Peers have firsthand experience with the challenges and triumphs of mental health recovery, which allows them to offer empathy, validation, and practical advice.

One of the most significant benefits of peer support is that it helps individuals feel less alone in their recovery journey. Mental health concerns can often make individuals feel isolated and misunderstood. By connecting with others who have gone through similar experiences, individuals can find comfort in knowing that they are not alone.

Peer support also provides a platform for individuals to share their stories and inspire others. By sharing their experiences, individuals can offer hope and encouragement to those who may be struggling. This sense of purpose and connection can be incredibly empowering and can contribute to an individual's overall mental wellness.

How Support Services Can Help You Navigate Life Transitions and Challenges

Life is full of transitions and challenges, and these can often take a toll on our mental health. Support services can provide guidance and support during these difficult times.

Support services can help individuals navigate life transitions such as starting a new job, moving to a new city, or going through a divorce. These transitions can be overwhelming and may trigger feelings of stress, anxiety, or depression. Support professionals can provide individuals with the tools and resources they need to manage these challenges effectively.

Support services can also help individuals develop coping strategies for challenging situations. Whether it's dealing with a difficult boss, managing conflict in relationships, or facing financial hardships, support professionals can offer guidance and support to help individuals navigate these challenges.

During times of change, support services can provide a sense of stability. They offer a safe space where individuals can express their concerns, receive validation, and gain perspective. This support can be invaluable in helping individuals maintain their mental well-being during times of uncertainty.

The Connection Between Social Support and Mental Health

Social support plays a crucial role in mental health. It has been shown to have a positive impact on mental well-being and can contribute to resilience and better stress management.

Social support provides a sense of belonging and connection. It allows individuals to feel understood, valued, and supported by others. This sense of belonging can have a significant impact on mental health, as it helps individuals feel less isolated and more connected to the world around them.

Social support also helps individuals feel more resilient and better able to manage stress. Knowing that there are people who care about them and are there to offer support can provide individuals with a sense of security and confidence. This can help individuals navigate difficult situations and bounce back from setbacks more effectively.

In addition to emotional support, social support can also provide practical assistance. Whether it's helping with daily tasks, providing financial support, or offering guidance and advice, social support can help individuals manage the practical challenges that often accompany mental health concerns.

The Role of Support Services in Reducing Stigma and Promoting Mental Health Awareness

Support services play a crucial role in reducing the stigma surrounding mental health and promoting awareness. By providing education and resources, support services can help individuals understand mental health concerns and encourage them to seek help.

Support services can help reduce the stigma surrounding mental health by providing a safe and non-judgmental space for individuals to discuss their concerns. This can help individuals feel more comfortable seeking help and sharing their experiences with others.

Support services also play a vital role in promoting mental health awareness. They provide information about mental health conditions, treatment options, and available resources. By increasing awareness, support services can help individuals recognize the signs of mental health concerns in themselves or others and encourage them to seek help.

By reducing stigma and promoting awareness, support services contribute to a more supportive and understanding society. This can have a significant impact on individuals' willingness to seek help for their mental health concerns and can ultimately lead to improved outcomes.

Why You Should Prioritize Support Services for Your Mental Health and Well-being

Prioritizing support services for your mental health is essential for overall well-being. Mental health is just as important as physical health, and seeking support is a crucial step towards managing your concerns effectively.

Support services provide a safe space for individuals to manage their mental health concerns. They offer tools, resources, and guidance to help individuals develop coping skills, build resilience, and navigate life's challenges.

By seeking professional support, individuals can access a higher level of care and expertise. Mental health professionals can provide a diagnosis, develop a treatment plan, and offer ongoing support and guidance.

Support services also play a crucial role in reducing stigma and promoting mental health awareness. By providing education and resources, support services can help individuals feel more comfortable seeking help and encourage them to share their experiences with others.

In conclusion, prioritizing support services for your mental health is essential for overall well-being. By seeking support, you are taking an important step towards managing your mental health concerns effectively and improving your quality of life. Remember, you are not alone, and there are resources available to help you on your journey towards mental wellness.

Chapter 39: Navigating the Choppy Waters of Transition: Tips for a Smooth Journey

Transition is a natural part of life that we all experience at various points. Whether it's a personal or professional transition, it can be a time of uncertainty and change. However, understanding and embracing transition is crucial for personal and professional growth. In this article, we will explore the importance of transition, how to recognize the signs that indicate a transition is needed, and strategies for planning ahead, developing a support system, staying focused on goals, embracing change, managing stress and anxiety, maintaining a positive attitude, learning from past transitions, celebrating successes, and preparing for future transitions.

Understanding the Importance of Transition

Transition is important in personal and professional growth because it allows us to evolve and adapt to new circumstances. Without transition, we would remain stagnant and unable to reach our full potential. Transition provides us with opportunities for learning, self-discovery, and growth. It pushes us out of our comfort zones and challenges us to develop new skills and perspectives.

In personal growth, transition can involve changes in relationships, lifestyle, or personal identity. It can be triggered by major life events such as marriage, parenthood, divorce, or the loss of a loved one. These transitions force us to reevaluate our priorities and make adjustments to our lives.

In professional growth, transition can involve changes in career paths or job roles. It can be triggered by factors such as job loss, promotion, or a desire for new challenges. These transitions require us to develop new skills, expand our networks, and adapt to new work environments.

Recognizing the Signs of Transition

Recognizing the signs that indicate a transition is needed is crucial for navigating through change successfully. Some common signs include feeling stuck or unfulfilled in your current situation, experiencing a lack of motivation or enthusiasm for your work or personal life, feeling overwhelmed or burnt out, or sensing a desire for something different.

It's important to pay attention to these signs and not ignore them. They are indicators that something needs to change in order for you to grow and thrive. By recognizing these signs, you can take proactive steps towards planning for a successful transition.

Planning Ahead for a Successful Transition

Planning ahead is essential for a smooth transition. It allows you to anticipate potential challenges and develop strategies to overcome them. Here are some tips for planning ahead:

1. Set clear goals: Define what you want to achieve during the transition and set specific, measurable, achievable, relevant, and time-bound (SMART) goals.

2. Create a timeline: Break down your goals into smaller tasks and create a timeline for completing them. This will help you stay organized and focused.

3. Research and gather information: Gather as much information as possible about the transition you are planning to make. This will help you make informed decisions and minimize uncertainty.

4. Seek guidance: Reach out to mentors, coaches, or professionals who have experience in the area you are transitioning into. They can provide valuable insights and guidance.

5. Develop a contingency plan: Anticipate potential obstacles or setbacks and develop a contingency plan to address them. This will help you stay prepared and resilient during the transition.

Developing a Support System

Having a support system during a transition is crucial for emotional support, encouragement, and guidance. Here are some ways to build a support system:

1. Identify your support network: Identify friends, family members, colleagues, or mentors who can provide support during your transition.

2. Communicate your needs: Clearly communicate your needs and expectations to your support network. Let them know how they can best support you during this time.

3. Seek professional help if needed: If you are struggling with the transition or experiencing significant stress or anxiety, consider seeking professional help from therapists or counselors who specialize in transitions.

4. Join support groups or communities: Joining support groups or communities of individuals who are going through similar transitions can provide a sense of belonging and understanding.

5. Be open to receiving support: Allow yourself to be vulnerable and open to receiving support from others. Remember that asking for help is a sign of strength, not weakness.

Staying Focused on Your Goals

Staying focused on your goals during a transition can be challenging, especially when faced with uncertainty and change. Here are some strategies to help you stay focused:

1. Prioritize your goals: Identify your most important goals and prioritize them. Focus your time and energy on the tasks that will have the greatest impact.

2. Break down your goals into smaller tasks: Breaking down your goals into smaller, manageable tasks can make them less overwhelming and more achievable.

3. Create a routine: Establishing a routine can provide structure and help you stay focused. Set aside dedicated time each day or week to work towards your goals.

4. Eliminate distractions: Identify and eliminate distractions that may hinder your progress. This could include turning off notifications on your phone or finding a quiet workspace.

5. Stay motivated: Find ways to stay motivated and inspired during the transition. This could involve reading books or articles related to your goals, listening to podcasts or TED talks, or surrounding yourself with positive and supportive people.

Embracing Change and Letting Go of the Past

Embracing change and letting go of the past is essential for a successful transition. It can be challenging to leave behind familiar routines, relationships, or identities, but it is necessary for growth. Here are some ways to embrace change and let go of the past:

1. Practice acceptance: Accept that change is inevitable and that it is necessary for personal and professional growth. Embrace the idea that change brings new opportunities and possibilities.

2. Reflect on the past: Take time to reflect on the lessons learned from past experiences and transitions. Use these lessons to inform your current transition and make better decisions.

3. Cultivate a growth mindset: Adopt a growth mindset, which is the belief that you can learn and grow from any situation. Embrace challenges as opportunities for learning and development.

4. Practice self-compassion: Be kind and compassionate towards yourself during the transition. Acknowledge that it is normal to feel uncertain or uncomfortable during times of change.

5. Seek new experiences: Embrace new experiences and opportunities that come with the transition. Step outside of your comfort zone and be open to trying new things.

Managing Stress and Anxiety During Transitions

Transitions can be stressful and anxiety-inducing, but there are strategies you can use to manage these emotions. Here are some tips for managing stress and anxiety during transitions:

1. Practice self-care: Prioritize self-care activities such as exercise, meditation, getting enough sleep, and eating nutritious foods.

Taking care of your physical and mental well-being can help reduce stress and anxiety.

2. Practice relaxation techniques: Incorporate relaxation techniques such as deep breathing exercises, progressive muscle relaxation, or mindfulness meditation into your daily routine.

3. Seek support: Reach out to your support system for emotional support and guidance. Share your feelings with trusted friends or family members who can provide a listening ear.

4. Manage your expectations: Recognize that transitions can be challenging and that it is normal to experience stress and anxiety. Be patient with yourself and set realistic expectations.

5. Seek professional help if needed: If you are struggling with managing stress or anxiety during the transition, consider seeking professional help from therapists or counselors who specialize in stress management.

Maintaining a Positive Attitude and Mindset

Maintaining a positive attitude and mindset during a transition is crucial for staying motivated and resilient. Here are some strategies for maintaining a positive attitude:

1. Practice gratitude: Cultivate a sense of gratitude by focusing on the positive aspects of your life and transition. Take time each day to reflect on what you are grateful for.

2. Surround yourself with positivity: Surround yourself with positive and supportive people who uplift and inspire you. Limit your exposure to negative influences or environments.

3. Challenge negative thoughts: Challenge negative thoughts or self-doubt that may arise during the transition. Replace them with positive affirmations or realistic perspectives.

4. Celebrate small wins: Celebrate small successes along the way to stay motivated and boost your confidence. Acknowledge and reward yourself for your progress.

5. Stay flexible and adaptable: Embrace the idea that things may not always go as planned during a transition. Stay flexible and adaptable, and be open to adjusting your goals or plans as needed.

Learning from Past Transitions

Past transitions can provide valuable insights and lessons that can inform future ones. Take time to reflect on past transitions and identify what worked well and what could have been done differently. Use these lessons to make more informed decisions and navigate future transitions more effectively.

Celebrating Successes Along the Way

Celebrating successes, no matter how small, is important during a transition. It helps to boost motivation, confidence, and overall well-being. Take time to acknowledge and celebrate your achievements along the way. This could involve treating yourself to something special, sharing your successes with loved ones, or simply taking a moment to reflect on how far you have come.

Preparing for Future Transitions

Transitions are a natural part of life, so it's important to prepare for future transitions. Here are some tips for preparing for future transitions:

1. Continuously learn and develop new skills: Stay curious and continuously learn new skills that can be valuable in future transitions. This could involve taking courses, attending workshops, or seeking out new experiences.

2. Build a strong network: Cultivate relationships and build a strong network of professionals and mentors who can provide guidance and support during future transitions.

3. Stay adaptable and open-minded: Embrace the idea that change is constant and stay adaptable and open-minded. Be willing to explore new opportunities and take calculated risks.

4. Reflect on past transitions: Continuously reflect on past transitions and identify what worked well and what could have been done differently. Use these insights to inform future transitions.

5. Set goals and create a plan: Continuously set goals for personal and professional growth and create a plan to achieve them. Having a clear direction can help you navigate future transitions more effectively.

In conclusion, transition is a natural part of life that provides opportunities for personal and professional growth. By understanding the importance of transition, recognizing the signs that indicate a transition is needed, planning ahead, developing a support system, staying focused on goals, embracing change, managing stress and anxiety, maintaining a positive attitude, learning from past transitions, celebrating successes, and preparing for future transitions, you can navigate through change successfully and embrace transitions as opportunities for growth. Embrace transition as a chance to evolve, learn, and become the best version of yourself.

Chapter 40: Why Choosing a Major Shouldn't Define Your College Experience

Choosing a major in college is a decision that many students feel pressured to make early on in their academic journey. The pressure comes from various sources, including parents, peers, and society as a whole. Students are often bombarded with questions about their future plans and career goals, which can be overwhelming and anxiety-inducing. However, it is important for students to remember that choosing a major is not a decision that needs to be made hastily or without careful consideration.

Exploring different fields of study before settling on a major is crucial for several reasons. It allows students to discover new interests and passions that they may not have been aware of before. It also provides them with the opportunity to gain a well-rounded education and develop a diverse skill set. By exploring different fields, students can make informed decisions about their future career paths and ensure that they are pursuing something that aligns with their interests and goals.

The Importance of Exploring Different Fields of Study

One of the greatest benefits of exploring different fields of study is the opportunity to discover new interests and passions. Many students enter college with a vague idea of what they want to study, but they may not have had the chance to explore all the options available to them. By taking elective courses in various disciplines, students can expose themselves to new subjects and topics that they may find fascinating. This exploration can lead to the discovery of a passion they never knew they had.

Another advantage of exploring different fields is the chance to gain a well-rounded education. College is not just about preparing for a specific career; it is also about developing critical thinking skills, communication skills, and a broad knowledge base. Taking courses in different disciplines allows students to develop these skills and acquire knowledge in areas outside their major. This well-rounded education can be valuable in both personal and professional contexts.

To make the most of their exploration, students should take advantage of the resources available to them, such as academic advisors. Academic advisors can provide guidance and support in choosing courses that align with a student's interests and goals. They can also help students navigate the requirements of different majors and provide information about potential career paths. By working closely with an advisor, students can ensure that they are making informed decisions about their academic journey.

The Benefits of Taking General Education Courses

General education courses are an essential part of a college curriculum, and they offer numerous benefits to students. These courses provide a well-rounded education by exposing students to a variety of subjects and disciplines. They often cover topics such as history, literature, mathematics, and the sciences, giving students a broad knowledge base that can be applied to various areas of their lives.

In addition to providing a well-rounded education, general education courses can also help students discover new interests and passions. Many students enter college with a limited understanding of what they want to study, and taking general education courses allows them to explore different fields before committing to a major. For example, a student who takes an introductory psychology course may discover a passion for the subject and decide to pursue it further.

Furthermore, general education courses can help students develop important skills that are applicable across disciplines. These skills include critical thinking, problem-solving, communication, and research skills. By taking courses in different areas, students can develop these skills in various contexts, making them more versatile and adaptable in their future careers.

The Value of Extracurricular Activities and Internships

Extracurricular activities and internships play a crucial role in a student's college experience and can have a significant impact on their future career prospects. These opportunities provide practical experience and allow students to build skills that are not typically taught in the classroom.

Participating in extracurricular activities such as clubs, organizations, or sports teams can help students develop leadership skills, teamwork, and time management skills. These activities also provide opportunities for networking and building relationships with peers, faculty, and professionals in various fields. By getting involved in extracurricular activities, students can expand their social and professional networks, which can be beneficial when it comes to finding internships or job opportunities.

Internships, on the other hand, offer students the chance to gain hands-on experience in their field of interest. They provide a bridge between the classroom and the real world, allowing students to apply what they have learned in a practical setting. Internships also give students the opportunity to develop industry-specific skills, build a professional network, and gain insight into potential career paths. Many internships also offer the possibility of being hired full-time after graduation, making them a valuable stepping stone into the workforce.

The Impact of Networking and Building Relationships

Networking and building relationships are essential skills that can greatly benefit students during their college years and beyond. College is a unique time when students have access to a diverse range of individuals, including peers, faculty members, alumni, and professionals in various fields. Building relationships with these individuals can open doors to new opportunities and provide valuable guidance and support.

Attending career fairs is one way for students to network and connect with professionals in their field of interest. Career fairs often bring together employers from different industries who are looking to hire interns or full-time employees. By attending these events, students can make connections with potential employers and learn more about different career paths.

Joining clubs and organizations related to their interests is another way for students to network and build relationships. These groups often host events, workshops, and guest speakers that provide valuable insights into specific industries or career paths. By actively participating in these organizations, students can meet like-minded individuals who share their interests and goals.

Connecting with alumni is also an important aspect of networking. Alumni can provide valuable advice and guidance based on their own experiences in the workforce. Many colleges and universities have alumni networks or mentorship programs that facilitate these connections. By reaching out to alumni, students can gain insights into potential career paths, learn about job opportunities, and build a network of professionals who can support them in their career journey.

The Role of Personal Growth and Development

College is not just about academics; it is also a time for personal growth and development. It is an opportunity for students to discover who they are, explore their interests and passions, and develop important life skills.

One way for students to engage in personal growth and development is by taking advantage of counseling services offered by their college or university. These services provide support for a variety of issues, including mental health, stress management, and career guidance. By seeking counseling, students can gain valuable insights into themselves and their goals, as well as develop strategies for managing the challenges they may face during their college years.

Leadership programs are another avenue for personal growth and development. Many colleges and universities offer leadership programs that provide training and opportunities for students to develop leadership skills. These programs often include workshops, seminars, and hands-on experiences that allow students to practice and refine their leadership abilities. By participating in these programs, students can gain confidence, learn how to work effectively with others, and develop important skills that are highly valued by employers.

The Significance of Diversity and Inclusion

Diversity and inclusion are crucial aspects of the college experience that should not be overlooked. College campuses are diverse communities that bring together individuals from different backgrounds, cultures, and perspectives. Embracing this diversity can lead to a richer and more inclusive learning environment.

Seeking out opportunities to learn about different cultures and perspectives is an important part of embracing diversity and inclusion. Many colleges and universities offer courses or programs that focus on multiculturalism or social justice issues. By taking these courses or participating in these programs, students can gain a deeper understanding of the world around them and develop empathy and respect for others.

Getting involved in clubs or organizations that celebrate diversity is another way for students to embrace diversity and inclusion. These groups often host events, workshops, or discussions that promote understanding and appreciation of different cultures. By actively participating in these activities, students can broaden their horizons, challenge their own biases, and develop a greater appreciation for diversity.

The Connection Between a Major and Career Path

While it is important to explore different fields of study and gain a well-rounded education, it is also crucial to consider the connection between a major and a potential career path. Many students enter college with a specific career goal in mind, and choosing a major that aligns with that goal can provide a solid foundation for their future.

Researching potential career paths is an essential step in making an informed decision about a major. Students should take the time to explore different careers, learn about the skills and qualifications required, and consider how their chosen major can prepare them for those careers. They should also consider the job market and the demand for professionals in their chosen field.

It is important to note that not all majors lead directly to specific careers. Some majors provide a broad skill set that can be applied to various industries, while others may require additional education or training beyond a bachelor's degree. Students should carefully consider their long-term goals and how their chosen major fits into those goals.

The Flexibility of Changing Majors and Career Paths

It is important for students to remember that choosing a major does not mean they are locked into that field for the rest of their lives. Many students change their majors multiple times during their college years, and it is not uncommon for individuals to pursue careers that are unrelated to their undergraduate degree.

Changing majors or career paths is a natural part of the learning process and personal growth. As students explore different fields of study and gain new experiences, their interests and goals may evolve. It is important for students to be open to these changes and not feel pressured to stick with a major or career path that no longer aligns with their interests or goals.

Colleges and universities often have resources and support systems in place to help students navigate the process of changing majors. Academic advisors can provide guidance and support, and there may be specific programs or requirements for students who wish to change majors. By seeking out these resources, students can make a smooth transition to a new field of study or career path.

The Influence of Life Experiences on Career Choices

Life experiences can have a significant impact on the career choices that individuals make. These experiences can include personal challenges, volunteer work, travel, or work experience. They shape our values, beliefs, and perspectives, and they can provide valuable insights into what we want from our careers.

Reflecting on their own life experiences can help students gain clarity about their career goals and aspirations. They can consider the skills they have developed through these experiences and how they can be applied to different career paths. For example, a student who has volunteered at a local animal shelter may discover a passion for animal welfare and decide to pursue a career in that field.

It is important for students to take the time to reflect on their life experiences and consider how they have shaped their career goals. By doing so, they can gain a deeper understanding of themselves and make more informed decisions about their future.

Embracing the College Experience Beyond a Major

Choosing a major is an important decision, but it is just one aspect of the college experience. It is crucial for students to embrace all that college has to offer and take advantage of the opportunities available to them.

Exploring different fields of study, taking general education courses, participating in extracurricular activities and internships, networking and building relationships, engaging in personal growth and development, embracing diversity and inclusion, considering the connection between a major and career path, and reflecting on life experiences are all essential components of a well-rounded college experience.

By embracing these aspects of college life, students can gain a deeper understanding of themselves, develop important skills, build a network of support, and make informed decisions about their future. College is a time for exploration, growth, and self-discovery, and students should make the most of this transformative period in their lives.

Chapter 41: Breaking the Stigma: Understanding Autism Spectrum Disorder

Autism Spectrum Disorder (ASD) is a neurodevelopmental disorder that affects communication, social interaction, and behavior. It is characterized by a range of symptoms and severity levels, which is why it is referred to as a "spectrum" disorder. ASD typically appears in early childhood, before the age of three, and lasts throughout a person's lifetime.

ASD affects individuals in different ways, but common symptoms include difficulties with social interaction and communication, repetitive behaviors, and restricted interests. Some individuals with ASD may have intellectual disabilities, while others may have exceptional abilities in certain areas, such as music or math.

The Prevalence of Autism Spectrum Disorder: Understanding the Numbers

The prevalence of Autism Spectrum Disorder has been on the rise in recent years. According to the Centers for Disease Control and Prevention (CDC), approximately 1 in 54 children in the United States has been diagnosed with ASD. This represents a significant increase from previous estimates.

There are several factors that contribute to the rise in numbers. One factor is increased awareness and improved diagnostic criteria. As more professionals become familiar with the signs and symptoms of ASD, more children are being identified and diagnosed.

Additionally, changes in diagnostic practices and increased access to healthcare services have also contributed to the rise in prevalence.

The Causes of Autism Spectrum Disorder: Debunking Myths and Misconceptions

There are many myths and misconceptions surrounding the causes of Autism Spectrum Disorder. One common misconception is that vaccines cause ASD. However, numerous scientific studies have debunked this myth and found no link between vaccines and ASD.

The exact causes of ASD are still not fully understood, but research suggests that a combination of genetic and environmental factors play a role. Certain genetic mutations or variations may increase the risk of developing ASD. Environmental factors, such as prenatal exposure to certain substances or complications during pregnancy or birth, may also contribute to the development of ASD.

Signs and Symptoms of Autism Spectrum Disorder: Identifying Early Warning Signs

Early identification and intervention are crucial for children with Autism Spectrum Disorder. There are several early signs and symptoms that parents and caregivers can look out for. These may include:
- Delayed or limited speech and language skills
- Difficulty with social interactions, such as making eye contact or understanding social cues
- Repetitive behaviors, such as hand-flapping or rocking

- Sensory sensitivities, such as being bothered by certain sounds or textures

- Fixation on specific interests or objects

It is important to note that not all children with ASD will exhibit the same signs and symptoms, and the severity of symptoms can vary greatly. If parents or caregivers suspect that their child may have ASD, it is important to seek a professional evaluation for an accurate diagnosis.

Diagnosis and Assessment of Autism Spectrum Disorder: Understanding the Evaluation Process

The evaluation process for Autism Spectrum Disorder typically involves a multidisciplinary team of professionals, including psychologists, pediatricians, speech therapists, and occupational therapists. The evaluation may include a variety of assessments and observations to gather information about the child's development, behavior, and communication skills.

The evaluation process may include:

- A thorough medical history review

- Developmental screenings

- Observations of the child's behavior in different settings

- Standardized assessments to measure cognitive abilities and social skills

- Speech and language assessments

Early diagnosis is important because it allows for early intervention and support services to be implemented. The earlier a child receives intervention, the better their long-term outcomes are likely to be.

Different Types of Autism Spectrum Disorder: From Asperger's Syndrome to Pervasive Developmental Disorder

There are different types of Autism Spectrum Disorder, each with its own characteristics and diagnostic criteria. Some of the most commonly recognized types include:

1. Autistic Disorder: This is the most severe form of ASD, characterized by significant impairments in social interaction, communication, and behavior.

2. Asperger's Syndrome: Individuals with Asperger's Syndrome typically have average or above-average intelligence and may have fewer difficulties with language and cognitive abilities. However, they may struggle with social interactions and have restricted interests.

3. Pervasive Developmental Disorder-Not Otherwise Specified (PDD-NOS): This diagnosis is given when an individual does not meet the criteria for Autistic Disorder or Asperger's Syndrome but still exhibits significant impairments in social interaction and communication.

It is important to note that the Diagnostic and Statistical Manual of Mental Disorders (DSM-5) no longer includes separate diagnoses for Asperger's Syndrome and PDD-NOS. Instead, these individuals are now diagnosed with Autism Spectrum Disorder.

Living with Autism Spectrum Disorder: Coping Strategies and Support for Families

Living with Autism Spectrum Disorder can present unique challenges for individuals and their families. However, there are coping strategies and support systems available to help navigate these challenges.

For families, it can be helpful to establish routines and provide clear expectations for the child. Visual supports, such as schedules or social stories, can also be beneficial in helping the child understand and navigate their daily routines. Additionally, seeking support from other families who have children with ASD can provide a sense of community and understanding.

Therapies such as Applied Behavior Analysis (ABA) can also be beneficial in helping individuals with ASD develop social skills, communication skills, and adaptive behaviors. Occupational therapy and speech therapy may also be recommended to address specific areas of need.

Treatment Options for Autism Spectrum Disorder: From Behavioral Therapy to Medication

There are various treatment options available for individuals with Autism Spectrum Disorder. The most common treatment approach is behavioral therapy, specifically Applied Behavior Analysis (ABA). ABA focuses on teaching individuals new skills and reducing problem behaviors through positive reinforcement and systematic teaching methods.

Other therapies that may be beneficial for individuals with ASD include speech therapy, occupational therapy, and social skills training. These therapies can help individuals develop communication skills, improve sensory processing, and learn appropriate social behaviors.

In some cases, medication may be prescribed to manage specific symptoms associated with ASD, such as hyperactivity or aggression. However, medication is not a cure for ASD and should be used in conjunction with other therapies and interventions.

The Importance of Early Intervention: Improving Outcomes for Children with Autism Spectrum Disorder

Early intervention is crucial for children with Autism Spectrum Disorder. Research has shown that early intervention can lead to significant improvements in communication skills, social interactions, and adaptive behaviors.

Early intervention services may include a combination of therapies, such as ABA, speech therapy, and occupational therapy. These services are typically tailored to the individual needs of the child and may be provided in various settings, including the home, school, or clinic.

By providing early intervention services, children with ASD have a better chance of reaching their full potential and achieving positive long-term outcomes. Early intervention can also help families navigate the challenges associated with ASD and provide them with the support they need.

Advocacy and Awareness: Breaking Down Stigma and Promoting Acceptance

Advocacy and awareness are crucial in breaking down the stigma surrounding Autism Spectrum Disorder and promoting acceptance.

It is important to educate the public about ASD and dispel myths and misconceptions.

One way to promote acceptance is by encouraging inclusion and understanding in schools and communities. This can be done by implementing inclusive education practices, providing training for educators on how to support students with ASD, and promoting acceptance and understanding among peers.

Advocacy efforts can also focus on increasing access to services and supports for individuals with ASD. This includes advocating for insurance coverage for therapies, promoting employment opportunities for individuals with ASD, and supporting legislation that protects the rights of individuals with disabilities.

Moving Forward with Understanding and Compassion for Autism Spectrum Disorder

In conclusion, Autism Spectrum Disorder is a complex neurodevelopmental disorder that affects individuals in different ways. It is important to understand the signs and symptoms of ASD, as well as the available treatment options and support systems.

By promoting awareness, acceptance, and understanding, we can create a more inclusive society for individuals with Autism Spectrum Disorder. With early intervention and support, individuals with ASD can lead fulfilling lives and reach their full potential. It is our responsibility as a society to ensure that individuals with ASD are given the opportunities and support they need to thrive.

Don't miss out!

Visit the website below and you can sign up to receive emails whenever Travis Breeding publishes a new book. There's no charge and no obligation.

https://books2read.com/r/B-A-CBXDB-GDFXC

BOOKS2READ

Connecting independent readers to independent writers.

Did you love *Unlocking the Spectrum: A Comprehensive Guide to Understanding and Thriving with Autism*? Then you should read *Celebrating Neurodiversity*[1] by Travis Breeding!

[2]

"Celebrating Neurodiversity" is not just a book; it's a manifesto for acceptance, understanding, and inclusivity. Breeding passionately advocates for the celebration of differences, urging readers to embrace the mosaic of neurodiversity that enriches our society. Through empowering stories of resilience, creativity, and innovation, Breeding showcases the immense potential that lies within the neurodivergent community.

From the unique ways in which neurodivergent individuals perceive the world to the invaluable insights they offer, "Celebrating Neurodiversity" is a thought-provoking exploration of what it truly

---

1. https://books2read.com/u/4DnjxP

2. https://books2read.com/u/4DnjxP

means to be neurodivergent. Breeding's empowering narrative inspires readers to challenge preconceived notions, foster empathy, and champion diversity in all its forms.

Whether you're a neurodivergent individual, a caregiver, or simply curious about the intricacies of the human mind, "Celebrating Neurodiversity" is a must-read that will leave a lasting impact. Join Travis Breeding on a journey of self-discovery, acceptance, and celebration as we embrace the kaleidoscope of neurodiversity and revel in the beauty of our differences.

Read more at breedingautismconsulting.com.

Also by Travis Breeding

Harmony in Flux: Navigating Bi-Polar Brilliance

The Friendship Rainbow

The Great Kindergarten Adventure: A Story about Going to School with Autism

The Magic Forest Adventure

Unlocking Brilliance: Navigating Autism and Applied Behavior Analysis Towards a Radiant Future

Decoding Love: Navigating Dating and Relationships on the Autism Spectrum

Echoes of a Late Diagnosis: Unveiling the Spectrum Within

From Theory to Practice: Implementing Effective Autism Interventions St

The Amazing Adventures of Aiden and His Asperger's Superpowers

The Magical Adventures of Lily and the Enchanted Forest

Unlocking Potential: A Journey Of Discovery Through ABA Therapy

Unlocking Potential: Navigating Employment for Neurodiverse Talent

Unlocking the Spectrum: A Journey through Applied Behavior Analysis from an Autistic Perspective

Unlocking The Spectrum: Navigating The Complexity Of Autism With Advanced Strategies And Insights

Beyond The Spectrum: Insights From Autistic Adults

Beyond The Stereotypes

Breaking Barriers: Navigating Autism With Therapeutic Insight

Celebrating Neurodiversity
Embracing Differences
From Diagnosis To Treatment
From Dreams To Reality: The Young President
Living With Autism: A Journey Of Triumph And Challenges
Neurodiversity Unveiled: Navigating The Spectrum Of Inclusion
Sunshine At Disney World
The Art Of Reinforcement
The Magical School Bus Ride: A Journey Of Understanding
ThroughThe Spectrum Of Love
Dancing With Shadows: How To Turn Your Fears Into Powerful
Allies
From Chaos To Control: How To Develop Strong Executive
functioning Skills
From Misunderstood To Mainstream
Unlocking the Spectrum: A Comprehensive Guide to
Understanding and Thriving with Autism
Unraveling The Mind: Understanding OCD, Autism, And
Obsession
Rise: Mastering Confidence, Mindfulness, And Self-Esteem
Twice Exceptional: Navigating Life with Autism and Gomez Lopez
Hernandez Syndrome
Unlocking The Spectrum: A Journey Of Discovery With Gomez
Lopez Hernandez Syndrome

Watch for more at breedingautismconsulting.com.

About the Author

Travis is the author of over 50 books about autism spectrum disorder. He travelst he country sharing the mission of making the world a better place for autistic individuals. In his spare time Travis enjoys writing, walking, and watching sports.

Read more at breedingautismconsulting.com.